Perspectives on Eternal Security

Perspectives on Eternal Security

Biblical, Historical, and Philosophical Perspectives

Edited by
Kirk R. MacGregor *and* Kevaughn Mattis

WIPF & STOCK · Eugene, Oregon

PERSPECTIVES ON ETERNAL SECURITY
Biblical, Historical, and Philosophical Perspectives

Wipf & Stock
A division of Wipf and Stock Publishers
199 W. 8th Ave., Suite 3
Eugene, OR 97401

www.wipfandstock.com

ISBN 13: 978-1-55635-870-8

Manufactured in the U.S.A.

Contents

About the Contributors

Jon Balserak (PhD, University of Edinburgh) is Research Fellow in Theology at the University of Birmingham. His publications include *Divinity Compromised: A Study of Divine Accommodation in the Thought of John Calvin* in the Studies in Early Modern Religious Reforms series (Kluwer Academic, 2006) and "Luther, Calvin and Musculus on Abraham's Trial: Exegetical History and the Transformation of Genesis 22" in *Reformation and Renaissance Review.*

Donna Bowman (PhD, University of Virginia) is Associate Professor of Interdisciplinary Studies and Associate Director of the Honors College at the University of Central Arkansas. Her publications include *The Divine Decision: A Process Doctrine of Election* (Westminster John Knox, 2002) and the *Handbook of Process Theology* (co-editor; Chalice Press, 2006).

James W. Bryant (PhD, Southwestern Baptist Theological Seminary; DD, Criswell College) is Senior Professor of Pastoral Theology at the Criswell College. His publications include *The New Guidebook for Pastors* (co-editor; Broadman and Holman, 2007) and essays in the *Holman Christian Standard Bible: Harmony of the Gospels* (Broadman and Holman, 2007).

Shawn L. Buice (PhD, Mid-America Baptist Theological Seminary) is Associate Professor of New Testament and Greek at the Mid-America Baptist Theological Seminary, Northeast Branch in Schenectady, New York. His publications include "The Parable of the Unjust Judge: Luke 18:1–8" (1997) and "The Great Commission Passages" (1998) in the *Mid-America Theological Journal.*

Harold R. Holmyard III (ThD, Dallas Theological Seminary) is an Old Testament translator and editor for the *Holman Christian Standard Bible.*

His publications include "Does Isaiah 33:23 Address Israel or Israel's Enemy?" (1995) and "Solomon's Perfect One" (1998) in *Bibliotheca Sacra.*

Francis Lyall (PhD, University of Aberdeen) is Emeritus Professor of Public Law at the University of Aberdeen. His publications include *Slaves, Citizens, Sons: Legal Metaphors in the Epistles* (Academie Books and Zondervan, 1984) and *An Introduction to British Law* (2nd ed.; Nomos Verlagsgesellschaft, 2002).

Kirk R. MacGregor (PhD, University of Iowa) is Assistant Professor of Religion at James Madison University. His publications include *A Central European Synthesis of Radical and Magisterial Reform* (University Press of America, 2006) and *A Molinist-Anabaptist Systematic Theology* (University Press of America, 2007).

J. Ramsey Michaels (ThD, Harvard University) is Professor Emeritus of Religious Studies at Southwest Missouri State University. His publications include commentaries on *1 Peter* in the *Word Biblical Commentary* series (Word, 1988) and *John* in the *New International Biblical Commentary* series (Hendrickson, 1989).

Georg Plasger (ThD, Universität Wuppertal) is Professor of Systematic and Ecumenical Theology at the Universität Siegen. His publications include *Die Not-Wendigkeit der Gerechtigkeit: Eine Interpretation zu „Cur Deus homo" von Anselm von Canterbury* (Aschendorff, 1993) and *Die relative Autorität des Bekenntnisses bei Karl Barth* (Neukirchener, 2000).

Verlyn D. Verbrugge (PhD, University of Notre Dame) is Senior Editor at Zondervan. His publications include *Early Church History* (Zondervan, 1998) and the *New International Dictionary of New Testament Theology: Abridged Edition* (editor; Zondervan, 2003).

Stephen Voorwinde (ThD, Australian College of Theology) is Lecturer in New Testament at the Reformed Theological College, Australia. His publications include *Wisdom for Today's Issues: A Topical Arrangement of the Proverbs* (P & R, 1996) and *Jesus' Emotions in the Fourth Gospel: Human or Divine?* (T. & T. Clark International, 2005).

Brandon G. Withrow (PhD, Westminster Theological Seminary) is Adjunct Professor at both Winebrenner Theological Seminary and Beeson Divinity School, Samford University. His publications include *Katherine Parr: A Guided Tour of the Life and Thought of a Reformation Queen* (P & R, 2008) and the critical edition of Peter van Mastricht's *Treatise on Regeneration* (Soli Deo Gloria, 2002).

Foreword

I was reared in a Christian home, for which I have been very thankful over the years. Nonetheless our religious orientation was Wesleyan Pentecostal, in which the doctrine of the security of the believer was viewed as false doctrine, if not a doctrine of Satan. Having placed my faith in Jesus as Savior at the young age of nine, my Christian walk was stunted, I believe, because I embraced my tradition's acceptance that one could "lose one's salvation" for failure to live a life without sin. Even as I chose to embrace Jesus of my own free will, I could as well cease to believe Him by the same means. From age 9 until 20, I have commented, I was "lost and saved" six times. When the frailties of the flesh overcame my commitment to Christ, I would fall from grace. Believing that I was no longer saved, I would then wait until the next youth camp or revival to embrace Christ once again.

It was in college, while a Greek major and studying the New Testament in the original language, that I came to believe a person who came to Jesus by faith was kept by the power of God and sealed with the Holy Spirit until the day of redemption. I came to understand in the first letter of John, that one should confess personal sins to maintain proper fellowship with God. Seminary only strengthened my acceptance of the doctrines of the Reformation built on the teachings of Jesus and the apostles, particularly Paul, taught by Augustine and other fathers, and reclaimed in the Reformation by Luther, Calvin, and taught by the great Reformed theologians since that time.

When I was attempting to evaluate the doctrine of eternal security in Christ, I read every book that I could find supporting the opposite view. I was especially impressed by Robert Shank and Guy Duty's books advocating that one could be truly regenerated by the Holy Spirit and justified by faith, yet cease to be a believer and be lost for eternity apart from God's grace. However, in spite of their arguments, I found that the force of the New Testament text would not sustain these arguments. Though those who wrote that Christians were not truly secure in their salvation made some forceful arguments and sought to bolster these by reference to the word meanings and grammar of the text, I found that the contexts of the passages cited, and the understanding of the Greek grammar, was superficial.

Having accepted the doctrine of the security of the believer, I have continued to be enriched by this doctrine for forty years. As time has gone by I have realized that this doctrine is not based merely on a reference to a few passages of Scripture but is embedded in the very notion of the grace of God—all of grace as Spurgeon said—so that God saves me forever by His love and grace, not because or through any works that I have ever done, or can ever do. The riches of God are granted to me, and the gift of eternal life, not the reward, because of His work through Christ and His choice of me from all eternity. What I once viewed as an accursed doctrine has become a blessed doctrine. What I once viewed as some easy way into heaven has become an understanding that it cost Jesus His life. To be saved is to be saved forever because the work of God begun in me due to Christ's death is continued in me by His life.

Since I began teaching theology, I have also envisioned that someday I would write a volume rigorously expounding the depths of this doctrine and defending the doctrine of eternal security from those who robbed Christians, like me, of their reason for comfort in the keeping power of God. With this new book edited by Kevaughn Mattis and Kirk MacGregor, much of my desire has been satisfied. They have brought together a remarkable team of scholars to argue this blessed doctrine, but in ways that I would probably have never considered. One may see in this work impressive scholarship exploring several unexplored avenues in setting forth the doctrine of security. The book is composed of exegesis of biblical texts as well as historical and philosophical analysis that is rare in books on doctrine. To this point those who have embraced eternal security reflect the vintage of Reformation thought. We think of Calvinists and Reformed scholars, and Baptists, who though rejecting most of Calvin, yet accept security. The scholars in this work demonstrate that the doctrine should not be viewed in an isolated manner but is part and parcel of other important doctrines of grace and salvation. Moreover, it is not simply a Reformation doctrine, but may be found in the first periods of the Church such as Clement of Rome. It is not only a New Testament teaching, but an Old Testament doctrine. It was not only argued by Calvin but believed by Luther.

I must confess that even though I have taught the doctrine of eternal security for more than 30 years, this volume of erudition has caused me to consider new ways to think about the topic. There is much fresh insight here, not only in a reexamination from a biblical and theological perspective but psychological and philosophical avenues that I have never fully explored. The reader of *Perspectives on Eternal Security* is offered a feast of analysis and synthesis, theology and philosophy that will challenge his or her thinking in ways unlikely to have been challenged before. I heartedly welcome the work and encourage you to read it carefully for new ways to think about and embrace the doctrine of the eternal security of the Christian.

H. Wayne House
Distinguished Research Professor of Biblical and Theological Studies
Faith Evangelical Seminary, Tacoma, Washington

Preface

THE ESSAYS WHICH COMPRISE this manuscript originated from *Testamentum Imperium* (TI), an online theological journal that affirms the irrevocable nature of Christian salvation. I am deeply grateful for the journal's reality, as it embodies an unfolding story of Christian generosity, divine favor, and hopeful perseverance. The journal's success depended upon commitments from authors via e-mail correspondence who had never heard of me before, and at the time I wrote them I had not yet secured a webmaster or website for the journal. However, by God's grace, invited scholars entrusted their pieces to me, and I happened to meet the charitable Dr. Michael G. Maness via e-mail requests for volunteers to create a website for the journal. Through this encounter, *Testamentum Imperium* acquired a committed managing editor and a permanent point of presence on the internet (http://www.preciousheart.net/ti). Through Dr. Kirk R. MacGregor, contributing author of TI (2009), a segment of the first volume of TI has metamorphosed into this book which you now read. To Drs. Maness and MacGregor, to all the journal authors and all those who have supported me with their prayers, thank you.

Perspectives on Eternal Security is an interdisciplinary reflection whose tone of writing is that of affirmation and hence avoids intense dispute with viewpoints adverse to those of the authors. This style of articulation is crucial for dislodging the concept of the irrevocable nature of salvation from its polemic locality, which often leaves many with the perception that it is merely a factious article of elaborate sixteenth- and seventeenth-century doctrinal systems that should now be avoided. This work seeks to unearth the innate value of eternal security as a doctrine whose careful attention engenders the spiritual virtue of orienting one's mind and affections toward the Divine in such a manner as to nurture confidence to face the unknown future through trust in the known God. Without a doubt, among the most persistent enquiries of the Christian are how the Triune God acts redemptively in this fallen world and what the implications of such activities are for human destiny. Pondering such questions in the tradition of thought affirmed in this book endeavors to lead us to unshakable hope, the hope of somehow seeing redemption as the victory of God given to us as a gift and promise.

It was through the existential angst of perceiving relationship with God as an unforgiving terrain that I developed an ardent interest in theological matters, particularly the soteriology of the Protestant Reformation. For me, therefore, this book is more than a theological enterprise; it engenders trust in the faithfulness of God, which is the premise upon which my spiritual life and that of countless others have effloresced. May this work ably shepherd you towards the Glory of God revealed in Christ.

Kevaughn Mattis, L.L.B. (Hons.)
Founder and Managing Director of *Testamentum Imperium*

Introduction

Kirk R. MacGregor

Throughout the biblical corpus and the course of the Christian tradition, the doctrine of eternal security has occupied a pivotal role as either an explicit object or underlying subtext of theological reflection. For personal assurance of salvation has preoccupied the psychology, and therefore daily praxis, of believers across the vocational spectrum from the lay through the ordained. The doctrine of eternal security holds that all persons who genuinely enter into a "spiritual marriage" of saving faith in God will ultimately reach glorification and will thus never lose their salvation; however, precisely *how* this state of affairs obtains has been, and continues to be, the subject of great controversy.

During the sixteenth century, eternal security received especial attention from the chief Protestant reformers Martin Luther (1483–1546) and John Calvin (1509–64), as it constituted a chief corollary to the former's rediscovery of justification by faith alone (*sola fide*) and the driving force behind the latter's profound reflection on the sovereignty, providence, and unconditional election of God. It is no accident, therefore, that Lutheran symbols such as the *Augsburg Confession* (1530) and the *Apology to the Augsburg Confession* (1530) make assurance of eternal security a necessary part of saving faith. Rooted in late-Augustinian monergism, Calvin proceeded in his *Institutes of the Christian Religion* (completed in 1559) to expound a model of eternal security henceforth denominated the perseverance of the saints, according to which God makes the elect persist in their Christian faith and lifestyle up to the moment of death by granting them irresistible grace, or grace which it is logically impossible to subvert. For Calvin, God could not control with certainty his decreed outcome of salvation, which entails not merely the justification but also the sanctification of the elect, without controlling with certainty the necessary means on which the outcome depends. The systematic nature and logical consistency of Calvin's model rendered it a quite attractive export to Reformed communities in the Netherlands, France, and Scotland. Moreover, in England the traditional quasi-Catholic exterior of the church received new life from the Calvinist doctrinal stream. This stream's perception of biblical fidelity led opponents of the Anglican Church who migrated to the New World, notably the Puritans and Particular Baptists, to place perseverance of the saints at the center of their theology.

Perseverance of the saints emerged to a position of prominence across the American religious landscape as a result of the First (*c.* 1730–1760) and Second (*c.* 1800–1830) Great Awakenings, nineteenth-century evangelical revivalism characterized by Charles G. Finney (1792–1875) and Dwight L. Moody (1837–1899), and the Princeton school of Calvinist orthodoxy (*c.* 1810–1920). Starting among the Calvinistic Dutch Reformed and Presbyterians of the middle colonies, the First Great Awakening spread to Congregationalist New England through the efforts of Jonathan Edwards (1703–1758), arguably the foremost American theologian. In his sermons and treatises, Edwards emphasized the sovereignty and the love of God, maintaining that all who have embraced Christ are continually and infallibly drawn by God's love to himself and to his service over the course of life.[1] Although unabashedly Reformed in his conviction that those who embrace Christ were first predestined to do so, Edwards' message, echoed as it was by Particular (or Regular) Baptist preachers, gradually became attached in the popular mindset to the notion of conversion: once individuals passed out of "nominal Christianity" through born-again experiences where they, by repentance and faith, became new creatures in Christ, they were forever sealed by the Holy Spirit for the day of salvation. By the time of the Second Great Awakening, pastors and theologians without Reformed persuasions proclaimed a new variant on eternal security representing a theological halfway house between synergism and monergism, where those who freely chose to respond to God's prevenient grace are then supernaturally preserved in faith until beatitude. This variant arose as a regular ingredient in the frontier preaching of camp meetings and tent revivals, alongside the Reformed model of perseverance which received fresh propagation at the hands of Princeton

1. Cairns, *Christianity*, 367.

Theological Seminary professors Archibald Alexander (1772–1851), Charles Hodge (1797–1878), A. A. Hodge (1823–1886), and Benjamin B. Warfield (1851–1921).

In the twentieth century, a third view of eternal security began to take shape which depended entirely on justification rather than on sanctification, often referred to by its proponents and detractors under the moniker of "once saved, always saved." Expanding upon the forensic justification introduced by Luther and codified by his successor Philip Melanchthon (1497–1560), this model avers that eternal security constitutes, within the internal logic of the Trinity, part of God the Father's decision to declare the believing sinner at the moment of personal faith "not guilty" on the basis of the infinite penalty that God the Son has paid on the sinner's behalf. Not only is this verdict irreversible, but, owing to the majesty of God's grace, it persists for all eternity regardless of how the individual proceeds to behave or even whether the individual renounces faith in Christ. Unlike the Reformed and the Second Great Awakening insistence that assurance of salvation and personal holiness of life amount to two sides of the same coin, proponents of this third view radicalize the Reformation maxims of *sola gratia* and *sola fide* by distinguishing between repentance and faith (through which grace comes), denying the necessity of the former at any point in life but affirming the necessity of the latter at some point in life for eternal salvation. Earl D. Radmacher expounds this perspective with all-desirable clarity:

> Don't confuse justification and sanctification. Tell unbelievers that if they simply believe in Christ they will at that moment have eternal life. That is justification by faith alone. . . . If an unbeliever asks if he must give up his sinful ways to have eternal salvation, tell him no. The only condition is faith in Christ. Tell him, however, that sin never pays, for the believer or the unbeliever, and that he should turn from his sinful ways whether or not he is convinced that Jesus gives eternal life to all who merely believe in Him for it. . . . Believe. Not repent. Not believe plus repent. Just believe. It's that simple.[2]

Accordingly, this model assigns to repentance a primarily ethical function, where repentance focuses more on the horizontal dimension of social influence than the vertical dimension of union with God.

2. Earl D. Radmacher, "Salvation: A Necessary Work of God," in *Understanding Christian Theology*, gen. eds. Charles R. Swindoll and Roy B. Zuck (Nashville: Nelson, 2003), 944.

Due to the prominence of the aforementioned three models throughout the past five centuries, it is little wonder that the vast majority of Western evangelicals associate eternal security with one of these. Nevertheless, these are far from the only ways Christians past or present have judged eternal security to be possible, as a plethora of views on theology proper, hermeneutics, and anthropology have produced numerous perspectives on eternal security from the biblical period onward. In an attempt to start remedying the knowledge gap, this first print anthology from Kevaughn Mattis' online journal *Testamentum Imperium* features thirteen essays from an international array of scholars which bring a wide scope of scriptural, historical, and philosophical perspectives to bear on the question of eternal security. While all the contributors subscribe to the doctrine of eternal security, they do so in various ways, with a balance between adherents to the first two models (Calvin's perseverance of the saints and the mediation between synergism and monergism) and exponents of other interpretations relatively unknown in the popular mindset.

For the first time, this volume maps out the contours of a wide trajectory of eternal security from its Hebraic origins to contemporary theological developments. To accomplish this goal, the book is divided into two parts. Part One, "Biblical and Exegetical Studies," analyzes and strengthens the canonical roots of eternal security which form the common foundation of all subsequent models of this doctrine. Part Two, "Historical and Philosophical Studies," considers issues of theological and social history as well as philosophy of religion which pertain to eternal security. Here we examine the understudied positions on eternal security of such thinkers and schools of thought as Clement of Rome (*c.* 40–99), Albrecht Ritschl (1822–1889), Karl Barth (1886–1968), and process theology, and we assess the practical impact of Calvin's preaching on predestination on the daily lives of his spiritual charges. Moreover, we philosophically delineate the permanent changes to the overall course of history and the human nature of individual believers accomplished by the dual event of Christ's death and resurrection as well as their implications for personal salvific assurance and Christian ethics.

PART ONE: BIBLICAL AND EXEGETICAL STUDIES

In chapter one, Harold R. Holmyard III carefully draws together the exegetical threads of many Psalmic texts to argue that, while not explicitly formulated, the concept that those who belong to Yahweh will be preserved by Yahweh forever, rescuing them from even the murky prospects of the prevailing Ancient Near Eastern Sheol afterlife model, is clearly affirmed. Contra the Documentarian source dating of the origin of belief in general resurrection to the Second Temple Period, Holmyard finds provocative traces of resurrection belief in such Davidic Psalms as 16 (vv. 9–10), 17 (vv. 14–15), 37 (vv. 10–13, 28–29, 35–38), and 49 (vv. 14–15). Furthermore, Holmyard examines the implications of the Hebrew vocabulary for "forever" to demonstrate that the righteous possess a permanent hope of consciously living in the presence of God beyond the grave (*e.g.* 23:6; 25:3; 30:12; 41:12–13; 121:7–8). Holmyard's panoramic treatment of the book of Psalms then turns to the eternality of God's love toward his faithful ones (*e.g.* 118:1–4, 29; 136; 138:8), revealing that its unfailing nature logically entails the permanent existence of all its objects. Since the Hebrew Bible does not deal with the theological issue of persevering in the faith with the same directness as the New Testament, Holmyard employs canonical synthesis to, in light of later revelation, unpack the ramifications of Psalmic motifs and images as they pertain to salvific endurance. Here Holmyard persuasively makes the case that the Psalms proclaim a God who enables all genuinely devoted to the Shema to persevere in their convictions throughout life, through his empowerment (*e.g.* 27:2–6; 31:19–24), forgiveness (*e.g.* 25:12–18; 40:4–12), care (*e.g.* 22:24; 36:5–7), and protection (*e.g.* 17:4–5; 37:17–28; 71:20; 91). For the Psalms simultaneously bestow assurance upon those struggling to endure and expect the righteous to endure, blossoming like a palm tree or cedar which continues to bear fruit into old age and so illuminating the majesty of God.

Chapter two, authored by J. Ramsey Michaels, broadly examines the prism of eternal security texts in John through the laser of an exceptional text-critical treatment of John 10:28–30, which greatly strengthens the connotations of both this foundational passage and the larger theme it represents. Reasoning from standard principles of textual criticism, Michaels conclusively establishes the impossibility that the common tautological translation of verse 29, "*My Father, who has given them to me, is greater than all*, and no one can snatch them out of my Father's hand," reflects the Johannine autograph. Rather, the original text of John pronounced, "*That which my Father has given to me is greater than all*, and no one can snatch it out of the Father's hand," indicating the supreme greatness of Jesus' sheep and their collective identity as a most precious gift by the Father to the Son. Due both to the irrevocable nature of the Father's gift to the Son and to the infinite worth of believers, both individually and collectively, in the Father's sight, the salvation of believers is forever secure. Relating it to John the Baptist's maxim that "a person can receive nothing unless it is given to him from heaven" (3:27), Michaels places this promise in the larger context of John's Gospel, where it is seen that God the Father decides the citizenship of his Kingdom by drawing disciples, who then validate their status as an intertrinitarian gift by coming to Jesus. In the high-priestly prayer of John 17, Jesus substantiates this reasoning by placing his disciples, past and present, in his list of gifts the Father has bestowed upon him (vv. 6, 9, 24). Given this assessment, Michaels closes his essay by displaying its added hermeneutical value for fully understanding the multilayered meanings of Christ's parables about the treasure in the field and the pearl of great price (Matt 13:44–46), which are now seen to span two vantage points. For believers, the treasure and the pearl connote the Kingdom of God; but for Jesus himself, the treasure and the pearl allude to the company of the redeemed, an insight corroborated by a rare but probable *logia Jesu* from the Gospel of Philip independent of the canonical Gospels.

Branching out from this *locus classicus* and building on the hermeneutical groundwork laid by Michaels, the next two chapters continue in Johannine studies with detailed analyses of individual pericopae furnishing unshakable assurance of the believer's salvation.

In chapter three, Shawn L. Buice probes John 6:38–40 for its ability to reveal the will of God, cognizance of which is vitally important for Christian discipleship and yet often seems a labyrinth incredibly difficult to decipher in particular life situations for laypeople and theologians alike. This confusion is increased by the nature of the scriptural witness itself: unlike such codes of religious law as the Jewish *Mishnah* or the Theravada Buddhist *Vinaya Pitaka*, the Bible features an absence of texts straightforwardly explaining what to do when faced with particular situations. However, John 6 explicitly identifies the will of God as, first, Jesus losing none of those the Father has entrusted him but resurrecting them on the last day, and second, the eternal life plus final resurrection, presented as an amalgamated whole, of everyone who puts their trust in Jesus. Buice relates this exposure to the pragmatic aspects of the larger Johannine Christology, which in part present Jesus as a divinely commissioned agent whose desire is to accomplish the Father's will. Admitting that a specific group of people, "those he has given me," are referred to in John 6:38–40, Buice follows R. C. H. Lenski by arguing that this concession does not demand limiting the number of persons who can acquire salvation to a divinely pre-selected company. Rather, Buice interprets the further description of this group, "everyone who sees the Son and believes in him," as a universal invitation which removes all religious and ethnic boundaries and places membership priority upon the hearer's decision. Standing in a Baptist tradition borne out of both Particular and General Baptist streams, Buice marshals John 6 as support for a view denominated "preservation of the saints," which mediates between synergism and monergism by drawing a distinction between the steps in the *ordo salutis* for which the individual and God are primarily, but not exclusively, responsible. Moreover, Buice maintains that a "preservation" model carries with it the pastoral advantage of preparing believers to rely exclusively upon God's strength for carrying out the good, so escaping the psychological damage caused by thrusting believers back upon themselves for the responsibility of achieving sanctification.

Chapter four treats the divine counsels reached prior to the creation of the space-time universe, as revealed by the high-priestly prayer in John 17. Here Jon Balserak insists that, far from an esoteric consideration with no practical relevance, a proper understanding of these counsels is imperative for the believer's security. Balserak sheds light on their significance by recalling the Patristic controversy between Heracleon (*fl.* 175), a Valentinian Gnostic who composed the first commentary on John's Gospel, and the prominent early church leader, philosopher, and exegete Origen (185–254). On the one hand, Heracleon proposed that, for John, faith in Christ was a matter predetermined by a person's conception by either God or the devil. On the other hand, Origen responded in his own Johannine commentary that belief was a matter of human free will. Dissenting from Heracleon's interpretation of the pre-temporal counsels while not necessarily agreeing with Origen, Balserak avers that John 17 evinces an overarching covenant of redemption, whose parties are the Father and the Son *sans* any creaturely envoy. Established before the world's foundation, this covenant stipulates that the Father will choose a people and entrust them to the Son, who will serve as their representative head; via his active and passive obedience, the Son will merit for this people all the treasures of beatitude. Therefore, it is the responsibility of Jesus to ensure that all believers ultimately obtain salvation, which proffers believers an inner peace that transcends the vicissitudes of contingency. In this light, Jesus' prayer can be seen as his request of confirmation that when he completes the Father's work, he and his people will receive the covenanted reward. Not merely content to verify this reward, Jesus displays supreme guardianship and compassion by adding a number of specific entreaties for the Father to prevent the flock from losing their salvation. Balserak points out that the covenant of redemption coupled with its dominical reinforcements furnish an unshakable ground for salvific assurance even amid believers' struggles with the gravest internal sense of sinfulness.

In chapter five, Stephen Voorwinde employs a close reading of Romans 8:31–39 to spell out precisely how God's love functions as the basis and substance for the security of the believer. Framed by three forensic questions and one relational question, Paul powerfully declares that nothing, including believers themselves, will break the chain of God's purpose for his adopted children, which extends from his foreknowledge to their glorification. Voorwinde shows the magnitude of this assertion by persuasively arguing, based on identifying the antecedent of "these things" (v. 31) with either Paul's treatment of divine grace covering chapters 5–8 or his argument in Romans up to this point, that it forms a conclusion to his entire discussion of Christian assurance. Voorwinde then explains how the provisions and promises of God shore up the assumptions behind each rhetorical question. For instance, Voorwinde notes that "God is for" believers in three different ways: he providentially arranges the circumstances of believers' lives; he ordains an eternal purpose for believers; and he gives believers his Son. Moreover, Voorwinde helpfully addresses several objections raised by Paul's opponents against his gospel which still comprise pressing matters for Christian praxis. Contrary to the perceived threat of antinomianism, Voorwinde highlights Paul's contentions that believers died to sin through participation in Christ's death, that believers died to the law and so are no longer yoked thereto, and that believers are therefore free to be yoked to Christ and share in the power of his resurrection through the Holy Spirit. To the issue of whether the word of God had failed as a result of its rejection by those first-century Jews who did not embrace the Way, Voorwinde unfolds Paul's joint lines of reasoning that not all who are descended from Israel are members of Israel, for whom God's priority in the gospel and promises in election still stand, and that the true Israel is revealed through the new way of the Spirit, the ultimate reality to which the Torah pointed. Voorwinde closes by illustrating how 8:35–39 utilize the twin foci of the death of Christ and the gift of the Spirit to draw together the threads of divine love in Romans, as God could never abdicate or refuse love to those in whom he has made such infinite investments.

In chapter six, writing from a Calvinist standpoint, Verlyn D. Verbrugge assesses the impact of 2 Peter 1:8–11 on the doctrine of election through analysis of the passage's socio-historical background, grammar, and structure. Regarding background, Verbrugge shows that Peter is addressing two distinct groups—believers and false teachers—the latter of which were once affiliated with the church but have now capitulated to worldly corruption. This breakdown is significant because it shows that Peter did not have a third "transitional" group in mind composed of persons gradually sliding out of the group of believers and into allegiance with the false teachers; for Peter, anyone who joined the false teachers thereby proved themselves to have never received the grace of God. Verbrugge cites approvingly the counterfactual insight of 1 John 2:19, which indicates that the false teachers never actually belonged to the church since, if they had, they would not have abandoned it. Placing 2 Peter 1:8–11 in its context, Verbrugge reveals that the preceding verses 1–7 display concern that believers escape sin and increasingly cultivate Christian virtues on the basis of the fact that they have received God's all-empowering gifts of faith, salvation, and the indwelling divine nature. This fact is corroborated by the use of ἐπίγνωσις in verse 8, indicating that those charged to display the eightfold virtues of verses 5–7 possess the decisive saving knowledge of God rooted in personal conversion, which is precisely the knowledge that Peter later claims the false teachers have ignored. In verse 9's description of the false teachers, Verbrugge maintains that the adverb πάλαι ("long ago, in the past") should not be linked with ἁμαρτιῶν ("sins"), as though the false teachers were previously cleansed of their sins, but is a temporal indicator of when the false teachers heard, and unfortunately ignored, the message of how to receive forgiveness. Upon examination of the major Greek terms in verse 10, Verbrugge concludes that "making sure" (ποιεῖσθαι . . . βέβαιος) of one's elective call means neither to cause nor to fortify one's eternal salvation, but rather to confirm in one's own heart the reality of God's gracious work through one's praxis, which could not transpire apart from one's previous election.

Chapter seven sees Francis Lyall use his unique background as a historian of law to delineate the particulars of the Pauline analogy of adoption, an analogy borrowed from Roman law instead of Jewish or Greek law, and its consequences for eternal security. Since Roman law dictated that a person could only be part of one family at a time, adoption required a change in formal legal relationship whereby someone left a previous family and became part of a new family. For male citizens, three possibilities existed for family status: *sui iuris* or independent; a *paterfamilias* who headed a family under his authority; and *alieni iuris* or part of a family controlled by a *paterfamilias* (female citizens could hold either the first or third status). When a *sui iuris* wished to become adopted into a family, s/he would commit the *detestatio sacrorum* by abandoning one's former deities and turn to the ritual worship of the new *paterfamilias*; similarly, when the neophyte turns from living independently to embracing the Lordship of Christ, the neophyte departs from the idolatry of exalting selfish and nationalistic concerns to the status of ultimacy and enters a spiritual priesthood offering up sacrifices of righteousness to God the Father. The adoption of an *alieni iuris* spelled termination of all legal ties with the former family and placement under the absolute authority of a new father, a situation which conjures up the notion of being transported out of the household of Satan and into the household of God. In both cases, the father owned all family members, which possession involved complete provision for their well-being and total responsibility for rectifying their mistakes. Such elements are clearly mirrored in the biblical imagery of Yahweh in general and Christ in particular as the good shepherd and the interrelated doctrines of forgiveness and atonement. Lyall is careful to note that while the analogy of adoption, by itself, does not demand that God will never reject his children, for Roman law in the New Testament period lacked controls on how an adopter might behave, it strongly points in the direction of the larger Scriptural witness that God cannot disclaim members of his family.

PART TWO: HISTORICAL AND PHILOSOPHICAL STUDIES

In chapter eight, Brandon G. Withrow investigates the controversial relationship between grace and works in the authentic first epistle of Clement of Rome, whose thought is representative of a larger stream of early Church Fathers which has, for the last two centuries, largely been branded as legalistic and so foreign to the Pauline gospel. Challenging this widespread opinion as based on anachronistically viewing Clement through Reformation lenses, Withrow insists that Clement's concept of salvation can only be understood against his first-century historical and theological backdrop. First, Withrow demonstrates that Clement was firmly entrenched in a Hellenistic Jewish tradition emphasizing moralism, as evidenced by the parallels between Clement's prayers and Jewish liturgy and the pragmatic manner in which Clement quotes the Septuagint and pseudipigraphal texts. Second, Withrow illustrates that Clement, while not a Stoic, understood Stoicism and freely appealed to Stoic ideas with which his audience would have been familiar to make Christian theological points. In sum, Clement's religio-historical context can best be described as a Second Temple interpretive tradition embracing a diversity of Jewish texts and Greek cultural traditions while simultaneously concerned to iron out their apparent contradictions. When explaining justification to the Corinthians, therefore, Clement works to harmonize two vital truths: genuine Christians must behave in a godly fashion and so perform good works; yet salvation is not based on these works. Due to the intersection of Clement's belief that the Corinthians were genuine Christians with the Corinthians' struggles with hubris, immorality, and schism, Clement naturally underscores the need for humility and obedience in his epistle, citing the faith and hospitality displayed by the Old Testament patriarchs. But this is not done at the expense of making salvation depend on works, for Clement insists that neither the patriarchs nor his believing contemporaries earn renown from their own righteousness, wisdom, or piety; rather, it is through faith that God has justified persons from the beginning of the world. Because divine justification is the wellspring from which good works flow, Clement goes on to assert that our good works do not ultimately belong to us but rather comprise the garments in which God adorns his children.

In chapter nine I propose that the practical thrust of Calvin's doctrine of predestination—to comfort and fortify believers in their salvation and thereby empower them to live righteously—should be reclaimed by the Christian tradition at large. Unfortunately, this motivation is often lost within perennial debates in evangelicalism between the theoretical consequences of Calvinism and Arminianism. In his sermons preached to the Genevan populace, Calvin made little (if any) effort to defend the disputed particulars of how he believed predestination operated; this he reserved for his systematic works and theological treatises. Rather, Calvin focused on the biblical purpose of election and its corollaries for daily life, which exhibit logical independence from his late-Augustinian doctrine of human freedom and therefore may be embraced by subscribers to other predestinary models. In other words, even if one does not agree with Calvin as to the *how* of predestination, one should agree with Calvin as to the *why*. This *why* included showing people that they could never save themselves or act in such a way as to compel God to save them, relieving believers of the anxiety to be good enough to retain the salvation they currently hold, guaranteeing the presence of God's cooperating grace throughout life, and enabling the panoramic perception of God's providence spanning one's past, present, and future. Readily understood and appropriated on a lay level, Calvin's doctrine of predestination fostered a veritable revolution in the morality of the citizens of Geneva, which was then safeguarded through the institution of the Consistory and its antithetical relationship between church discipline and sacramental reception. I further amplify the ethical value of predestination through a case study of the sixteenth-century Huguenot community, which discloses how the implications of this doctrine supplied the Huguenot spiritual life-blood and sustained their existence during the persecutory Wars of Religion. Giving the lie to the thesis that the unconditional nature of Calvinist predestination inevitably spawns worry as to whether believers find themselves among the elect, Huguenot spirituality considered predestination as an exhibition of the love God showers upon believers and his care for their salvation.

In chapter ten, turning to anthropological concerns, I appraise the evidential value for eternal security of the necessary changes in human nature accomplished by the Holy Spirit at the moment of regeneration. Since the Holy Spirit promises to eternally indwell each regenerated believer and seal the believer for the day of redemption by making certain internal changes, I contend that believers can be sure of their salvation by apprehending the Spirit within via the *sensus divinitatis* and by perceiving the reality of those changes in their souls. The tenor of the chapter builds philosophically upon the anthropological categories expounded in the Pauline corpus, where each individual alienated from God is a ψυχικός ἄνθρωπος ("soul-ish human," or a human dominated by the selfish desires of one's own soul) and where each individual in good standing with God is a πνευματικός ἄνθρωπος ("spiritual human," or a human dominated by the Christlike desires of the Holy Spirit). The transformation from a ψυχικός to a πνευματικός ἄνθρωπος cannot be accomplished by human effort, such as religious affiliation or acts of social justice, since no one can alter the fundamental inclination of one's soul. Exclusively the work of the Spirit, I explain the precise nature of the associated changes to the believer's soul and why they effect a habitual harvest of good spiritual fruit, as opposed to the occasional good fruit which the unregenerate may yield. Moreover, these changes infuse the believer with a spectrum of theological virtues, classically summarized in Galatians 5:22–24, sufficient for acting righteously in all circumstances. All in all, the believer is marked as such by citizenship in the Kingdom of God, or adherence to the philosophy of life where God is the ruler over all earthly affairs but, when God rules, he does so as a servant leader who comes up alongside others with unconditional love and expects his followers to do the same.

In chapter eleven, Georg Plasger examines the "negative side" of eternal security or the danger from which believers are secure, namely, God's coming wrath, from the perspectives of Albrecht Ritschl (1822–1889), Martin Luther, and Karl Barth (1886–1968) and then considers each of these perspectives in light of the Pauline doctrine of redemption. Aiming to correct the past clerical abuses of placing inordinate guilt upon perceived transgressors, Ritschl severely de-emphasized God's wrath to the point of objective nonexistence, such that God never exhibits anger and expresses only love toward humanity. Thus, the wrath of God is reduced to a psychological construct whereby individuals who have not yet embraced Christ fail to feel God's ubiquitous love. By contrast, Luther regards God's wrath as real and accounts for it by finding within the divine constitution a behavioral dualism, in which God displays his alien nature of judgment against sinful people but exhibits his true nature of love and mercy toward believers. Luther also felt that believers experience the underbelly of wrath when God progressively destroys the old person of sin or "flesh" still resident within. Synthesizing Ritschl's exclusivity of love with Luther's veridicality of wrath, Barth understands God's wrath as an expression of his love, since God does not direct his wrath toward creatures but toward the demonic forces of futility which threaten to destroy them. The exemplification of God's wrath as a necessary component of his love occurs at the cross, thereby concurring with Luther that wrath only makes sense within a soteriological context. When analyzing the relevant Pauline passages, Plasger discloses that, for believers, the Day of the Lord serves as the vehicle for deliverance from divine wrath and expands the reconciliation implemented through Jesus' death and resurrection to the entire created order. Intriguingly, Plasger finds in Ephesians 5:6 and Colossians 3:6 an admonition against believers placing salvific confidence in their own act of belief rather than perceiving that belief is simply the means for appropriating salvation, a helpful corrective of new religious movements which teach people to "have faith in their faith." According to Plasger, Paul views divine wrath as separation or alienation from God; however, God, in obedience to his covenant, takes such alienation upon himself in the person of Christ to forever set believing sinners free, a model best approximated by the thought of Barth.

Chapter twelve bridges anthropology with philosophy of history, as James W. Bryant illuminates the uniqueness of the Hebraic view of human nature within the spectrum of ancient and modern views and then unfolds the significance of its time-space implementation. Unlike metaphysical dualisms between a good soul and evil body or vice versa, the Hebraic model was notable for its unitary quality, predicated upon the spiritual value of the material world. Since the Hebrews perceived God alone as infinite, humans were taken as finite and therefore mortal in and of themselves; however, everlasting human life followed from the divine attributes of justice and relationality. Employing empirico-logical thought and intuition, the Hebrews surmised that justice demanded the ultimate vindication of righteousness and ultimate retribution against wickedness, which is typically not accomplished during the pre-mortem state. Moreover, they sensed the intrinsic constancy of relationship with God and its character as a link or channel supplying finite beings with the supernatural vitality that could permanently sustain them. Like Holmyard, Bryant finds anticipations of the general resurrection model of the afterlife sprinkled throughout the Hebrew Bible and not simply in later books such as Ezekiel and Daniel. Through his miracle-working ministry consummated at the resurrection, Jesus both validated the reality of, and proved his control over, the general resurrection, marking a new center of history as the start of the transfigured creation to be continually renewed by a Spirit-empowered church until the Day of the Lord. Bryant delineates how the resurrection stands as the pinnacle of a long line of disclosure situations, or historical revelations of God's superintendence over history, which harked back to God's defeat of the Egyptians in the Exodus and gave rise to Israel's linear conception of time. Finally, Bryant postulates an inextricable relationship between Jesus' resurrection and eternal security grounded in the notion of promise. Considering the resurrection as the divine imprimatur of the new covenant, the one overarching vow made between Jesus and believers embodying many component promises, Bryant reasons deductively that God's raising Jesus from the dead vindicates Jesus' promise to forever preserve the covenantal beneficiaries.

Chapter thirteen rounds out the collection with Donna Bowman's inventive perspective, namely, a constructive account of the doctrinal content and usefulness of eternal security within process theology. Bowman begins by outlining the basic tenets of process theology as pertaining to theology proper and divine foreknowledge, a framework within which salvation may be conceived negatively and positively. Negatively, salvation means deliverance from the structures of human life which constrain human becoming or the actualization of human potentialities. Positively, salvation spells the eternal effectiveness of our lives, choices, and endeavors within the perpetual time-space stream which God and humans coinhere. Consequently, the Process mechanism of salvation consists of three interrelated steps. First, God presents each person with a spectrum of prearranged and prevalued possibilities for daily decision-making. Second, God invites each person to share in the creation of the future through creative reordering and adaptive revaluing of those possibilities, an enterprise that God infuses with the value and purpose without which all human endeavors would be doomed to futility. Third, God forever conserves in, and continually presents to, the world each person's value-laden accomplishments, which, in contradistinction to the traditional notion of perpetuity of personal consciousness, forms the Process notion of eternal life. In this system, eternal security amounts to the twofold affirmation that God always upholds the divine promises and that salvation constitutes God's work rather than ours. Bowman points out that such an affirmation exhibits tremendous pedagogical value in conveying the permanent and unswerving divine purpose to cultivate beauty and intensity of feeling through partnership with free creatures, a purpose which God always does everything in God's power to fulfill. Moreover, it reminds us that, although meaningless in and of themselves, our lives are sewn by the divine Weaver as integral threads into the fabric of the world's glorious restoration.

LAUNCHING AN ONGOING SCHOLARLY CONVERSATION

This book makes a number of important contributions to the theological academy. It illuminates the trajectory of eternal security as a significant theological locus throughout the history of the development of Christian doctrine, alongside such classic loci as sin, grace, and revelation, so releasing it from being perceived as exclusively a matter of Reformed interest. Eternal security is a glacier sweeping all eras of Christian thought whose surface has barely been scratched and upon which much fruitful scholarly labor is waiting to be accomplished. To give but a few examples, theological models of eternal security and their social implications during the Patristic and Medieval eras remain to be explored, as well as the psychological effects and lifestyle consequences of belief and disbelief in eternal security among members of modern denominations.

Eternal security is an interpretive prism through which the thought of major individuals and schools can be assessed, thereby opening up fresh readings from historical texts and new constructive possibilities from contemporary theological systems. On the one hand, innovative readings create a mutually beneficial relationship for historians and exegetes, undergoing refinement by engaging Scripture via the hermeneutical circle and unearthing ever-present but previously undiscovered biblical truths and insights. On the other hand, new constructive possibilities serve as grist for the philosophical mill, calling upon philosophers of religion to evaluate their plausibility and, if deemed coherent and valid, to work out their logical infrastructures. For these reasons, these articles and their brothers and sisters in the completed online 2007 edition shed tremendous light on the single most important matter of practical theology in the Christian tradition. Our sincere hope is that this volume expands the scholarly conversation on eternal security recently commenced in *Testamentum Imperium* across the landscape of religious and theological disciplines and builds bridges between Christians of various confessions by facilitating greater awareness of, and respect toward, a multiplicity of positions on our great testament, the assurance of our salvation.

Abbreviations

AB	*Anchor Bible Commentary Series*
BDAG	*A Greek-English Lexicon of the New Testament and Other Early Christian Literature*, 3rd ed.
BECNT	*Baker Exegetical Commentary on the New Testament*
EBC	*The Expositor's Bible Commentary*
EDNT	*Exegetical Dictionary of the New Testament*
JSNTSup	*Journal for the Study of the New Testament Supplement Series*
NAC	*New American Commentary*
NICOT	*New International Commentary on the Old Testament*
NIVAC	*NIV Application Commentary*
REBC	*The Expositor's Bible Commentary, Revised Edition*
TNTC	*Tyndale New Testament Commentaries*
WBC	*Word Biblical Commentary*
WMANT	*Wissenschaftliche Monographien zum alten und neuen Testament*

PART ONE

Biblical and Exegetical Studies

1

The Psalms

Eternal Security and Perseverance

Harold R. Holmyard III

The Psalms speak directly to issues regarding the eternal security and perseverance of believers in just a small portion of their material. Both these doctrines pertain to eternal life, and the psalmists' overwhelming concern was the present life. But many additional passages have suggestive value for these doctrines.

Eternal security teaches that "a person truly saved will never be lost, either by sinning or by ceasing to believe." The maintenance of eternal security is grounded in the perseverance of God. "Perseverance of the saints" is the "teaching that the saints will definitely persevere in the faith, both in belief and in action."[1] God expects a person to persevere or endure to the end if that person is to be saved (Matt 10:22; 24:13; Mark 13:13; Jas 5:11). What follows is a study of psalmic texts that bear directly or indirectly on the doctrines of the believer's eternal security and perseverance.

ETERNAL SECURITY

The approach taken to eternal security will involve a maximization of the possibilities of meaning inherent in the Psalms' wording, given the recognized belief of Israelites in a general resurrection. This belief is apparent not only in OT passages like Dan 12:2–3, Isa 25:7–8, and Isa 26:19, but

1. Arnold Fruchtenbaum, "Perseverance," <http://www.ariel.org/qapersev.html>, accessed April 12, 2008.

in the NT record of OT faith in places like Heb 11:13–22. Accordingly, a method of canonical interpretation sympathetic to belief in resurrection is warranted. When Jesus argued for the reality of resurrection with Sadducees, he derived the doctrine from the words, "I am the God of Abraham, Isaac, and Jacob" (Exod 3:6). The Sadducees might have rejected resurrection because it was not mentioned in the Pentateuch.[2] So Jesus extracted it from the fact that God was not a God of the dead but the living (Matt 22:23–32). Christians have the mind of Christ (1 Cor 2:16), and God the Father and the Holy Spirit can illuminate the implications of Scripture for them (Eph 1:17–18). Readers can obviously apply some Psalms to the topic of eternal security. Other passages are debatable, but the effort will be to observe texts that encourage such a hope.

David wrote Psalm 2 about a future king of Israel ruling over the entire world (v. 8; cf. Acts 4:25). The NT indicates that he wrote with conscious knowledge of a mighty descendant who would follow him and rise from the dead (Acts 2:25–31). Jesus explained that David viewed this Messianic king as his Lord, something not really possible unless they were contemporaries (Matt 22:42–45; Ps 110:1). David may have prophesied of that one here, promising that everyone trusting in him would be blessed (Ps 2:12). If that king would rise from the dead, his subjects like David evidently would too. The NT quotes Ps 2:9 in just such a context (Rev 2:27).

Psalm 4:3 offers the comforting thoughts that the Lord has set apart the godly person for himself and will hear when such a person prays. So he can have peace, trusting in the Lord (vv. 8, 5). The psalm may not look beyond this life, but it is suggestive in that God is likely to preserve what he sets aside for himself.

Psalm 5 speaks of God's destruction of the wicked (vv. 4–6, 10) but, in contrast, prays confidently about believers (vv. 11–12):

> But let all who take refuge in You rejoice;
> let them shout for joy forever.
> May You shelter them,
> and may those who love Your name boast about You.
> For You, Lord, bless the righteous one;
> You surround him with favor like a shield. (HCSB)

2. Josephus, *Antiquities of the Jews*, 18.1.4.

Again, the psalm's horizon may be this world, but it describes God's enduring care.

Psalm 6:5 states, "For there is no remembrance of You in death; in Sheol who will praise You?"[3] "In Sheol, persons were believed to exist in a form of semi-life, at rest, yet not in joy, for they had not the fullness of life which made possible the richness of relationship with the living God."[4] The Jews put their hope in the general resurrection, not in the intermediate state.

Psalm 9 is confident that God will defeat David's enemies (v. 3), uphold David's cause (v. 4), and destroy the wicked (vv. 5–6, 15–17). God is a refuge for the oppressed and does not forsake those who trust in him (vv. 9–10). He will judge the world in righteousness (v. 8) so that the wicked retreat to Sheol and the needy are not forgotten forever (vv. 17–18). These ideas may not require a final judgment but are quite compatible with one.

Psalm 16 is significant for eternal security. While the psalm might concern David's temporal well-being, the apostle Peter, guided by the Holy Spirit, said that David, being a prophet and knowing that God by oath had sworn to him about seating a descendant on his throne, looked ahead and spoke concerning the resurrection of Christ, that he was neither abandoned to Hades nor did his flesh see corruption (Acts 2:30–31). Peter began by saying that David spoke about Christ: "I saw the Lord before me always" (Acts 2:25; Ps 16:8). Does Peter mean that the "I" is David and "the Lord" is Christ? Or does he mean that the "I" is Christ and "the Lord" is the Father? It seems possible that in the original context the "I" was David, who saw the Christ as the "Holy One" of verse 10.[5] Jesus explained that David used "my Lord" in Psalm 110:1 of the Christ (Mark 12:36–37). Because the Holy One would not suffer decay, David would not be abandoned to Sheol (Acts 2:27; Ps 16:10). But when Peter applied the words to Christ (Acts 2:31), he referred both clauses of Ps 16:10 to Christ, because of course Christ was neither abandoned to Sheol nor did he suffer corruption.[6] Other prophets spoke about the death and resurrec-

3. Sheol was the underworld of the dead and was closely associated with the grave. A transliteration of the OT Greek rendering of the word is "Hades."

4. Craigie, *Psalms 1–50*, 93.

5. The demons later called Christ the "holy one" (Luke 4:34). The equivalent term in Hebrew can be applied to other human beings (Deut 33:8; Ps 89:19).

6. It is hard to believe David intended that a psalm of his, speaking in the first person without a clear reference to a Messianic figure, should have no reference at all to David himself.

tion of Christ (1 Pet 1:11), but the first-person form of Psalm 16 suggests that David saw the implications it held regarding his own future state. It seems that David identified his fate with that of his descendant, holding that his descendant's victory over death implied his own. So David did not just have a short-term deliverance from Sheol in mind, but a permanent one. David knew that the Lord upheld his destiny (v. 5). His body rested securely, knowing that God would not leave him in the grave (vv. 9–10). David concluded this psalm with the idea that God had revealed to him the way of life (rather than death). He expected that God would fill him with joy in the divine presence, and with eternal pleasures at God's right hand (v. 11).

Psalm 17:14–15 ends with a powerful contrast between two types of satisfaction:

> With Your hand, Lord, [save me] from men,
> from men of the world,
> whose portion is in this life:
> You fill their bellies with what You have in store,
> their sons are satisfied,
> and they leave their surplus to their children.
> But I will see Your face in righteousness;
> when I awake, I will be satisfied with Your presence. (HCSB)

The term "awake" may refer to waking after death (Isa 26:19; Dan 12:2; Eph 5:14; *cf.* Job 14:12; Jer 51:39, 57). David's enemies have their portion in this life and in material well-being. But David's desire is to see the Lord, even after death. The expectation of seeing God is sometimes an after-death or eschatological expectation (Job 19:26–27; 1 John 3:2). David's portion is the Lord, and it will last beyond this life.

Psalm 18 is about God saving David from his enemies, yet the language is so absolute that for a man with hopes of life after death, the words could be suggestive. David shows such hopes in Psalms 16–17 and here calls God his fortress and deliverer, the horn, or strength, of his salvation (v. 2), who rescues him from sorrows of death and hell (vv. 4–5). God moves heaven and earth to secure safety for one who trusts in him. God shows mercy to his anointed forever, to David and his offspring (v. 50).

Eternal hopes might be present in David's Psalm 21:

> Life he asked of You; You have given it to him,
> length of days forever and ever. . . .

> For You bestow on him blessings forever;
> You make him rejoice with gladness in Your presence. (vv. 4, 6)

David's Psalm 22 has been considered a prophecy of the Messiah through heightened expressions that surpassed David's experience and through his identification with the coming One.[7] Hebrews 2:12 applies Psalm 22:22 to the resurrected Christ. Could Psalm 22 concern death and resurrection? The psalm begins with the words Jesus cited from the cross, "My God, My God, why have You forsaken Me" (Mark 15:34), and verses 8 (*cf.* Matt 27:43), 18 (*cf.* Jn 19:23), and others seem prophetic of his death. The person in 22:1–21 is in mortal danger yet is restored to almost idyllic conditions in 22:22–31. The afflicted eat and are satisfied. The psalmist tells them to let their hearts live forever (v. 26). The entire earth will turn to the Lord as a result of what happened to this figure (v. 27). All who are perishing, who cannot keep themselves alive, will bow before the Lord (v. 29). Since the NT invites us to read the psalm of the resurrected Christ, it certainly could have been the Spirit's intent to speak of the ultimate blessedness of believers in Ps 22:22–31, possibly in the millennium after the first resurrection.

Psalm 23, traditionally the most popular psalm, has given multitudes comfort concerning this life, but it certainly seems to hint beyond this life. If God will be with believers in the "darkest valley," isn't the darkest valley the approach of death (v. 4)? If they will be with God for the length of their days, will that fellowship cease forever when they die (v. 6)? Since God is a loving Shepherd (v. 1), hope arises that death will not be the end.

Psalm 24 presents God as the One who founded and established the earth (vv. 1–2), whose fellowship is to be sought by the believer, with the result of blessing and "vindication from God his Savior" (vv. 3–5). Such a person is among "the generation of those who seek Him." Next the city gates are described as "ancient doors" that should open to let in the "King of glory," who is evidently coming in, perhaps to Jerusalem. The psalm draws a contrast between the life of believers and the God of generations who enters the ancient city gates. If this everlasting God is the believer's Savior, might that salvation not extend beyond this brief life?

Psalm 25 could describe this life only, but verse 3 claims, "No one who hopes in You will be put to shame." Paul took up these words in his

7. Franz Delitzsch, *Psalms*, 3 vols. in 1, in *Commentary on the Old Testament*, by C. F. Keil and F. Delitzsch (Grand Rapids: Eerdmans, 1986), 1:306–7.

hope that he would not be put to shame in anything, but that Christ would be magnified in his body, whether by life or death (Phil 1:20). Isn't it the confidence of resurrection that gives a person certainty that neither life nor death can permanently put him to shame? Christ despised the shame of his death for the joy that was set before him (Heb 12:2). The psalmist fixes his hope on God (vv. 3, 5, 21). God is his merciful and loving Savior (vv. 5–6). He entreats God to forgive his sin, guide him, guard his life, and redeem Israel from all its troubles. God confides in those who fear him, and reveals his covenant to them. The existence of such an atmosphere of trust renders it incongruous for its promises to cease forever at death.

David in Psalm 28:9 asks God to save his people, bless his inheritance, be their Shepherd, and carry them forever. Again, while the words could regard just this present life, they can be suggestive of hope beyond this life. Psalm 29 presents God as awesomely powerful, One who sat enthroned at the Flood and sits enthroned forever. Everyone in God's temple cries, "Glory!" God strengthens his people and blesses them with peace (vv. 9–11). If God is to sit forever as King over his people and they are to be more than a passing show, his power must strengthen them beyond this life.

The Davidic Psalm 30, for the dedication of the temple, is a hopeful personal testimony of deliverance. It ends, "O Lord, my God, I will praise You forever" (v. 12). The word "forever" (*olam*) could mean the foreseeable future, the rest of one's life, but it could suggest limitless time as well. David in Psalm 31:5 wrote words that Jesus cited as he was about to die: "Into Your hand I commit my spirit." Jesus certainly felt David's words had implications beyond the time of death. Such absolute consigning of oneself to God will be rewarded at death by God keeping one's spirit. Psalm 31 is about divine rescue from enemies, and 1 Cor 15:26 assures that the last enemy to be destroyed is death. "The Lord preserves faithful ones" (Ps 31:23).

The Davidic Psalm 32:1–2, quoted in Romans 4:7–8, says that a person is blessed if one's transgression is forgiven, one's sin is covered, and the Lord will not count iniquity against that one. Might this not be a great comfort even for an OT saint? Death was the punishment for sin (Gen 2:17; Rom 6:23), but if God had forgiven one's sin, perhaps death was not to be feared. Paul in Romans 4 applies Psalm 32:1–2 in a context of eternal justification from sin.

Psalm 33 opens the way Psalm 32 closes, with the righteous rejoicing in the Lord for his unfailing love (vv. 1, 5). The Lord's counsel stands forever, his purposes through all generations, and that means the people he chose for his inheritance are blessed (vv. 11–12). While the horizon could be this life, a God who cares that much and has unfailing love may want to preserve his inheritance longer than this life only.

David's Psalm 34 closes with pregnant words: "The Lord redeems the life of His servants, and none of those who take refuge in Him will be condemned" (v. 22). Romans 8:1 teaches that "there is no condemnation for those in Christ Jesus," who redeemed us to God by his blood (Rev 5:9). David did not know those details but expressed full confidence in God by the Spirit. God would deliver him from all his troubles (v. 19). Peter cites Psalm 34:8 with regard to the NT saint, who in Christ has tasted that the Lord is good (1 Pet 2:3).

David shows expansive optimism in Psalm 36:5–9. God's lovingkindness extends to heaven, his faithfulness to the skies. Thus people find refuge in God and drink fully from the wealth of his house and the river of his pleasures. The fountain of life is with God, and they see light in his light. The OT believer is encouraged to think that God will do everything for him that can possibly be done.

In Psalm 37 David contrasts the destinies of the righteous and the wicked. Amid many comforting words David five times repeats that the righteous will inherit the land (vv. 9, 11, 22, 29, 34) while the wicked are cut off (v. 38). The wicked have no future like the righteous do (vv. 37–38). The inheritance of the blameless will endure forever (v. 18); twice David says they will dwell in the land forever (vv. 27, 29). The word translated "land" can also be rendered "earth," and that is how Jesus used it in the Beatitudes, citing Psalm 37:11 in the context of the kingdom of heaven (Mt 5:5). The Beatitudes look beyond this life, so Jesus suggests that gentle souls will inherit eternal life. It is hard to know whether David thought in those terms, but the expression "forever" certainly allows it. Was there any cognitive dissonance about Psalm 37 that might point the OT saint beyond this life? Were the wicked always cut off (Ps 37:34)? The prophets describe wicked men ruling the land, as does Ecclesiastes (Eccl 3:16). Doubtless there were evil old men (Ezek 9:6). But in the context of eternity all transgressors will be destroyed (Ps 37:38), and the gentle will inherit the earth.

David, oppressed by enemies and by sin in Psalm 39, speaks of the fleeting quality of life, his days being a mere handbreadth. The span of his years is as nothing before God. His life is a breath, and he himself a phantom (vv. 4–6). Immediately he adds, "So now, Lord, for what do I hope? My hope is for You." But if David's present life is so little, how can he hope much in God unless that hope extends beyond this life? David later repeats that he is a breath and reminds God that he lives with God as a stranger, an alien, like all his forefathers (vv. 11–12). This language goes back to Abraham (Gen 23:4), who lived with God as an alien in Canaan. The Book of Hebrews explains that all the patriarchs lived this way, having a hope for a permanent home in heaven beyond this life (Heb 11:9–16). It seems natural to expect that David had this hope, too.

In Psalm 41 David prays for healing from sickness in order to requite the enemies that slander him, betray him, and hope for his death (vv. 2–10). He trusts that God will support him because of his integrity and establish him in the divine presence forever (v. 12). The word "forever" (*olam*) might signify "continually," but David uses it again in the next sentence where it describes the Lord as blessed from *olam* to *olam*, "everlasting to everlasting" (v. 13). There is a definite article before it in verse 13 which might change the connotation, but the reader cannot miss the close connection.

Psalms 42–43 can be read together as a single psalm describing David under affliction and away from the temple, longing for God's presence. God was the health of his countenance and his God (42:5, 11; 43:5). He prayed to the God of his life (Ps 42:8). Would God cease to be his God at the time of death?

Psalm 46 might suggest God would not, in its double assurance that "the Lord of armies is with us; the God of Jacob is our refuge" (Ps 46:7, 11). Believers would not fear if the earth changed and the mountains tumbled into the sea. Their quiet confidence was this reality: Yahweh is God (v. 10).

Psalm 49 teaches that the believer can be fearless in days of calamity when the wickedness of his foes surrounds him (v. 5). Their wealth cannot redeem them so that they live forever and do not see the Pit. The price is too high, and they should not even think of buying their way out of God's justice (vv. 8–9). The wise as well as the foolish die, leaving their wealth to others (v. 10). Their grave is their home forever (v. 11). Despite their riches, they are like animals that perish (v. 12). Those who have confidence in themselves, and others who trust in them, are destined for Sheol like sheep; death will be their shepherd (vv. 13–14). In contrast, the believer's confidence is his hope of an afterlife. When the psalmist says the upright will rule over such self-confident ones in the morning (v. 14), morning may refer to the resurrection, since the OT describes resurrection as awakening from sleep (Isa 26:19; Dan 12:2). While the worldly will molder in the grave, far from their earthly mansions, the believer has One who is willing and able to redeem his life from the power of Sheol, for God will take him (vv. 14–15). The word "take" or "receive" points to God's reception of the soul in heaven. Genesis 5:24 states that Enoch walked with God and then no longer existed on earth because God took him. Hebrews 11:5 explains that Enoch was removed so that he would not experience death, because he pleased God. Elijah was "taken" to heaven in a chariot, not seeing death. Both Elijah and the prophetic disciples knew before it happened that God would "take" him (2 Kgs 2:3, 5, 9). So being taken by God symbolized being welcomed into his fellowship after this life. We are not to be in awe when a man becomes rich, for he will take none of his wealth with him at his death (Ps 49:16–17). People praise others during this life for doing well, but worldly people eventually go where their dead ancestors are. They will never see the light (vv. 18–19). People without understanding are like the animals that perish (v. 20). The psalmist contrasted himself with such people. He had understanding to put his trust in the Lord. Since God would redeem him, he was not like the animals. When animals die, that is the end for them, but death would not be the end for the psalmist.

In Psalm 52 David contrasts himself with Doeg the Edomite, who represents evil persons. God will tear down forever someone who boasts of evil, uprooting him from the land of the living (vv. 1, 5). David, on the other hand, is like a green olive tree in the house of God. He will trust in the Lord's lovingkindness forever and ever (v. 8). He will praise the Lord's name forever for what God has done and will hope in that name (v. 9). The psalm could speak of this life only, but the contrast between everlasting ruin and praising the Lord's name forever certainly hints at a permanent distinction in destiny between the evil man and one who trusts in the Lord. The olive tree can live for two thousand years and so could be a symbol of permanence.[8]

8. As agriculturist Geoff Lawton points out, "Individual olive trees have seen not only generations, but entire kingdoms, come and go on the earth's surface" ("About Olives," <http://www.permaculture.org.au/topics/olives.php? page=2>, accessed April 12, 2008).

Psalm 56, composed when David was held by the Philistines in Gath, calls upon God to save him from enemies, particularly the nations. While he has utmost confidence that God will preserve his life, one wonders whether the psalm goes further. Delitzsch felt that the hope of walking before God in the "light of life" in verse 13, contrasted with death and perhaps the darkness of Hades, spoke of more than this present life.[9] Part of the refrain (vv. 4, 11) is: "What can mortal man do to me?"

Psalm 61 seems to peer beyond this life in its last five verses. David desired to dwell in God's tent for ages, to take refuge in the shelter of his wings (v. 4). For God had heard his vows and had given him the heritage of those who fear his name (v. 5). David asked that God add days to his life, increasing his years to span generation after generation (v. 6). He wished to sit before God forever and asked God to appoint lovingkindness and truth to guard him (v. 7). Then he would sing praise to God's name forever, paying his vows day by day (v. 8). What this heritage comprised is uncertain, and one can think of the land of Israel, since David wrote "from the ends of the earth" (v. 2). But possibly David considered his God-fearing forefathers, who were heirs of eternal promises (Heb 11:8–16, 39–40). Christians are heirs of God, too, the expectation being eternal glorification (Rom 8:17). Such a state would enable David to sit before God forever (Ps 61:7).

Psalm 62 has a refrain that only in God is there rest for David's soul, for his salvation and hope come from him (vv. 1, 5). "He alone is my rock and salvation. He is my fortress; I will not be greatly shaken" (v. 2; *cf.* v. 6). David asserts that people are only a breath and that one should not set one's heart on riches (vv. 9–10). God will reward a person according to his work (v. 12). Since in this life we do not necessarily see everyone rewarded this way, one thinks of an equitable judgment beyond this life.

In Psalm 63:3 David asserts that God's love is better than life. But isn't God's love a part of his life? So how can David make this distinction unless he can separate God's love from life? David could do that if he envisioned God's love for him continuing after the end of his physical life.

Psalm 71 is keenly aware of the issues of aging. The psalmist still requires protection from enemies and depends on the Lord. He asks God not to cast him away at the time of old age or abandon him when his strength is gone (v. 9). Though he realizes that death must come (v. 18), he will

9. Delitzsch, *Psalms*, 2:171.

"continually have hope" and will praise God more and more, telling of his righteousness and salvation, though he does not know the sum of them (vv. 14–15). God will bring him up again from the depths of the earth (v. 20). This person, whom God has redeemed, will sing for joy (v. 23). The author may have spoken of earthly troubles and rescue in verse 20. But since he was cognizant of eventual death, perhaps his hope extended so far as to be brought up from the earth's depths. He may have mentioned not knowing the full measure of God's salvation (vv. 14–15) partly because he believed there was more to it than his experience in this life.

Psalm 73:16–28 is one of the clear passages about the believer's confidence of eternal life. The psalmist began with his envy of the prosperity of the wicked (vv. 3–12). By comparison, he felt his godliness had no reward (vv. 13–15). Yet in God's sanctuary he realized that wicked people had no future except ruin (vv. 16–20). Fortunately, he was always with the Lord, despite his senseless attitude (vv. 21–23). God guided him with his counsel, and "afterward you will take me into glory" (v. 24, NIV). Or one might read the last words as "take me up in glory" (HCSB). The Hebrew can also be understood as "and after glory You will take me," but the Masoretic reading tradition, which may date to the first centuries CE, isolates "afterward" and joins "glory" with the verb. So "glory" must function adverbially as the place to which (NIV), or the manner in which (HCSB), God would take the man. And "afterward" must contrast with this present life, in which God guided the psalmist with his counsel. We have seen at Psalm 17 that God's taking a person can involve receiving him into fellowship after this life. The psalmist had no one in heaven but God and desired no one on earth besides him (Ps 73:25). This thought can distinguish heaven and earth as different places where he could be. His heart and flesh might fail, but God would be the strength of his heart and his portion forever (v. 26). The stark juxtaposition of his heart failing but God nonetheless being its strength implies a wordplay. The heart was not only the physical organ but the central part of a human. God would be the strength of his being after its physical end. The psalmist evidently looked beyond his earthly life to an eternal destiny, or portion, with God. The author closed by distinguishing two destinies: inevitable destruction for those far away from and unfaithful to God versus goodness experienced by one close to God who had made God his refuge (v. 27). The contrast shows that all believers will not perish since they have a refuge from destruction.

Psalms 49 and 73 seem to be plain expressions of an assurance of life beyond the grave for one who trusts in God. These explicit affirmations indicate the presence of this hope within worshiping Israel. In view of all that Scripture communicates, they do not seem isolated convictions. Therefore, many other psalms that may not deal with this subject directly might allude to it less directly or assume it. In other words, it was probably a shared hope among OT believers even if we find only scattered direct expressions of it.

Psalm 86:12b–13 contains a typical but ambiguous expression:

> I will honor Your name forever,
> for Your lovingkindness towards me is great,
> and You have delivered my life from Sheol beneath.

Does the psalmist by "forever" simply refer to the rest of his life? Does the deliverance from Sheol only indicate a temporal rescue from imminent death? One response is that the trust of the writer in God is so absolute that it does not seem to find death as a looming end to everything.

But Psalm 88 might seem to contradict any limitless confidence. Heman finds himself near Sheol (v. 3). He is regarded as one soon to go to the Pit (v. 4). He is like the slain in the grave "whom You no longer remember and who are cut off from Your strength" (v. 5). Heman bemoans his afflicted state, saying (vv. 10–12):

> Will you do wonders for the dead?
> Will the shades arise to praise You? Selah
> Will Your lovingkindness be recounted in the grave,
> or Your faithfulness in Abaddon?[10]
> Will Your wonders be known in the darkness,
> or Your rightousness in a land of oblivion?

Heman pleads that he not die, and his words represent a typical perspective on Sheol. It seems that the state of the righteous dead was different before the cross. Jesus described them as being in Abraham's bosom, which may have been a compartment of Sheol (Luke 16:22).[11] But the hope of the OT saint was resurrection. Although the dead were temporarily inactive and even insignificant, this would not always be the case. The righteous dead

10. The Hebrew word transliterated as Abaddon means "destruction" and was another name for the realm of the dead.

11. Browning, *A Dictionary of the Bible*, *s.v.* "Abraham's Bosom."

would wake up from their sleep. So Heman's downcast words throw no doubt on the hopeful expectations of so many psalms.

Psalm 89, written by Ethan, uses "forever" twice within two verses in a way suggesting the meaning might be the same in both.[12] We have seen David's hope in an afterlife. Verse 28 quotes God saying that he will maintain his love to David forever; his covenant with David is sure. The Lord adds that he will establish David's line forever, his throne as long as heaven endures (v. 29). God distinguishes between David and his line. If David's line will literally be established forever, then perhaps God will literally maintain his lovingkindness to David personally forever.

Psalm 92 compares the fate of evildoers with that of the righteous. The brutish man does not understand that the wicked spring up like grass only to be destroyed forever, while God is exalted forever (vv. 6–8). God's enemies will perish (v. 9), but he will exalt the psalmist's horn, that is, increase his power (v. 10). The same root word for "exalt" is used of God and the psalmist. The righteous, in contrast to the wicked, will spring up like a palm tree or cedar (v. 12). Transitory grass is unlike the enduring palm or cedar. The righteous will bear fruit even in old age to show that the Lord is upright. The circumstances could pertain only to this life, but the eternal perishing of the wicked hints at an eternal flourishing for the righteous.

The first part of Psalm 103 (vv. 1–9) recounts all the Lord's benefits as a motive for blessing him. The first listed is forgiveness of iniquities. He redeems lives from destruction and crowns them with lovingkindness and mercy (vv. 3–4). David returns to the initial benefit to explain that the Lord has not compensated believers according to their sins and iniquities, for his mercy to them is as great as heaven is high above the earth (vv. 10–11). The transgressions are as far removed from them as the east is from the west (v. 12). David next speaks of the Lord's fatherly pity for those who fear him, based on his knowledge of our bodies, that they are dust (vv. 13–14). Dust connotes perishing because the curse on sin was that as humanity came from the dust, so humanity would return to it (Gen 3:19). Each human flourishes like grass or a flower. A wind passes over it, and it is gone (Ps 103:15–16). Grass is another familiar image for a human's short-lived existence (Pss 90:5; 92:7; 129:6; Isa 40:6–7). Against these images of fleeting life, David says that God's lovingkindness is from

12. The terms for "forever" in the two verses are different but synonymous.

everlasting to everlasting towards those who fear him, and to children's children (Ps 103:17). David might only contrast God's everlasting kindness with the brief lives of human beings. Yet his stress on the removal of sin and its consequences (vv. 3–4, 10–12), the greatness of God's mercies, the impermanent nature of this present life, and the promise of everlasting lovingkindness for those who fear God encourages hope that he may ultimately set aside death as sin's punishment for forgiven believers.

Jesus' interpretation of Psalm 110:1 reveals complex meanings in OT prophecy, suggesting the complexity that may lie beneath the surface elsewhere. Jesus said that here David by the Spirit called the Messiah his Lord (Matt 22:43–45; Mark 12:35–37; Luke 20:41–44):

> The Lord said to my Lord, "Sit as My right hand
> Until I make your enemies a footstool for Your feet."

David saw a human figure in heaven and called him his Lord. Psalm 110:4 adds that the Lord had sworn that this person would be a priest forever after the order of Melchizedek. We know that the fulfillment is in Jesus Christ, who is a priest forever (Heb 7:11–28). The apostle Peter showed from Psalm 16:8–11 (Acts 2:25–31) and Psalm 132:11 (Acts 2:30) that David had supernatural revelation about the future and the Messiah. Peter continued by citing Psalm 110:1 as speech about the ascension of Christ (Acts 2:34). It seems natural to conclude that David took such revelation as a partial basis for confidence that the Lord would not abandon him to the grave (Ps 16:10).

The first four verses of Psalm 118, and the last verse, repeat that the love of the Lord endures forever. Israel was to give thanks to God because he was good and his love endured forever. This inspires all the more thanksgiving if eternal love is relevant for individuals, which the NT proves to be the case. The OT saints could have rejoiced in this fact by faith.

The last two verses of Psalm 121 (vv. 7–8) suggest such rejoicing:

> The Lord will guard you from all evil; He will guard your life.
> The Lord will guard your going out and coming in, from now until forever.

Psalm 133:3 also suggests such rejoicing. In speaking of Mount Zion, the psalmist asserts: "For there the Lord commanded His blessing, life forevermore."

The phrase "His love is forever" occurs 34 times in the Psalms, 26 times in Psalm 136 alone. It would be an important idea for earth even if life ended in the grave, but it is so much more powerful in the reality that life continues beyond the grave. The believers in Israel were to sing Psalm 136 because the eternal love of God was very pertinent to them, a matter for rejoicing.

David in the last verse of Psalm 138 (v. 8) certainly applies to himself the words about the Lord's love being eternal:

> The Lord will fulfill [His purpose] for me.
> Lord, Your lovingkindness is forever;
> Do not forsake the work of Your hands.

On the basis of God's eternal love, David pleads with the Lord not to forsake him.

The last verse of Psalm 139 (v. 24) evokes similar thoughts. David pleads:

> See if there is any offensive way in me,
> And guide me in the everlasting way.

David uses comparable language in Psalm 145:1–2:

> I will exalt You, My God the King,
> And I will bless Your name forever and ever.
> Every day I will bless You
> And praise Your name forever and ever.

David goes on to say that God's kingdom is an everlasting one (v. 13), and he stresses God's love and care for each believer (vv. 18–20). David closes the psalm by exhorting every creature to praise his holy name forever and ever (v. 21). In light of NT truth, it is best not to limit these many expressions to hyperbolic affirmations of merely temporal care. The one who trusts God should do so on the basis of the fact that his love endures forever and so will not leave the believer even at the time of death.

PERSEVERANCE

The ancient Israelites did not grapple with exactly the same theological issues that concern us. The NT speaks of every believer's need to "stand firm" or "endure" in their faith throughout life (e.g. Matt 10:22; 24:13; Mark 13:3; 2 Tim 2:12; Rev 3:10). The OT may not frame a requirement in the same terms, but OT saints would have understood that they could never outlive the obligation to love the Lord with all their heart, mind, and strength (Deut 6:5). Their duty was to serve Yahweh. Many delighted in the prospect, declaring their heart's loyalty to God.

The Psalms record their various life challenges and display their tenacious faith in counting on God to answer prayer, rescue them, and provide for them. While the Psalms may not declare explicitly that God's people will maintain their faith until the day they die, the psalmists' attitudes and their trust in the Lord exhibit a faith that the worst trials were unable to eradicate. The Psalms show that those who truly trust God will do so no matter what problems they face.

Psalm 1 does not amount to a general statement of perseverance but underscores that the blessed person is defined by particular actions. Somebody who does not avoid wickedness (v. 1) or delight in God's word (v. 2) cannot take assurance from the psalm. But one with those qualities can be sure of persevering. His leaf will not wither (v. 3), unlike the ungodly, who are like chaff driven by the wind (v. 4). Chaff is associated with divine judgment in the Bible.[13] Although the ungodly will perish, God knows the righteous, who by implication will not perish (v. 6). Being known by God is a characteristic of the saved as opposed to the lost.[14]

Unfortunately, many psalms do not express convictions about believers in general. Often David or somebody else expresses what he trusts God will do for him personally. God answers according to one's faith (Matt 9:29), yet since he does not show partiality (Jas 3:17; Acts 10:34; Rom 2:11), any Israelite of like faith could potentially have counted on the same divine help as David hoped to receive.

Psalm 3, though written by David, expresses many thoughts that any Israelite could have experienced. It asserts (v. 8):

> Salvation belongs to the Lord; Your blessing is upon Your people.

The context concerns temporal danger and rescue, and the NT concept of spiritual salvation evidently developed from this practical use of the term "salvation." David calls God a shield, sustainer, and deliverer, who answers prayer. The psalmists attribute many such qualities to God, which naturally suggest that the believer will stand his ground throughout this

13. Job 21:18; Ps 35:5; Isa 5:24; 17:13; 29:5; 33:11; 41:15; Dan 2:35; Hos 13:3; Zeph 2:2; Matt 3:12.

14. Gen 18:19; Exod 33:17; Matt 7:23; 25:12; Luke 13:25, 27; 2 Tim 2:19.

life. Although in NT terms they had to "endure," Israelite psalmists did not consider doing this in their own strength but depended on the presence and power of Yahweh.

David in Psalm 6 asks God not to rebuke or discipline him in divine anger and wrath but to be gracious. He trusts that God will answer his supplication and save him because of his unfailing love (vv. 1–2, 4, 9–10). So his consciousness of sin did not dampen his confidence in God.

David claims that God saves those whose hearts are upright (Ps 7:10) and judges the wicked (vv. 11–16). The king prays for God to save him (7:1) and expects God to judge him according to his righteousness and integrity (7:8). David saw perseverance as a matter involving full participation by the believer.

Psalm 10 describes the evil man in detail, giving assurance that God is aware of him and will ultimately judge him. He hears and strengthens the humble (v. 17). Such sentiments encourage believers to persevere, since God will be with them.

Psalm 11:7 promises that the Lord keeps his eye on the upright person. Verses 1 and 7 together suggest that one perseveres in the face of threat by trusting God to see and come to one's aid. Intervening verses describe God's ultimate defeat of the enemy.

Psalm 12 promises divine protection to godly persons when oppressed by enemies. God sets them in safety from foes (v. 5), keeping and preserving them (v. 7). David counts on God's mercy and salvation despite his foes (Ps 13:4–5), confident that God will deal well with him (13:6). For God is with the righteous as a refuge for the afflicted (Ps 14:5–6).

Psalm 15 gives a list of things a righteous person does. Such a person will never be shaken in life (Ps 15:5). David in Psalm 16:1 asks God to keep him safe on the basis that he takes refuge in God. Conversely, he trusted that because God was at his right hand, he would never be shaken (v. 8).

Psalm 17:4–5 suggests that the believer's confidence in persevering will be steady as he applies God's word to his life. It is by this word that David kept watch to avoid the ways of the violent. So his steps held to God's paths; his feet did not slip. Psalm 18 likewise shows that one keeps the Lord's ways by attention to his laws and decrees (vv. 21–23), and that God rewards such faithfulness with faithfulness on his part (vv. 24–26). Believers call for God's help (v. 6) when enemies are too powerful (v. 17), and the Lord saves those who humbly trust him (v. 27). It is he who gives them strength to fight life's battles (vv. 32–42).

Psalm 19:7–11 stresses the same value of God's word for the believer's perseverance in the faith, recounting how it revives and instructs, bringing joy and light. It creates a reverence towards God that lasts forever, and it is full of truth and righteousness. It is the most precious and sweet commodity, giving warning to God's servants. Obedience is richly rewarded.

Psalm 20:7–8 claims that those who trust in this world will be brought to their knees and fall, while those who trust in the Lord will rise and stand firm. Psalm 22 is a testimony that God does not abandon his own in the worst of circumstances. He does not disdain a believer's suffering or hide from him but responds to his cry for help (v. 24). Psalm 23 indicates that the Lord is with the trusting one in the darkest circumstances; she or he will always dwell with the Lord (vv. 4, 6).

Psalm 25, written by someone struggling with sin (vv. 7, 18), nevertheless declares that the person who fears the Lord will spend days in prosperity (vv. 12–13). The author's confidence of persevering is based on the Lord's goodness, which leads God personally to instruct sinners (vv. 8, 12), guiding the humble in his ways, which are loving and faithful for those who keep them (vv. 9–10). Psalm 26 shows that perseverance involves an active obedience on the part of the believer.

David in Psalm 27 expresses confidence no matter what foes he may face (vv. 2–3, 6):

> For he will conceal me in His shelter in the day of adversity;
> He will hide me under the cover of his tent;
> He will set me high on a rock (v. 5, HCSB).

Yet he continually prays to God that this be true in his case (vv. 4, 7–9, 11–12). In Psalm 28 he says that his heart trusts in the Lord, and he is helped, adding that the Lord is the strength of his people (vv. 7–8). Psalm 29 glorifies the Lord's power and closes by repeating this idea that the Lord gives strength to his people (v. 11).

Psalm 30 is a testimony of God's deliverance that invites all saints to praise God because his anger lasts only for a moment but his favor for a lifetime (vv. 4–5). The implication is that all saints can hope for such deliverance and ability to persevere when they call on God.

Psalm 31 is like Psalm 27 in its prayerful confidence of deliverance despite difficult circumstances. David believes that God will hide him in his shelter from human troubles (31:20; 27:5). Persevering is often tough, but God preserves the faithful (Ps 31:23).

Psalm 32 again describes God as a hiding place for David, protecting him from adversity, surrounding him with songs of deliverance (v. 7). God's unfailing love surrounds the person who trusts in him, inspiring the righteous to rejoice (vv. 10–11). Sin should not prevent one from persevering, since the Lord is willing to forgive it (vv. 1–5).

Psalm 33 teaches that God considers everything earthlings do (v. 15), and that his eyes are on those who fear him and hope in his unfailing love to deliver them from death and preserve them in famine (vv. 18–19). So perseverance entails waiting on the Lord, the believer's help and shield (v. 20). Psalm 34 also shows the Lord's eyes on the righteous (v. 15). The psalm assures them that they will persevere because of all God will do for them. He answers prayer; he delivers from fear, a crushed spirit, trouble, and enemies; and he gives joy, food, and every good thing.

Psalm 35 is clear that human enemies cannot prevent the saints' perseverance because God will defeat enemies and rescue the poor from those too strong for them. The psalm is a prayer for such deliverance. Psalm 36 speaks of God's love, faithfulness, righteousness, and justice as essentially limitless and as preserving humanity. God's unfailing love is precious (vv. 5–7). Since his love reaches heaven and is unfailing, there is no situation where it will not reach his people.

Psalm 37 promises that for those who trust him, God will make righteousness and justice shine as bright as the noonday sun (vv. 5–6). The Lord upholds the righteous (v. 17). They will not be put to shame in times of adversity (v. 19). The Lord steadies the steps of those with whom he is pleased. Such people will not fall, for God holds their hands (vv. 23–24). He loves the upright and will not forsake those faithful to him (v. 28). He helps them and delivers them (v. 40). The whole psalm involves such assurances.

Psalm 38 concerns David troubled by sin and guilt (vv. 4, 18), yet he is certain that God will answer his prayer (v. 15). He has faith to pray to the Lord even when being disciplined for sin (vv. 8–9). For according to Psalm 40, a person who trusts in the Lord is blessed (v. 4), despite trouble due to sin (v. 12). Notwithstanding David's sin (Ps 41:4), God upheld him because of his integrity (v. 12). Even when David feels rejected by God under adversity (Pss 42:7, 9; 43:2), he trusts that he will again be able to praise God as his Savior (Pss 42:5, 8, 11; 43:3–5).

God made a striking promise regarding perseverance in Psalm 50:15, telling OT believers that they should call on him in a day of trouble and he would deliver them. As a result, they would honor him in the testimony of their deliverance.

Psalm 51:17 declares, "You will not despise a broken and crushed heart, God." David has faith that God will receive his repentance and forgive him. David had committed terrible sin in adultery (Ps 51 superscription) but still had this assurance, so there is no reason why sin should prevent believers from persevering.

Psalm 52 shows that David, who is an example, intends to trust in the Lord's lovingkindness forever and ever (v. 8). Someone with that attitude will persevere. Psalm 53 implies that victory will eventually come to God's people. David asserted that surely God was his help; the Lord was the One who sustained him (Ps 54:4). Every believer can have this confidence.

In Psalm 55:22 David writes out of much experience in being rescued by God. He tells the righteous person to fling his burden on the Lord because God will sustain him. God will never allow the righteous person to be shaken. "Shaken" here implies a disastrous instability bringing collapse. David, taken captive by an enemy (Ps 56 superscription), three times repeats that he trusts, or will trust, in the Lord (Ps 56:3–4, 11). Similarly, when on the run from Saul (Ps 57 superscription), David's heart was steadfast (v. 7) because he knew that the Lord worked on his behalf (v. 2). When Saul's men tried to kill him (Ps 59 superscription), David watched for the Lord to act and considered God his strength, fortress, and shield (vv. 9, 11, 16–17). Facing enemies in Psalm 62, David shows a spirit of perseverance by repeating four times that God is the source of his salvation (vv. 1–2, 6–7).

David regularly praises God and expects that at the end of his ordeal he will praise God further, rejoice, and sing to his name (Ps 63:3–7, 11). Another concept assisting perseverance is deep appreciation of God's grandeur and his provision of what humanity needs (Psalm 65). The testimonies of those God has rescued are an encouragement (Ps 66:5–6, 9–20). So is a conviction of his sovereignty (Ps 67:4).

Psalm 68 conveys an overwhelming sense of God's victorious greatness operative on behalf of his people. The final verse intones that "the God of Israel gives power and strength to His people" (v. 35). With such a God on one's side, defeat seems out of the question, for God listens to the needy (Ps 69:33).

Psalm 70:4 is a typical psalmic sentiment: "May all who seek You rejoice and be glad in You. May those who love Your salvation continually say, 'Let God be exalted.'" So prevalent are ideas like this that one feels they are the true expectation for saints. This is what God intends and what believers should anticipate.

Characteristic of persevering believers is their faith that God will bring them out of trouble. The psalmist says (Ps 71:20):

> Although You have shown me many and bitter troubles,
> You will again revive me,
> And from the depths of the earth You will again bring me up.

Psalm 73:1 testifies that God is good to those who are pure in heart. In their troubles believers remember that their God is the mighty Creator of the world (Ps 74:16–17). They rejoice that his name, which implies God himself, is near (Ps 75:1). God promises that the horns of the righteous will be lifted up (Ps 75:10), which implies being victorious. God is a mighty warrior on his people's behalf (Psalm 76). In their distress they remember his long history of acting for their deliverance (Pss 77:5–20; 83:9–12). They take warning from the many who have failed to believe despite God's marvels (Ps 78). They note that tribulation is often God's discipline (Pss 79–82, 89–90).

Psalm 84 expresses the faith of a persevering believer who considers a person "blessed" "whose strength is in You," and "who trusts in You" (vv. 5, 12). He characterizes God as a "sun and a shield" who "grants favor and honor" and withholds nothing good from those who live with integrity" (v. 11). Psalm 85 adds that "He promises peace to his people" (v. 8), and "His salvation is near to those who fear Him" (v. 9). Also associated with God are love, faithfulness, and righteousness (v. 10).

The Lord declared his character to Moses (Exod 34:6), and the psalmist describes God in exactly the same terms, having learned from experience that he is "a compassionate and gracious God, longsuffering and abounding in love and truth" (Ps 86:15).

Psalm 91 gives assurance to one struggling to persevere. The psalmist had learned that God protects his people and elevates them to ultimate success. Many statements reflect God's actions or promises to believers according to the Mosaic covenant.[15] The repeatedly assuring promises

15. *Cf.* God as a refuge (Ps 91:2; Deut 33:27); God's sheltering wings (Ps 91:4; Exod 19:4); protection from hostile weapons (Ps 91:5; Lev 26:6); not being afraid (Ps 91:5; Lev

resemble even stronger new covenant promises of God's unfailing love (*e.g.* Rom 8:28–39).

Psalm 92:12–15 expects the righteous to persevere, flourishing like a palm tree or cedar, still bearing bear fruit in old age, fresh and green. They will magnify the Lord. They have a vision of the majestic, eternal God (Ps 93), of the God who avenges wickedness to rescue his people (Ps 94). They realize he is the Creator who must be obeyed (Ps 95), the one true God and Judge over all the earth (Ps 96). Other gods are idols, while Yahweh controls all the forces of nature and guards his faithful ones (Ps 97). All creation should sing to One who reveals his salvation and righteousness (Ps 98). The nations should worship the One who is holy (Ps 99:3, 5, 9), loving, and good (Ps 100).

Psalm 101, though from a king's perspective, outlines a lifestyle that will honor the Lord. A genuine believer does not completely despair, no matter how destitute he or his nation may be (Ps 102). He counts his blessings, naming them one by one, remembering to praise the Lord (Ps 103). The believer meditates on God's revelation of himself in all aspects of the natural world he created (Ps 104).

Psalms 105–106 show the heart of the Israelite faith. It was fixed on a God who had worked among a chosen people through the centuries. Psalm 107 expands the range of his care to all humanity. David focuses on this universal God in Psalm 108, only at the end mentioning Israel's military defeats. When David does concentrate on his predicament, it is with serene confidence that the Lord will punish murderous enemies and rescue the needy righteous (Ps 109:29, 31).

Psalm 110 is a prophetic psalm about God's empowerment of his king, whom the NT identifies as Christ Jesus (Mark 12:35–37; Acts 2:34–35; Heb 1:13). So the springs of David's faith ran deep into mysteries of the future.

Each statement of Psalm 111 magnifies some aspect of the Lord. Each statement of Psalm 112 depicts some blessing that comes to a righteous man who trusts in the Lord. God stoops from heaven to assist the lowliest people (Ps 113). His care for Israel shook nature (Ps 114). This people praised the God who constituted its help and shield (Ps 115).

26:5); freedom from disease (Ps 91:6; Deut 7:15); one overcoming a thousand (Ps 91:7; Deut 32:30); no plague (Ps 91:10; Exod 12:13); angels guarding in the way (Ps 91:11; Exod 23:20); protection from wild beasts (Ps 91:13; Lev 26:6); God setting believers on high (Ps 91:14; Deut 28:1); God delivering believers (Ps 91:15; Deut 23:14); provision of long life (Ps 91:16; Deut 5:33).

The testimony of one person whom God has helped can encourage all his people (Ps 116). Israel praises a God of mercy and truth (Ps 117). Psalm 118, another personal testimony of divine deliverance, stresses that God works through his people and that trust in God is better than any human source of help (Ps 118:8–9).

Psalm 119 contains 176 verses in honor of God and his word. Almost every verse mentions God's word in some way. This psalm displays the importance of meditating on divine revelation. The psalmist felt it was vital to his life.

Psalms 120–134 are "songs of ascent," generally short, that worshipers might sing on their way to Zion for the annual religious festivals. God rescues his own from those who destructively speak evil (Ps 120). He watches to guard them from all harm (Ps 121). Jerusalem symbolized God's presence (Ps 122), which is now always with Christians (John 4:21–24). Believers constantly look to Yahweh for mercy (Ps 123), for he is a God of deliverances (Ps 124), surrounding his people with protection (Ps 125). He brings joy out of sorrow (Ps 126), enables one to build a meaningful life (Ps 127), and blesses those who fear him (Ps 128). He judges those who assault believers (Ps 129); our hope should be in him (Ps 130). Even one who is a king can have a childlike faith (Ps 131). Associated with Jerusalem are the Davidic promises, which God will keep, as he keeps all his promises (Ps 132). He unites believers (Ps 133) and blesses his servants (Ps 134).

Psalm 135 encourages the faithful of every generation to praise the Lord for his goodness and greatness (vv. 3–5). He vindicates his people and has compassion on his servants (v. 14). Psalm 136 enumerates the many facets of his eternal love, and Psalm 137 conveys the sad loss of blessing under judgment. Psalms 138 and 139 are respectively David's personal testimony of God's praiseworthiness and his acknowledgement of God's sovereign supervision over his life.

The persevering saint has confidence that God will protect him from evil men (Pss 140, 142–44) and evil temptations (Ps 141). Psalms 145–50 call for praise of the Lord and catalogue many reasons for it. The attitude of the psalmists is almost uniformly one of active trust in God's love and saving power. This belief in a living relationship with God is met by proofs of God's deliverance, so the Psalter calls all believers to have the same attitude.

2

"What My Father Has Given Me"

Believers as God's Gift in the Gospel of John

J. Ramsey Michaels

The text most commonly introduced in support of the so-called "security of the believer," or "perseverance of the saints," is John 10:28–30. There Jesus speaks about those whom he calls his "sheep," defined as those who, he says, "hear my voice, and I know them and they follow me" (v. 27). He then adds, "And I give to them eternal life, and they will never perish. No one will snatch them out of my hand. What my Father has given me is greater than all else, and no one can snatch it out of the Father's hand. The Father and I are one" (vv. 28–30, NRSV; see also the NIV margin, the Good News Bible, and Richmond Lattimore's translation).

The more familiar reading of John 10:29 begins differently. Instead of "What my Father has given me is greater than all else," the text is usually remembered as "My Father, who has given them to me, is greater than all" (NIV, and most English versions). The notion that God the Father is "greater than all" is surely true in any Jewish or Christian context, and the Greek text acknowledges this by placing "my Father" first in the sentence. But in a number of the earliest and most reliable Greek manuscripts, Latin versions, and patristic quotations, the word for "greater" (μεῖζον) and the pronoun that goes with it (ὅ) are neuter, and therefore cannot refer to "Father," which is masculine. Thus, a literal translation of the Greek text would be, "My Father, that which he has given to me is greater than all, and no one can snatch [it] out of the Father's hand."[1] The more common reading "My Father who has given them to me, is greater than all" is by far the "easier" reading, so "easy" in fact that it would seem to go without saying. Because it was the reading of the majority of later Greek manuscripts from the Byzantine and medieval periods, it became part of the King James Version and most subsequent English versions.[2] But a basic rule of textual criticism is that the more "difficult" reading (unless it makes no sense at all) is more likely to be original than a smooth or "easy" reading. That is, would early scribes have changed "My Father . . . is greater than all" (which makes perfect sense) to "What my Father has given me is greater than all" (which raises as many questions as it answers)? It is easier to imagine a change in the opposite direction, clarifying a pronouncement that on the face of it seems hard to understand.[3]

The point of the pronouncement, then, is not simply that God the Father is "greater than all," but that because the Giver is "greater than all," the "gift" (that is, "what he has given") is "greater than all" as well. The context makes it clear that the Father's "gift" consists of Jesus' "sheep," who "hear his voice," whom he knows and who follow him (see v. 27)—in short, all who believe. They are secure in Jesus' hand because they were first of all secure in the Father's hand, and, as he concludes, "I and the Father are one" (v. 30). The neuter singular signals that they are being viewed corporately, as "that which" the Father has given. The text as a whole views them both individually ("no one will snatch *them* out of my hand," v. 28),

1. This reading (that of the NRSV) is the reading of B (Vaticanus, from the fourth century, our best single witness to the Greek text of the New Testament), plus a number of old Latin versions and the Latin Vulgate, the Bohairic Coptic version, and a number of the church fathers, including Tertullian, Hilary, Ambrose, Jerome, and Augustine. Certain other very early manuscripts (including the fourth century Codex Sinaiticus, or א, as well as the slightly later manuscripts L, W, and Ψ have the neuter pronoun (ὅ), yet with a masculine adjective for "greater" (μείζων), which Bruce Metzger calls "impossible Greek" that "cannot be construed" (*Textual Commentary on the Greek New Testament*, 232). This reading, confused though it may be, confirms the reference not only to the Father as Giver but to a neuter singular "gift" that the Father has given to the Son.

2. In addition to the majority of later manuscripts, however, this reading has very early support in one ancient papyrus (P^{66}, from the third century), and a few other somewhat later manuscripts (including A, Θ, and a later scribal corrector of B).

3. Metzger, *Textual Commentary*, 232.

and corporately ("no one can snatch [*it*][4] out of my Father's hand"—"it" referring to the Christian community as a single entity, v. 29).

This classic promise of "eternal security" must be set in a wider context within John's Gospel. The principle on which it is based comes first from the lips of John the Baptist, who, when his disciples reminded him that Jesus was baptizing and that "everyone is coming to him" (John 3:26), replied: "A person can receive nothing unless it is given him from heaven" (3:27). The broad principle he expressed has a variety of applications. First of all, he meant that *he, John*, could receive only what God gave him, for he added, "You yourselves can testify that for me that I said I am not the Christ, but that I am sent on ahead of him" (3:28). But more than that, it implied that *even Jesus* could receive only what God the Father gave him "from heaven." If Jesus was baptizing, and people were flocking to him in great numbers, it was because God wanted it so, and it was not John's place to question God. Moreover, the principle applies to *everyone*, for no one can receive salvation or eternal life unless God gives it. As Paul would later ask the Corinthians, "What do you have that you did not receive?" (1 Cor 4:7).

Three chapters later, Jesus himself endorses exactly the same principle: "*All that the Father gives me* will come to me, and the person who comes to me I will never cast out" (6:37, italics added). The same interplay evident in John 10:29 between the corporate and individual nature of Christian salvation is in play here as well. "All" in Greek (πᾶν) is neuter and singular (literally "everything"), referring to all believers *corporately*, while the participle, "the person who comes" (ὁ ἐρχόμενος) is masculine singular, focusing on *individuals* who "come to Jesus" in the sense of believing in him, or giving him their allegiance. God decides who they are, for they are God the Father's gift to Jesus, and they prove it precisely by "coming to him." Jesus will make the same point negatively a few verses later ('*No one* can come to me *unless* the Father who sent me draws him," v. 44), and yet again further on in the chapter ("This is why I have told you that *no one* can come to me *unless* it is given him from the Father," v. 65, italics added). Thus when Jesus goes on to promise that "the person who comes to me I will never cast out" (v. 37b), he is not issuing a gener-

4. As the brackets indicate, the pronoun "it" is not in the Greek text, but must be supplied (more literally, "no one can snatch out of my Father's hand"). But "it" has to be supplied and not "them" because of the neuter singular "what" (ὅ) or "that which" the Father is said to have given.

alized "Whosoever Will" invitation. Even as staunch a Calvinist as John Bunyan, at the very end of his classic *Grace Abounding to the Chief of Sinners*, thought that he was,[5] but in fact the title of the old gospel song is based rather on Revelation 22:17, "And let him that is athirst come. And whosoever will, let him take the water of life freely" (KJV). Here in John's Gospel, Jesus is referring not to those who come on their own whim or initiative, but quite specifically to those whom the Father has "given" or "drawn" to him.[6] Earlier he said that the person who "practices wicked things hates the Light and does not come to the Light, for fear his works will be exposed" (3:20), while the person who "does the truth comes to the Light, so that his works will be revealed as works wrought in God" (3:21). In this Gospel, coming to Jesus in faith is clear evidence that a person has been "drawn" to him by the Father's love.

The basis of the so-called doctrine of "eternal security" is that those who are so "drawn" are the Father's gift to the Son, and this gift, Jesus insists, is an irrevocable gift. It cannot be "lost" or wasted. "And this is the will of the One who sent me," he continues, "that of all he has given me I might not lose any of it, but raise it up at the last day" (6:39).[7] These verses in John 6 form the essential background to the startling notion in 10:29 that "What my Father has given me is greater than all else, and no one can snatch it out of the Father's hand." The "security" of the believer is clear in both passages, but what is surprising in the second is the phrase "greater than all," with its strong accent on the immense *value*, or *worth* of the Father's gift to the Son, that is, on the value or worth of Christian believers. The doctrines of grace have taught us that in ourselves we are worthless sinners—and "in ourselves" this is true. But value, like beauty, is

5. Bunyan wrote: "The scripture also did now most sweetly visit my soul, *And him that cometh to me I will in no wise cast out* (John 6:37). O the comfort that I have had from this word, *in no wise*! . . . But Satan would greatly labour to pull this promise from me, telling of me, that Christ did not mean me. . . . But I should answer him again, Satan, there is in this word no such exception, but *him that comes*, *him*, any *him*, him that cometh to me, I will in no wise cast out" (*Grace Abounding*, 55, par. 215).

6. Perhaps a different gospel song is more appropriate here: "I've found a friend, O such a friend. He loved me ere I knew him. He drew me with the cords of love, and thus he bound me to him."

7. Again, notice the neuter "all" (πᾶν) and "it" (αὐτό), but here again it is balanced by the generic masculine in the following verse: "For this is the will of my Father, that *every person* (πᾶς) who sees the Son and believes in him might have eternal life, and I will raise *him* (αὐτόν) up at the last day" (v. 40, italics added).

in the eye of the beholder, and in this case the Beholder is Christ, who sees believers as a treasured gift, "greater than all" because it comes from the Father and must therefore have had great value in the Father's eyes.

Jesus picks up the thread of the Father's gift and its immense value not only in chapter 10 of John's Gospel, but again in his long prayer to the Father in John 17, where he enumerates several things the Father has "given" him, including "authority over all flesh" (17:3), "words" to pass along to his disciples (v. 8), God's own "name" (vv. 11–12), and God's own "glory" (vv. 22, 24). Pre-eminent among these gifts from God, not surprisingly, are the disciples themselves, and ultimately all Christian believers. "I have revealed your name," he recalls, "to the men[8] you gave me out of the world. *They were yours,* and you gave them to me, and they have kept your word" (17:6). And again, "I pray for them. I do not pray for the world but for those whom you gave me, because *they are yours* (and all mine are yours and yours mine), and I am glorified in them" (17:9–10). The words in italics remind us that Christian believers belonged to the Father *before* they belonged to the Son ("They were yours," v. 6), and that in being given to the Son they nevertheless still belong to the Father ("they are yours," v. 9). This is true both corporately and individually, for Jesus finally prays, "Father, *that which* you have given to me, I want *them* to be with me where I am,[9] that they may see my glory which you have given me, because you have loved me before the creation of the world" (v. 24, italics added).

Jesus affirms in this last great prayer that his stated intention "that of all he has given me I might not lose (μὴ ἀπολέσω) any of it" (see 6:39) has in fact been realized, for "none of them is lost (ἀπώλετο) except the son of destruction" (that is, Judas Iscariot), and the only reason for that single exception was "so that the scripture might be fulfilled" (17:12).[10] Jesus' prayer confirms that both the principle itself (that "none of them is lost") and the one exception to it (Judas) are grounded in the eternal plan of God. When Jesus is arrested in the following chapter, he tells the arresting officers, "I told you that it is I, so if you are seeking me, let these [that is, his disciples other than Judas] go" (18:8). He did this, we are told, "so that

8. "Men" is appropriate here for ἀνθρώπους here because Jesus is referring in all likelihood to the all male "Twelve" (see 6:70).

9. Yet again, notice the interplay between the neuter singular ("*that which* you have given me") and the masculine plural ("I want *them* to be with me"), reflecting both the individual and corporate aspects of election and salvation (see above, n. 7).

10. The "scripture" is evidently Psalm 41:10 (see John 13:18).

the word he had spoken, that 'I have not lost any of those you have given me' might be fulfilled" (18:9). In John's Gospel, the temporal safety of the disciples God had given Jesus becomes a sign of their eternal safety in the Father's hand.[11]

What conclusions can be drawn from this brief survey of the evidence? First, the so-called "security of the believer" does not emerge in a vacuum in the Gospel of John. Rather, it is a corollary of the often-repeated claim that believers are God the Father's gift to Jesus the Son. They belonged to God before they belonged to Jesus. Without using the verb "to choose," or the noun "election,"[12] John's Gospel makes the point that God has taken the initiative in human salvation. Those who "come to the Light" do so not because they are sinners. Sinners in fact habitually avoid the light (John 3:19–20). They come rather *despite* being sinners, because at some point in their lives they "do the truth" (3:21). They do so because God the Father is *already* at work in them, drawing them to his Son (see 6:44). Coming to Jesus merely *reveals* "the works of God" in a person's life (again, see 3:21). A prime example in the Gospel is the man who was born blind in order that "the works of God might be *revealed* in him" (9:3)—not by the restoration of his sight so much as by coming to believe in Jesus and worshiping him (9:38). Turning Reformation theology on its head, one could say that they prove their good works (not *their* good works exactly, but God's work in them), by their faith.[13] A second conclusion is that those so drawn and so given to Jesus are of immeasurable worth and value ("greater than all," 10:29), not in themselves or on their own merits, but in the eyes of the Father who loved them and made them his own, and in the eyes of the Son who received them as his greatest treasure. And this value is their intrinsic value, for what could be more

11. This is the case in spite of the shame associated with their desertion of Jesus in the Synoptic Gospels (see, for example, Mark 14:27), and even in John's Gospel itself (see 16:32).

12. The language of choice or election is used in John's Gospel, but in relation to Jesus' *selection* of the Twelve to accompany him during his ministry and continue his work thereafter (see 6:70, 13:18, 15:16), not in relation to God the Father's *election* of individuals or of a people to salvation.

13. See my article, "Baptism and Conversion in John: A Particular Baptist Reading," in *Baptism, the New Testament and the Church. Historical and Contemporary Studies in Honour of R. E. O. White*, JSNT Sup 171, ed. S. E. Porter and A. R. Cross (Sheffield: Sheffield Academic Press, 1999), 136–56.

"intrinsic" than the value assigned to a person by God the Creator and Redeemer?

Having looked closely at the relevant passages in John 3, 6, 10, and 17, it is legitimate at the end of this essay to allow ourselves a bit more range, and our imaginations a bit more room. Take, for example, Jesus' parables (in Matthew, not in John) about the "treasure hidden in the field" which a man discovered, and sold all that he had in order to buy the field and the treasure in it (Matt 13:44), or the "one precious pearl" which a merchant admired so much that he sold everything in order to make it his own (Matt 13:45–46). These are commonly understood as incentives to Jesus' hearers to seek the "highest good," the Kingdom of Heaven. But what if the pearl or the treasure, or both, represent instead those whom God the Father loves, redeems, and entrusts to his Son? If that were the case, it would not be so different from the way in which Jesus in John's Gospel views believers as "greater than all," a gift of matchless worth from the Father who sent him. Ironically, such an idea comes to expression even in a document judged heretical by the later church, the apocryphal *Gospel of Philip*, probably Gnostic in origin, from the second or third century:

> When the pearl is cast down in the mud it does not become dishonoured the more, nor if it is anointed with balsam oil will it become more precious. But it has its worth in the eyes of its owner at all times. So with the sons of God wherever they may be. For they have the value in the eyes of the Father. (*Gospel of Philip* 48)[14]

It should be noted, however, that this is by no means a characteristically "Gnostic" interpretation. The *Gospel of Thomas*, for example, moves in exactly the opposite direction, interpreting not only the parables of the treasure and the pearl (*Thomas*, 76, 109), but also the lost sheep (*Thomas*, 107) and the net (*Thomas*, 8) as referring to humans seeking and valuing the "highest good," rather than God seeking and valuing a people for himself.

Finally, it may not be accidental that one of the first of Jesus' disciples, the first who was said to "believe" in him (John 1:50) was named "Nathanael," a name that means "gift of God." Jesus recognized Nathanael's worth as a gift from the Father when he addressed him as "a true Israelite in whom is no deceit" (1:47), and told him, "Before Philip called you when you were under the fig tree, I saw you" (1:48). With this, he echoed the

14. For the translation, see R. McL. Wilson, *The Gospel of Philip* (London: A. R. Mowbray, 1962), 109.

prophet's words about God's joyful discovery of his people Israel long ago: "Like grapes in the wilderness, I found Israel. Like the first fruits on the fig tree, in its first season, I saw your ancestors" (Hosea 9:10, NRSV).

Such random thoughts "outside the box" are admittedly speculative and by no means capable of proof, yet they are consistent with the main point that in John's Gospel the "security" of Christian believers rests on their profound value in God's sight, and on the Father's work in their lives long before they ever came consciously and willingly to the Son in faith.

3

The Security of the Believer as the Son's Fulfillment of the Father's Will

(John 6:38–40)

Shawn L. Buice

INTRODUCTION

Understanding God's will, on both a practical and theological level, is one of the most important biblical issues believers face. On the practical level, Christian men and women desire to know God's will for their lives (*i.e.*, which job God wants them to have, which person God wants them to marry, etc.). Yet, many struggle to find that specific will. Part of the difficulty in being able to discern God's will is that the Bible does not call each of us by name and say specifically what we should or should not do. However, guidelines exist to help believers understand God's will for their lives.[1]

On the theological level, theologians wrestle with the various components of God's will, too. For example, they desire to know the will of God as it relates to salvation (*i.e.*, what is God's role—since he is sovereign, what is man's role—since he possesses free will, can salvation be lost, etc.). Here, as on the practical level, difficulty exists. Part of the problem

1. Two resources which have become quite popular are Rick Warren's *The Purpose Driven Life*, and Henry Blackaby's *Experiencing God*. Warren's book has sold more than a million copies in twenty languages. Blackaby's book is fifteen years old and has sold more than 4 million copies.

seems to be that there are so few passages that explicitly state "this is the will of God."[2] Even where there are texts that make this assertion, their interpretation has given rise to various opinions.

One example of a text that speaks about God's will appears in John 6:39–40. In the midst of this "bread of life" discourse, Jesus claimed:

> This is the will of Him who sent Me: that I should lose none of those He has given Me but should raise them up on the last day. For this is the will of My Father: that everyone who sees the Son and believes in Him may have eternal life, and I will raise him up on the last day.[3]

On this occasion, as Jesus spoke, he described the nature of the will of his Father. According to Jesus, God's will meant two things. First, that he (Jesus) would "lose none of those" God had given him; and second, that he would "raise them up" on the last day.

This passage makes several assertions. First, God does have a role in salvation. He is the one who "gives" some[4] to his son Jesus (6:37, 39). Second, those whom the Father gives, Jesus will never cast out (6:37). Third, not only will Jesus not cast them out, he will also not lose any of them (6:39). Last, not only will Jesus not lose any of them, but he will raise them up "on the last day" (6:40).

Based on this text and others like it, many have derived the concept of the security of the believer. What does this concept mean? Is this the correct understanding of the words of Jesus? What truly is God's will as it is presented here? These are some of the questions that we will seek to answer as we examine this portion of John's Gospel.

ANALYSIS OF THE TEXT

Context

John 6:39–40 comes in a section of John's Gospel that has become known as the "Bread of Life" discourse. This particular discourse falls within the

2. A sampling of such texts is 1 Thess 4:3; 5:18; and 2 Pet 3:9.

3. Unless otherwise noted, all Scripture references in this chapter come from the HCSB.

4. The use of the neuter relative pronoun at this point is interesting. If anything, we would expect the masculine pronoun to be employed, but it is not. More will be said about this later.

first half of John's Gospel which describes the public ministry of Jesus.[5] The discourse itself extends from John 6:22–71 and includes the first of many "I am" sayings of Jesus as recorded by John.[6]

As the narrative begins in verse 22, one notes that Jesus and his disciples have gone to the other side of the Sea of Galilee (6:22). They had been in Galilee, where the 5,000 had been fed (6:1–15). A crowd gathered and asked Jesus a simple question, "Rabbi, when did You get here?" (6:25). Jesus responded, "I assure you: You are looking for Me, not because you saw the signs, but because you ate the loaves and were filled" (6:26). Interestingly enough, Jesus did not answer their question directly, but moved to address the real issue at hand—"food that lasts for eternal life" (6:27).

This reply leads to further discussion (6:28–29) in which the crowd asked Jesus what sign he was going to perform for them because their fathers had eaten manna in the wilderness (6:30–31). Jesus responded by speaking of the "real bread from heaven" (6:33). The mention of this type of bread caused the crowd to exclaim, "Sir, give us this bread always!" (6:34) It was this statement that prompted Jesus to begin the discourse on the fact that he himself was this bread.

The theme of Jesus as the bread of life continues until verse 58 (6:47–58). In fact, as the discussion progresses, Jesus speaks of eating his flesh and drinking his blood! Because of the nature of this concept, many of Jesus' disciples "turned back and no longer walked with Him" (6:66). The chapter closes with two final statements. First, Peter affirms the commitment of the twelve to follow Jesus because only he had "the words of eternal life" (6:68) and they had come to know and believe that he was "the Holy One of God" (6:69). Second, Jesus noted the fact that one of them was "going to betray Him" (6:71).

5. Many commentators have well noted the basic structure of John's Gospel, where Raymond Brown's analysis has influenced many. See Brown, *Gospel According to John*, cxxxviii. In brief, Brown described the divisions of John's Gospel in this manner:

a) Prologue (1:1–18)
b) The Book of Signs (1:19—12:50)
c) The Book of Glory (13:1—20:31)
d) Epilogue (21:1–25)

6. The other "I am" sayings found in John are: "I am the light of the world" (8:12); "I am the door" (10:7); "I am the good shepherd" (10:11, 14); "I am the resurrection and the life" (11:25); "I am the way, the truth, and the life" (14:6); and "I am the true vine" (15:1, 5).

Analysis

When we focus on John 6:35–40, the focus of this article, we note a highlighted emphasis on the will of the Father. In fact, three times in these verses Jesus referred to God's will. In verse 38, Jesus claimed that he came "not to do (His) will, but the will of Him who sent (Him)." In verses 39 and 40, Jesus clarified what this will was by stating twice that "this is the will" of my Father. The Greek word used at this point is the noun θέλημα. Generally, θέλημα is used with one of two ideas in the New Testament. It can be used in a subjective manner indicating "the act of willing or desiring."[7] One example of this is found earlier in John's Gospel. In John 1, the Apostle John wrote, "But to all who did receive Him, He gave them the right to be children of God, to those who believe in His name, who were born not of blood, or of the *will* of the flesh, or of the *will* of man, but of God" (vv. 12-13; italics mine). The subjective connotation at this point indicates that the action, becoming children of God, finds its basis not with humanity but God.

Θέλημα may also have a more objective sense meaning "what one wishes to happen."[8] This is the meaning in John 5:30 where Jesus said: "I can do nothing on My own. Only as I hear do I judge, and My judgment is righteous, because I do not seek My own *will*, but the *will* of Him who sent me" (italics mine). The objective sense of θέλημα in this passage is highlighted by Jesus' commitment to carry out what God wanted to happen. It is this second sense that should be understood as the connotation in John 6.

This particular word is found about sixty-two times in the New Testament. Of those uses, thrity-five are found in John (eleven times) and Paul (twenty-four times) combined. D. Müller explained that since "θέλημα is the more theologically significant word (generally used for the will of God), the theological emphasis lies primarily in Paul and John who focus on this theme."[9] Certainly, Muller's observation applies to John's Gospel. Whether one sees explicit statements to this affect or the idea is implied, one of the notable emphases in John is Jesus' desire to carry out the Father's will.[10]

7. *BDAG*, s.v. "θέλημα."

8. Ibid.

9. *NIDNTT*, s.v. "Will, Purpose."

10. See also John 5:30, 6:38–40, and 7:16.

This theme is introduced in John 4 and is interspersed throughout John's narrative until its climax in John 17. For instance, in John 4:34 Jesus stated: "My food is to do the will of Him who sent Me and to finish His work." Jesus' desire to finish the work his Father had given him is described in John 17:4 where Jesus prayed: "I have glorified You on the earth by completing the work You gave Me to do." Perhaps the most intense illustration of Jesus finishing the work he was given to do is his climatic cry from the cross—"It is finished" (John 19:30). Commenting on this aspect of John's theology, D. A. Carson noted that "The Fourth Gospel does not record the agony of Gethsemane (*cf.* Mt. 26:36–46), including the resolute 'Yet not as I will, but as you will,' but its entire Christology is an expression of that same resolution."[11] It is the will of God, then, that Jesus explains he came to do.

The will of God that Jesus came to do is explained in John 6:39–40 with two very similarly structured statements. Understanding these verses is vitally important to grasping what it is that Jesus came to do. Therefore, one must ask a few questions at this point: Do verses 39 and 40 describe two different components of God's will? And, if they are different, how are they to be reconciled? Or, could it be that some type of grammatical construction is employed here by John to show that both verses work together?

At first glance, it might appear that verses 39 and 40 are making a distinction between two different aspects of God's will. Further analysis, however, reveals that both verses are carefully linked. For instance, both verses begin with similar predicate nominative structures placing the demonstrative pronoun τοῦτο (this) with the third declension noun θέλημα (will). Both verses use purpose clauses to express the purpose of God's will. The sense of purpose is expressed by the use of the conjunction ἵνα followed by a verb in the subjunctive mood. Finally, both verses also end in the same manner stressing the fact that Jesus will raise up on the last day those whom the Father gave him.

These similarities are such that many have noted the connection between the two and the way they clarify exactly what is the will of the Father. Barclay Newman and Eugene Nida recognized a connection explaining that "both verses 39 and 40 stipulate the will of God; verse 40

11. Carson, *The Gospel According to John*, 291.

simply amplifies what is already in verse 39."[12] Gerald Borchert arrived at a similar conclusion saying that verse 40 "serves as a kind of summation to vv. 35–39."[13]

While noting the connection between the two verses, William Hendriksen explained that verse 39 employed a figure of speech called "litotes" to highlight its emphasis. According to Hendriksen, a litotes is an "affirmation produced by the denial of the opposite."[14] The understanding of verse 39, then, would be that since Jesus would lose none of those who had been given by the Father, he would "guard them to the very end."[15] Hendriksen explained that verse 40 was "a further definition of the will of the Father."[16] Based on these observations, a more detailed analysis of this text reveals that verses 39 and 40 are inextricably linked to describe the will of God that Jesus came to fulfill. This will can be understood, then, as containing two parts. Furthermore, both components should be understood as working together and in no way contradicting each other. The first part is that Jesus should lose none of those that God has given him (further clarified in verse 40 as those who see the Son and believe in him). The second part is that he will raise them up on the last day.

Another question arises at this point—since Jesus will not lose any that the Father gives him, who are these that will not be lost and raised up on the last day? Twice in these verses, Jesus refers to a specific group with the use of the neuter singular relative pronoun where one would expect a masculine plural form to be used (vv. 37, 39). Newman and Nida noted that this "is a strange expression in Greek," although it "is a stylistic feature of the Gospel of John."[17] Even though the expression may be strange and somewhat difficult to translate,[18] most commentators are agreed to its meaning. F. F. Bruce commented on this construction explaining that

12. Newman and Nida, *Translator's Handbook*, 201.

13. Borchert, *John 1–11*, 266.

14. Hendriksen, *John*, 234. Carson also noted the used of the litotes in this passage at verse 37. See Carson, *John*, 290.

15. Hendriksen, 235.

16. Ibid.

17. Newman and Nida, *Translator's Handbook*, 199. Other examples of John's use of this construction can be found in 17:2 and 17:24.

18. The New King James Version, the New American Standard Updated, and the New International Version translate the neuter pronoun as "all" in both verses 37 and 39. The NET Bible translates verse 37 with "everyone" and uses the phrase "one person of every one" in verse 39.

"the pronoun 'all' is neuter singular, denoting the sum-total of believers."[19] The tendency by some is to look at this passage as support for the idea of an elect group. Hendriksen boldly stated his belief that "the expression 'all that' views the elect as a unity; they are all *one* people" (emphasis his).[20] Carson agreed with Hendriksen's conclusion affirming that the relative pronoun here "is used to refer to the elect collectively."[21]

While one must agree that a specific group of people is being referred to in this passage, this admission does not necessitate that s/he need attempt to limit the number of individuals to an "elect" group. For the specific group about which Jesus speaks is further described in verse 40 as "everyone who sees the Son and believes in Him." R. C. H. Lenski stated that "The neuter singular is used as an abstract expression and as such sums up the whole mass of believers of all ages and speaks of them as a unit."[22] According to Lenski, one can look at these words of Jesus without developing an idea of an elect or limited group. Certainly, then, there are some given to Jesus by the Father (6:37). These he will never cast out (6:37) nor lose (6:39). Moreover, he will raise them up on the last day (6:40).

Summary

The words of Jesus at this point must be understood as affirming the security of the believer. It is God's will, in other words, that those whom he has given to the Son be raised up on the last day. Jesus will keep them and not lose any of them. The believer's assurance, then, lies not in his or her own work or power, but in the work of Jesus.

Such security is emphasized in this passage in a variety of ways. First, the act of God's giving must not be minimized. Grant Osborne recognized that here in this passage, "the sovereign control of salvation by God is given greater stress than anywhere else in John."[23] Second, the commitment of Jesus to complete the will of his Father and his promise to raise

19. Bruce, *Gospel of John*, 1983), 154. See also Borchert, *John 1–11*, 265; Hendriksen, *John*, 234; Kostenberger, *John*, 211, fn. 61; Lenski, *Interpretation of St. John's Gospel*; and Newman and Nida, *Handbook*, 199.

20. Hendriksen, *John*, 234.

21. Carson, *John*, 290.

22. Lenski, *Interpretation*, 463. Later, Lenski further clarified his thinking, noting there "is not a fixed number, in some mysterious way chosen by an absolute decree of God to be such a gift to Jesus" (464).

23. Osborne, "Soteriology in the Gospel of John," 247.

up on the last day those who have believed in him must be given its due weight. Last, the emphasis on the individual responding by seeing and believing should not be overlooked either. Raymond Brown commented on this topic, stating:

> The stress in vs. 37 that God destines men to come to Jesus does not in the least attenuate the guilt in vs. 36 of those who do not believe. One might conjecture that the reason that they do not believe is because God has not "given" them to Jesus. Yet, it would be unfair to NT thought-patterns to elaborate this as a psychological explanation of the refusal to believe.[24]

Based on Brown's conclusion, one sees the need to properly evaluate all components of this text and attempt to keep from elevating one aspect over another. All three of the previously mentioned concepts, then, must be understood as working together. Now, based on these summary statements, one must ask, "What are the implications of these words for our theology?"

IMPLICATIONS OF THE TEXT

Having analyzed John 6:39–40, now one must consider the claims of these verses and how they apply to our understanding of the will of God. As was stated at the end of the previous section, this writer believes that this portion of John's Gospel affirms the security of the believer. It still remains, however, for us to explain what this means.

Definitions

When we examine a theme like the security of the believer, we must be careful to define our terms clearly. For example, some refer to this concept as the "security of the believer;"[25] others prefer the designation the "perseverance of the saints;"[26] and yet others opt for a different descriptive phrase such as the "preservation of the saints."[27] While some might

24. Brown, *John*, 276.

25. This is the description adopted by Southern Baptists. See *The Baptist Faith and Message* (Nashville: LifeWay Christian Resources, 1998).

26. This is the designation adopted by Calvinists and represents the "P" in the acrostic "TULIP."

27. One recent proponent of this terminology is Olson, *Beyond Calvinism and Arminianism*. Olson explained "that the truth of eternal security in Christ is not identi-

think these three phrases are synonymous and describe the same thing, certain differences exist.[28] Consider, for instance, what the Southern Baptist understands the security of the believer to be.[29] *The Baptist Faith and Message* says "All true believers endure to the end. Those whom God has accepted in Christ, and sanctified by His Spirit, will never fall away from the state of grace, but shall persevere to the end."[30] In other words, Southern Baptists believe that if a person is truly saved, they cannot lose their salvation. They are secure in their relationship with Jesus and this security depends solely on God.

The emphasis on the work of God is also understood by those who prefer the designation "preservation of the saints." C. Gordon Olson confessed that he preferred the term preservation "because the emphasis is upon the work of the triune God, not upon the works of man."[31] Olson argued that the difference between the ideas of "perseverance" and "preservation" was not simply one of semantics. He continued, "The nub of the difference is that Calvinists have generally put the onus upon the saints to persevere, while a biblical concept of eternal security puts the responsibility upon God to preserve the saved."[32] Olson's observations fit nicely with the analysis of John 6 offered already in this article. The security of the believer rests in the fact that Jesus, in accordance to the will of God, will raise them up on the last day.

As was just mentioned, the perseverance of the saints, as commonly understood by Calvinists, contains two components. One component emphasizes God's part and the other places responsibility on the believer himself. Taking note of both aspects, Wayne Grudem defined perseverance as the idea that "those who are truly born again will be kept by God's power and will persevere as Christians until the end of their lives, and that

cal to the traditional Calvinistic doctrine of the *perseverance* of the saints" (295; emphasis his).

28. For a detailed and very pointed analysis of the distinction between the ideas "the security of the believer" and "the perseverance of the saints" see Vance, *Other Side of Calvinism*, 562–63.

29. This writer understands that all Southern Baptists are not completely united on this issue. In fact, there are many Southern Baptists who do agree with the five points of Calvinism. He is speaking in general terms, however, to highlight a fundamental difference between these two concepts.

30. *The Baptist Faith and Message*, 12.

31. Olson, *Beyond*, 295.

32. Ibid.

only those who persevere until the end have been truly born again."[33] In Grudem's definition, one sees both emphases highlighted. First, true believers will be kept by God's power. Second, the evidence that one is a true believer is revealed in the fact that they remain or persevere to the end.

It is this second emphasis that distinguishes the phrase "perseverance of the saints" from the phrases "security of the believer" or "preservation of the saints." The latter two recognize the sole responsibility of security as resting with the fulfillment of God's will, not the contribution of humanity or the fact that the believer perseveres. Again, in accordance with the words of Jesus in John 6, the security of the believer lies in the Son's fulfillment of the Father's will.

Implications

Having sought to properly define the various terms used to describe a specific theological understanding of the security of the believer, we turn now to draw out the implications of John 6 for our theology. To put it another way, what does it mean that a believer has security in his salvation?

To reiterate, a believer can find great comfort in John 6 knowing that they are secure and that their security lies not in what s/he does, but in the fulfillment of God's will as carried out by the Son. Jesus affirmed this idea himself in this text, noting that he would never cast out those the Father gives him (6:37); that he would lose none of those the Father had given him (6:39); that those who see him and believe in him would have eternal life (6:40); and that he would "raise them (him) up on the last day" (6:39–40).[34]

To state that the believer's security rests in the work of Christ is not to deny that the believer should live a life in accordance with God's will for him or her. In fact, at this point, some have misunderstood what "security of the believer" actually means. For instance, John MacArthur appeared to lump those who defend the designation "security of the believer" in with those whom he would describe as having an easy believism. This understanding follows from his observation that some advocate a "once saved, always saved" message that places no emphasis

33. Grudem, *Systematic Theology*, 788.

34. The scope of this article does not permit in-depth analysis of other Johannine texts that speak to the issue of the security of the believer. See other essays in this book for further discussion. The point that needs to be expressed here briefly, however, is that this is a theme given some emphasis in John's Gospel (see also John 10:25–30).

on personal holiness or the need for the believer to conduct his life in a manner worthy of the Lord (Col 1:10). MacArthur claimed that "Any doctrine of eternal security that leaves out perseverance distorts the doctrine of salvation itself."[35]

MacArthur's comments need to be addressed. First, proponents of the term "eternal security" do not deny the need for righteous living on earth. While they recognize that some believers may fall into sin and even "bring reproach on the cause of Christ,"[36] they are firmly committed to the biblical idea of a faith that is vibrant, alive, and shows itself in good works. Or to state it another way, they affirm what Paul said in Ephesians 2:10 when he wrote "we are His creation—created in Christ Jesus for *good works*, which God prepared ahead of time so that we should walk in them" (italics added for emphasis). Second, in contrast to what MacArthur stated, one can forthrightly affirm a proper biblical understanding of the security of the believer without holding to the idea of perseverance of the saints. In fact, Laurence Vance openly confessed that eternal security and perseverance of the saints "have no connection whatsoever."[37] A proper understanding of security notes the necessity of the believer living a godly life without placing an overemphasis on his "persevering" as a necessary component of security.

CONCLUSION

One of the central truths related to the soteriology of the New Testament is called the security of the believer. One of the key passages from which this concept is derived is the "bread of life" discourse as recorded in John 6. The assurance possessed by the believer is affirmed in this passage in a number of ways. First, God the Father gives some people to his son Jesus. Second, the ones whom the Father gives will not be cast out by Jesus. Third, Jesus will *not* lose any. Last, Jesus will raise them up on the last day. Because the work of the Son constitutes a response to the Father's will, the security of the believer is certain.[38]

35. MacArthur, "Perseverance of the Saints," 13.

36. *The Baptist Faith and Message*, 13.

37. Vance, *Other Side*, 562.

38. This author wishes to express his gratitude to two colleagues, Tim Christian and Michael McDill, for their helpful suggestions with editing this article.

4

The Prayer of Jesus in John 17 and the Security of the Believer

Jon Balserak

One of the most impressive qualities about the Gospel of John is that it beckons us to contemplate the pre-temporal counsels of the Almighty. John 17 is no exception, setting before us decisions made between the members of the Godhead before the foundation of the world. Although such esoteric considerations may appear quite unconnected to the issue of a believer's assurance of salvation, this paper will argue that the exact opposite is the case.[1] In order to do so, it will begin by considering a dispute which arose in the early church.

AN EARLY CONTROVERSY: ORIGEN VS. HERACLEON

John's gospel has often been entangled in controversy. One of the first involved Origen and a Gnostic named Heracleon, who wrote what is the earliest known commentary on the Gospel of John.

Heracleon's commentary argued, among other things, that the Gospel of John discusses human anthropology, and particularly the question of belief and unbelief, in terms of what Jeffrey Trumbower has helpfully

1. In preparing this essay, the following commentaries were consulted: Origen, *Commentary on the Gospel according to John*; Chrysostom, *Commentary on Saint John*; Augustine, *Tractates on the Gospel of John*; Aquinas, *Catena Aurea*, 4:2; Calvin, *Commentary on the Gospel according to John*. It is apparent that there are innumerable commentaries on John which we could have been consulted. These, however, are surely some of the best ever produced by the Christian Church.

called the "fixed origins of human beings."[2] By this phrase, Trumbower explains that Heracleon held that in John's Gospel belief was a matter determined by one's origin—that is, by whether one was "born from above," or "of your father the devil"; whether one is "of the world" or "not of the world"; and so forth. These origins, Heracleon believed, were fixed prior to Jesus' coming and incapable of change.

Origen argued in his own commentary on John against Heracleon. To Origen, the views of Heracleon wrongly denied the freedom of human beings to choose either to accept or reject, to follow or not follow, Jesus.

The controversy, though forgotten today, is a useful one on account of what it teaches us. For one thing, it draws attention to the curious language and themes found in John. Expanding slightly upon the Origen–Heracleon debate, we find in John the following themes or ideas:

> *Regarding Jesus and the Father:*[3]
>
> Jesus has come from above, having been sent by the Father to complete a task—3:31; 13:1, 3; 16:28; 17:8, 18
>
> More specifically,
>
> > Jesus received commands from his Father—10:18; 12:49; 14:31; 17:4
> >
> > Jesus did not come to do his own will but the will of the one who sent him—5:30; 6:38
>
> Accordingly,
>
> > Jesus did not honor himself, nor seek his own glory —8:49–50, 54
> >
> > Jesus' teaching was not his own—7:16; 12:49; 14:24
> >
> > Jesus confessed that the Father was greater than him—14:28
> >
> > Jesus pleased the Father—8:29, 46
> >
> > When he finished his work, Jesus would be glorified—17:1, 4–5

2. Trumbower, *Born from Above*.

3. This twofold structure—Jesus and the Father, and Jesus and believers—was suggested to me by Donald Macleod; see his *A Faith to Live By*, 119–32.

Regarding Jesus and believers:

Jesus knows who will come to him and who will not—6:64

In fact, believers are given to Jesus by the Father—6:37; 17:2, 6

Accordingly, all those who are given to Jesus come to him—6:37—and those who are of the truth (his sheep) hear Jesus' voice—10:4–5; 18:37

In keeping with this, Jesus says he does not pray for the world but for those who believe, or would in the future, believe in him—17:9

As for the world, it hates Jesus—7:7; 15:18–19

Jesus is not of the world—8:23

Also believers are not of the world—17:16

Similarly, people are described in a variety of ways: "born of God"—1:13; "born from above"—3:3; "from below"—8:23; "of the world"—8:23; "not of the world"—17:14; "of your father the devil"—8:44; "my sheep" or "not of my sheep"—10:26–27; "of the truth"—18:37

Many of these themes open for us a window into the counsels of eternity. Of course a number of them are not exclusive to the Gospel of John. Nonetheless they are expressed in a particularly powerful way in John.

Secondly, by drawing attention to these ideas, this controversy beckons us to consider the divine counsels towards the end of understanding them and being edified by them. The Gnostics, represented by Heracleon, sought to understand these counsels. The Christian church, however, has argued that they did so wrongly and has sought to articulate a correct understanding of them. What, then, is this understanding? How ought these themes and issues arising in John to be understood? Once this general question is answered, attention can be turned to John 17.

THE COVENANT OF REDEMPTION

To answer this, we must examine the covenant.[4] Arising from the early work of theologians like Irenaeus, Augustine, and a host of others, was an

4. Our thinking on this issue has been stimulated not only by Donald Macleod, but also by Michael S. Horton, "A Classic Calvinist View," 23–42. For a fuller treatment of the

idea which would be developed through the Middle Ages, with the *pactum* theology, *sine qua non* causality, and *meritum de congruo*, and would further mature during the Reformation and post-Reformation periods, from which emerged what is now known as covenant theology.

Traditionally, covenant theologians have spoken of three distinct covenants: a covenant of works, a covenant of grace, and a covenant of redemption. The precise number of covenants varies depending on which writer one consults. But for our purposes it is not essential that we settle, or even look at, the dispute.

The covenant of works, also known by other names such as the covenant of creation, originates in time between God and humankind in the Garden of Eden. Adam is given stipulations which he is to obey and which, if obeyed, will result in the confirmation of him and his posterity in everlasting life. Of course, he breaks these, as is recorded in Genesis 3, and brings the curses of the covenant upon his, and his posterity's, heads.

The covenant of grace is, as it were, God's response to Adam's fall. It has as its contracting parties God and the elect, or believers.[5] This is the covenant through which believers are restored, or brought back into relationship with God. It is, to put it another way, the covenant which promises salvation. It is a covenant which makes demands of human beings, namely, faith: "Believe on the Lord Jesus Christ and you shall be saved" (Acts 16:30). It is likewise a covenant which makes demands of God.[6] In it God binds himself to believers. He promises to be their God. Accordingly, God and believers live in covenant with one another; a bond which will, quite literally, never be dissolved.

Then there is the covenant of redemption. This originated before time and represents, one might say, the background to the covenant of grace. The parties in this covenant are God the Father and God the Son. Notice that there is no creaturely representative in this covenant. The re-

covenant, see the standard works from the post-Reformation period such as Herman Witsius, *De oeconomia foederum Dei cum hominibus* (*Economy of the Covenants Between God and Man*). The debate on the covenant between Voetius and Cocceius will be familiar to any student of the period and need not be entered into here.

5. It may also be, perhaps, that the contracting parties are God and Christ, as the second Adam, and all the elect in him. This is the position stated in the Larger Catechism (Ans. 31); see Macleod, *Faith*, 123–24.

6. There has been considerable debate about the character of this covenant and whether it is unilateral or bilateral. For a sane consideration of the matter, see Muller, *After Calvin*.

quirement is obedience, specifically the obedience of the Son, who obeys on behalf of his people. As Donald Macleod states:

> The stipulation is that Christ will do everything that is necessary for the salvation of His people. What we receive freely in the Covenant of Grace Christ earned by His compliance with the Covenant of Redemption.[7]

What is understood here, then, is that before the foundation of the world God the Father elects and entrusts a people to God the Son, who will be their head. God the Son, of course, agrees to these terms. He will be the head of this people and their representative. He will obey on their behalf, will be their guardian and will ultimately die and rise from the dead on their behalf. By doing so, he will merit for them all the riches of salvation.

It is, of course, this covenant that seems to be alluded to in so many ways by the passages already cited above from John's Gospel. Or, stated in another way, the Gospel of John contains material which requires us to postulate the covenant of redemption. To give just one example, in John 5:30 Jesus explains, "I seek not to please myself but him who sent me." Here, in this one sentence, we have stated that Jesus was sent, that someone other than himself sent him (presumably God the Father), and that Jesus works to please the one who sent him. From the last of these points, we may easily infer that Jesus was given guidance (commands) on pleasing the one who sent him. From all of these points, we may infer that decisions on all these matters were taken, at the very least, before Jesus' incarnation and, given the character of other statements—both Johannine and extra-Johannine—found in Scripture (for example, Eph 1:4), most likely before the foundation of the world. Thus the lineaments of a pre-temporal covenant between the members of the Godhead begin to appear even from this one sentence. Were we to have more time and space, a fuller account of this covenant of redemption could be outlined.

Although this introduction has been exceedingly brief, it shall have to suffice. Now John 17 can be taken up.

7. Macleod, *Faith*, 126.

JOHN 17 WITHIN THE CONTEXT OF THE COVENANT

In John 17 we find Jesus speaking to his Father prior to Jesus' death. The topic of conversation, we discover, is the plans they had made before the foundation of the world—in other words, the covenant of redemption. A quick overview of the chapter reveals discussion of the following:

> That Jesus had come from the Father and was now returning to him—17:8, 11–13
>
> Specifically, that Jesus had been sent from the Father to complete a task given to him by the Father—17:4
>
> That Jesus had been given power in order that he should give eternal life to all those who had been given to him by the Father—17:2
>
> The request to be glorified (17:1, 5), which Jesus makes on the basis that he had completed the work given to him by the Father—17:4
>
> Some of the specific things Jesus had done at the Father's behest—17:6, 8, 12, 14, 19, 26
>
> The faith of his people (17:25), who are continually identified as those whom the Father had given to Jesus—17:2, 6, and so forth
>
> Assertions which point to a union between Jesus and believers—17:10, 14, 18–19
>
> Prayers made on behalf of those whom the Father had given him—17:9, 11, 15, 17, 20–24

That all this fits perfectly into the outline of the covenant of redemption provided above should be evident. What is discovered here is that Jesus has been commissioned by the Father to give eternal life to a specific group of people, who have been chosen by the Father and entrusted to the Son. In keeping with this commission, the Son has been given commands by the Father which he has now completed. On the basis of this accomplished obedience, the Son is now requesting that he be rewarded. This is, one can only assume, in accordance with the arrangements made beforehand. The Father and the Son had agreed that if the Son obeyed perfectly, he would merit a reward. This is the reward he is now requesting. This reward is, of course, not won for himself but for those whom he represents and is, in effect, eternal life in all its fullness. Thus, Jesus has earned through his obedience the riches which he now requests from the Father and would lavish on his people. Jesus, moreover, as his people's guardian and shepherd, prays for their safety, that they would be guarded from danger, that the Father would keep them in his name, sanctify them, make them one, and bring them to join the Son at a later date in heaven.

THE SECURITY OF THE BELIEVER WITHIN THE CONTEXT OF JOHN 17

Thus, as was stated in this essay's introduction, contemplation of the pretemporal counsels of the Almighty, far from being a matter of no practical benefit to the believer, is in fact intimately connected to the issue of a believer's assurance of salvation. This should be apparent from our brief consideration of the contents of John 17, and may be elucidated further by noting the simple truth that such contemplation highlights and impresses upon the conscience of the Christian the remarkable fact that her or his salvation is entirely the work of the Son of God. It is, to put it another way, the responsibility of the Lord Jesus to see to it that all believers are saved. That is at the very heart of the covenant of redemption, which was agreed upon before the foundations of the world. That, moreover, can be seen most plainly in the expressed intent of so much of John 17. It is evident there that Jesus' concern is to give eternal life to as many as the Father had given him (v. 2), and that what he is doing in this prayer is returning to the Father near the climax of his work on earth and requesting (making sure, as it were) that when he has completely finished the work of his Father, he and his people will receive the reward which was agreed upon. This is what he seems to mean when he declares: "I have finished the work which you gave me to do. Now, O Father, glorify me . . ." (v. 4). In other words, "Glorify me, the head of the church. Glorify the head so that the members may benefit." Admittedly he speaks of the work as already completed; exegetes, however, seem to concur with the idea that he is speaking of the matter as if it were an already accomplished fact, even though he had still to go through with his death, burial and resurrection.[8] Yet even though this is so, the force of his request is in no way diminished. Jesus plainly declares: "Father, I have finished the work; now reward me." And since he is earning that reward on behalf of the church, his gain is theirs; his recompense means payment for them.

8. See, for example, Calvin, *Commentary on John*, 2:168.

Indeed Jesus can be seen to be at pains to ensure the safety and salvation of his people. So he is not only intent upon discussing the agreed-upon reward, but also adds a number of specific requests—that his people should be kept from the devil, sanctified, made one, and so forth—the sum of which is the safeguarding of his people. Not only, then, has he merited the salvation which he then gives to his people, but he acts as their guardian and shepherd in order to ensure that they are kept in the way of faith so that their salvation will not be a gift which they forfeit by falling away.

In this regard, we can also note the tenderness of Jesus. For when he does turn to mention the obedience of his people, he simply declares that "they have kept your word" (v. 6)—a statement which is patently inaccurate, if a strict sense of "kept" is intended. For up to that point Jesus' disciples had been as thickheaded and unbelieving as one could possibly imagine, and of course they were, in a matter of hours, going to disown and deny Jesus. These were remarkably flawed men. And yet Jesus glosses over all such flaws and declares simply that they had obeyed the Father. If one were, then, to attempt to oppose one's disobedience with the salvation won by Jesus on his or her behalf—as if to say, "irrespective of what Jesus has done on my behalf, I am not worthy to have salvation because of my disobedience"—Jesus' answer is ready: "they have kept your word." That is to say, the church's disobedience can never disqualify them from the reward earned for them by their head.

CONCLUSION

Such then is the character of Jesus, and such the character of the security of all believers as it is treated in this passage from John's Gospel. John 17, precisely because it opens up to its readers the secrets of the pre-temporal decisions made between God the Father and God the Son concerning the community of believers, provides a remarkably stable ground for assurance even in the midst of the deepest internal sense of sinfulness on the part of the believer. This is so because it reveals in the clearest possible way the fact that one's salvation is not the result of (*i.e.* does not rest upon) one's believing but of (or upon) the work of the Son, who took it upon himself to be one's representative head.

5

Eternal Security and the Saving Love of God

An Exposition of Romans 8:31–39[1]

Stephen Voorwinde

INTRODUCTION

The relationship between the eternal security of the believer and the saving love of God is nowhere stated more compellingly than in Romans 8:31–39. This is Scripture's *locus classicus* for the doctrine of the perseverance of the saints or the eternal security of the believer:

> 31 What, then, shall we say in response to this? *If God is for us, who can be against us?* 32 He who did not spare his own Son, but gave him up for us all—how will he not also, along with him, graciously give us all things? 33 *Who will bring any charge against those whom God has chosen?* It is God who justifies. 34 *Who is he that condemns?* Christ Jesus, who died—more than that, who was raised to life—is at the right hand of God and is also interceding for us. 35 *Who shall separate us from the love of Christ?* Shall trouble or hardship or persecution or famine or nakedness or danger or sword? 36 As it is written:

1. Originally published in *Vox Reformata* 71 (2006): 5–27. Reprinted by permission of the publisher.

This article is dedicated to the memory of my friend and colleague John Peet (1940–2005). Before he went to be with the Lord, John was the pastor of the Christian Reformed Church of Cobden, Victoria, Australia. As he struggled with cancer during the last year of his life John drew great comfort from this passage, which was also the text for my sermon at his funeral on January 28, 2005.

> "For your sake we face death all day long;
> we are considered as sheep to be slaughtered."

> 37 No, in all these things we are more than conquerors through him who loved us. 38 For I am convinced that neither death nor life, neither angels nor demons, neither the present nor the future, nor any powers, 39 neither height nor depth, nor anything else in all creation, will be able to separate us from the love of God that is in Christ Jesus our Lord.[2]

These verses are dominated by four controlling *who?* questions, which in turn determine the structure of the passage:

1. "If God is for us, *who* can be against us?" (v. 31)
2. "*Who* will bring a charge against those whom God has chosen?" (v. 33)
3. "*Who* is he that condemns?" (v. 34)
4. "*Who* shall separate us from the love of Christ?" (v. 35)

Questions 1–3 are legal or forensic in nature, while the fourth question is relational. In v. 35 the language of law makes way for the language of love. Hence the passage divides neatly into two constituent parts:

a) The legal section (vv. 31–34). Here the language of the law court is most prominent, namely "delivered (for sentencing)" (v. 32), "bring a charge against," "justifies" (v. 33), "condemns," and "intercedes" (v. 34).

b) The relational section (vv. 35–39). These verses are embraced by a neat inclusio of love—"the love of Christ" (v. 35) and "the love of God, which is in Christ Jesus our Lord" (v. 39). It is from this love that the elect are declared to be inseparable, no matter what natural or supernatural forces may be arrayed against them (vv. 35, 38, 39).[3]

2. Unless otherwise indicated, all Scripture quotations in this chapter are from the NIV.

3. *Cf.* Schreiner, *Romans*, 458: "Most scholars divide the verses into five sections (vv. 31a, 31b–32, 33–34, 35–37, 38–39) . . . A more persuasive analysis splits the text into two sections (vv. 31–34 and 35–39) in which the first part has a judicial emphasis and the second focuses on love." Thus also Moo, *Epistle to the Romans*, 538: "I think it is simplest and most natural to divide the paragraph into two parts: vv. 31–34 and vv. 35–39. The first is dominated by judicial imagery . . . In vv. 35–39, Paul expands the picture by adding to our assurance for the 'last day' assurance for all the days in between."

The transition from a legal to a relational emphasis in these verses becomes more comprehensible in the light of Paul's earlier emphasis on adoption (vv. 14–17). Here Paul draws an illustration from a practice that was common in the Roman world. Under Roman law adoption involved a legal transaction by which the adoptee was released from his natural father's legal authority (or *potestas*) and was then transferred to the *potestas* of the adoptive father.[4] A son who was thus adopted received all the rights of the new family and became heir to his adoptive father's estate.[5] If his new father had natural sons, the adoptee was treated as their equal. "The debts of his old life were cancelled," writes David Williams, "and no claim could be made against him in the courts on that account. In the eyes of the law, he was no longer the person he had been. He was a new man."[6] This practice has obvious parallels to the adoption of the believer into the family of God. Paul develops this metaphor most fully in Romans 8:12–17. As Williams further explains:

> There was a time when we were under the *potestas* of sin (Paul has argued this, although not in these terms, in the earlier chapters), but God, in his mercy, has made us God's children by adoption. The past has no claim on us now. Our adoptive Father, on the other hand, has an absolute claim (*e.g.*, we have no right to our assets; they are rightfully his). The past is no more; our debts have been cancelled; a new life has begun. We are heirs, Paul declares, "heirs of God and fellow heirs with Christ." (v. 17)[7]

The background of Paul's thinking in a practice that would have been well known to his Roman readers explains his easy transition from legal to relational language in vv. 31–39. Because all the legal requirements for the believers' adoption into God's family have been met, God is able to lavish his love upon his children without let or hindrance. Because we are God's very own through the process of adoption, no counter-claims can be lodged against us. Our opponents have had their day in court and none of their accusations will stand. Nothing from our past life can be

4. Williams, *Paul's Metaphors: Their Context and Character*, 64.

5. See Cary, *Oxford Classical Dictionary*, 7: "The classical form of adoption gave to the adopted the position of a *filius familias* in the new family with all its duties and rights, especially in regard to inheritance . . . He received his adoptive father's name and rank: a plebeian adopted by a patrician became a patrician and vice versa."

6. Williams, *Paul's Metaphors*, 64.

7. Ibid., 65.

held against us. Just as under Roman law the adoptee's old life was left behind, so for the believer his adoption into God's family brings with it a new legal status. As a son of God nothing can come between him and the love of his adoptive Father. It is only within this strongly legal-relational context that the doctrine of the eternal security of the believer can be fully appreciated.

Important as this feature of Paul's immediately preceding argument is for understanding of the doctrine of eternal security, verses 31–38 can be more deeply understood in the light of the overall context. Precisely how these verses fit into Paul's overall argument has been a matter of some dispute among scholars. Yet it is imperative that this matter be resolved if we are to adequately examine the meaning of the passage before us.

THE QUESTION OF CONTEXT

The passage opens with a crucial question: "What then shall we say to *these things*?" (v. 31 NASB) But what precisely is the antecedent to *these things*? The question is pivotal. How far back is Paul reaching into his earlier argument? In our paragraph Paul is clearly drawing an argument to a close. But precisely what argument is it? It is obvious that *these things* should include the teaching of vv. 28–30, which embraces God's providence and his eternal purpose. Yet these doctrines are not stated *de novo* in these verses, but are firmly anchored in Paul's earlier discussion. But how far back does this discussion go, and to what argument is Paul now giving such a resounding conclusion? On this point there seem to be two major schools of thought:

a) There are those who hold that Rom 8:31–39 forms an inclusio with 5:1–11, as both passages, according to Thomas Schreiner, "feature the confidence that comes from the hope of believers."[8] Moreover, "Paul reflects back on 5:1—8:30 and considers the greatness of what God has accomplished on behalf of believers."[9] This inclusio does not exclude the fact that in these verses Paul is also bringing chapter 8 to a climax. The point is more fully developed by Douglas Moo:

> [T]he similarity between the language and contents of this passage and Rom. 5 suggests that this paragraph, while responding immedi-

8. Schreiner, *Romans*, 456.

9. Ibid.

> ately to what Paul has been saying in chap. 8, and especially 8:18–30, is intended to cap Paul's many-sided discussion of Christian assurance in chaps. 5–8 as a whole. Thus, we hear again, as in 5:1–11, of the love of God in Christ for us and the assurance that that brings to us; of the certainty of final vindication because of the justifying verdict of God; and of how these great forces render ultimately impotent and unimportant the tribulations of this life.[10]

While this view has an obvious appeal because of the symmetry that it uncovers in Paul's argument, there is a more convincing alternative. The phrase *These things* has an even further reach than either Moo or Schreiner seems willing to allow.

b) There is a loud chorus of commentators who believe that *these things* points not only *to* the immediately preceding context (especially vv. 18–30) but *through* that context to Paul's entire argument up to this point. Leon Morris, for example, makes a bold claim: "The whole [of vv. 31–39] should be seen as the conclusion and summing up not only of the immediately preceding section, but of the whole of the letter up to this point."[11] Charles Hodge has argued the same case with equal emphasis: "The conclusion of the chapter is a recapitulation of all his former arguments, or rather the reduction of them to one, which comprehends them all in their fullest force; God IS FOR US."[12]

10. Moo, *Romans*, 538; *cf.* Snyman, "Style and Rhetorical Situation of Romans 8:31–39," 218–31. Snyman seeks to make the same point on the basis of rhetorical criticism: "However it gets argued, most commentators and scholars agree that Rom 8:31–39 forms the concluding (perorative) section of the unit chapters 5–8. The (elite) audience, as one type of implied reader, has gone through the argument of Rom 5–8, an argument of which much is quasi-logical and convincing. In Rom 8:31–39 as concluding (perorative) section, Paul is no longer seeking to convince his audience, but now—in this peroration—he makes a final appeal which is based on the elite audience's agreement and aims at evoking a full and emotionally charged consent to the shared affirmation. The emotional, affective impact of the passage is a well-established fact, recognized by all commentators" (227). Snyman's argument that our passage is a conclusion to chapters 5–8 depends on the rather dubious assumption that 4:23–25 is a peroration of the same order as 8:31–39 and 11:33–36. Nevertheless, he has correctly highlighted the affective nature of these verses. Paul is making an emotive appeal based on his earlier argument. Such an appeal at the end of an argument conforms to Greek rhetorical practice.

11. Morris, *Epistle to the Romans*, 334.

12. Hodge, *Commentary on the Epistle to the Romans*, 287.

James Dunn has likewise argued that our passage serves to sum up Paul's whole argument in Romans 1–8. "What shall we then say to these things?" (v. 31) evokes the following comments:

> The question obviously introduces a conclusion, certainly to the final section 8:18–30; but since 8:18–30 is itself the climactic conclusion of the whole sequence of chap. 6–8 (matching the role of 5:12–21 in the section 1:18—5:21 . . .), the ταῦτα ["these things"] can be taken to refer to the whole developed line of argument in chaps. 6–8; and since 8:18–30 effectively rounds off the argument so far (1:18—8:30) it is not going too far (despite Wilckens, n. 767) to refer the ταῦτα to the whole (*cf.* Cranfield). NEB catches the mood well, "With all this in mind, what are we to say?"[13]

Although some of the more recent commentators view our passage as the conclusion only of Paul's argument in chapters 5–8, there is much to be said for these verses being a rousing appeal to Paul's readers to personally appropriate all of his teaching up to this point. He is passionately urging his readers—whatever their circumstances—to make his gospel of God's love their own. As such, this passage occupies a central position in the epistle as a whole and has a climactic place in the mainstream of Paul's overall argument.

The Broader Context

In the exordium (1:1–7) Paul introduces himself to his readers in terms of his gospel. The heart of this gospel was the message of justification by faith, a doctrine for which Paul argues strenuously in chapters 1–5. All human beings, whether Jews or Gentiles, lack the righteousness that God requires (1:18—3:20). Therefore their only hope lies in God providing that righteousness through Christ by means of the propitiation in his blood (3:21—5:21). Hence the only way that people can be right with God is through faith in Christ. But before Paul applies that doctrine to life in 12:1*ff.*, he addresses two major objections that might be raised against it.

Objection 1: If salvation is by faith, rather than by works, doesn't that lead to a careless (and perhaps even lawless) way of life? This objection is stated quite explicitly at the beginning of chapter six: "What shall we say, then? Shall we go on sinning so that grace may increase?" (6:1). Paul gives the short answer in the very next verse: "By no means! We died to sin; how

13. Dunn, *Romans 1–8*, 499.

can we live in it any longer?" This short answer is then unpacked in the remainder of chapters 6–8:

a. We died to sin by being raised with Christ to newness of life (ch. 6).
b. We also died to the law which merely succeeds in identifying and diagnosing our sin, not in overcoming it (ch. 7).
c. We live in the newness of resurrection life by the power of the indwelling Holy Spirit (ch. 8).

In chapters 6–8, therefore, Paul demonstrates the transforming power of God's righteousness. Justification leads to sanctification.

Objection 2: The second major objection to Paul's teaching is met in chapters 9–11: If the message of justification by faith is true, and if it demonstrates God's justice, then why was it rejected by those for whom it was originally intended? If, by and large, the gospel was rejected by Israel, how can it demonstrate the justice of God? If Israel fails to believe, how can the gospel be "the power of God for the salvation of everyone who believes: first for the Jew, then for the Gentile" (1:16)?[14] Have not Paul's own missionary journeys disproved the principle of Jewish priority? And—most seriously—haven't God's purposes failed, if Israel remains in unbelief?

Objection 1 seems to have been raised by Paul's opponents (3:7–8). The second objection also deeply affected the apostle himself. For him Jewish unbelief was a very personal and heart-rending issue (9:1–5). "I have great sorrow and unceasing anguish in my heart," he writes. As Paul pens these words, his emotions are deeply stirred. He then addresses the turmoil of his own soul by way of a clear and cogent argument. At the outset he states the proposition that he is about to defend: "It is not as though God's word had failed. For not all who are descended from Israel are Israel" (9:6). In the chapters that follow he both explains and develops this claim, and supports it from Scripture.

14. *Cf.* Harding, "The Salvation of Israel and the Logic of Romans 11:11–36," 57: "Paul's argument in 1:18—8:39 has cast a shadow over his claim that the gospel is for Jew first since it is clear that the Jews have largely insisted on keeping the Torah when confronted by gospel preaching. They need to be persuaded that Paul's message is to be believed, and that it comprises God's diagnosis and prescription for the Jew first. It is therefore totally expected that Paul, having declared at the outset that this is the case, should open the issue to a large-scale discussion as to why Israel has not been persuaded and what her destiny might be."

Hence Romans 8:31–39 comes at a crucial juncture in Paul's overall argument. He has just answered one major objection and is about to tackle a second. In this passage he not only draws his entire earlier argument to a close, he also lays the groundwork for meeting the second major objection raised against his doctrine of justification by faith. If no one can bring any charge against God's elect because God is the one who justifies (v. 32), then what will become of God's elect in the Old Testament, the chosen nation of Israel? We have seen how God deals with his adopted sons, but now what about his "natural" sons?[15] How does God propose to deal with his ancient covenant people? As Schreiner explains:

> Israel was God's chosen people and the only one foreknown among the nations (Amos 3:2), and yet now the church is said to be foreknown and chosen by God (Rom 8:29–30). Yahweh had promised never to forsake Israel (Deut 31:6), yet now this promise is extended to the church (Rom 8:38–39; *cf.* also Heb 13:5). With the application of so many OT promises to the church in chapters 5–8, the relationship of Israel to God's saving plan cries out for resolution, and Paul turns to that question next.[16]

The place that our passage occupies in this epistle is therefore pivotal. It brings Paul's earlier argument to both its logical conclusion and climactic crescendo. Clearly his argument peaks at this point. As a compelling preacher Paul drives home the point of his argument with driving force. He also sets the stage for meeting the second major objection to his gospel. More modestly, he is also drawing chapter 8 to a fitting close.

The Narrower Context

In chapter 8 Paul is still answering the objection raised in 6:1: "What shall we say, then? Shall we go on sinning that grace may increase?" In chapter 6 he has begun to answer this question by appealing to the new life that the believer has in Christ. Not only has such a person been united to Christ in his resurrection (vv. 3–15), he has thereby also become a slave to righteousness (vv. 15–23). Yet this new slavery does not mean bondage to the law (7:1–6). Rather, the believer has died to the law. As Paul further

15. The language of adoption/sonship remains prominent throughout chapter 9. See vv. 4, 7–9, 26–27.

16. Schreiner, *Romans*, 467. Dealing with the question of Israel is of course beyond the scope of this article. The interested reader is referred to my essay, "Rethinking Israel," 4–48.

explains in 7:6, "But now, by dying to what once bound us, we have been released from the law so that we serve in the new way of the Spirit, and not in the old way of the written code." This verse proves to be a watershed for the chapters that follow. *The old way of the written code* is graphically described in the remainder of chapter 7. There Paul depicts the man who in his struggle against sin calls upon the law as his ally, and the outcome is ignominious defeat. Then Paul describes the better way—*the new way of the Spirit*. This is the subject of chapter 8.

Those who live according to the Spirit are those in whom the righteous requirements of the law are fully met (8:4). Through Christ Jesus the law of the Spirit of life has set them free from the law of sin and death (v. 2). They therefore have set their minds on what the Spirit desires (v. 5). Their minds are controlled by the Spirit, resulting in life and peace (v. 6). Hence God will give life to their mortal bodies through the Spirit who lives in them (v. 11). Those who by the Spirit put to death the misdeeds of the body will live (v. 13). It is in this context that believers are first called "sons of God" (v. 14) and "children of God" (vv. 16–17) in Romans. They are defined as "those who are led by the Spirit of God" (v. 14). It is here that Paul's adoption theology comes to its finest flower:

> 15 For you did not receive a spirit that makes you a slave again to fear, but you received the Spirit of sonship.[17] And by him we cry, "*Abba,* Father." 16 The Spirit himself testifies with our spirit that we are God's children.[18] 17 Now if we are children, then we are heirs—heirs of God and co-heirs with Christ, if indeed we share in his sufferings in order that we may also share in his glory.

The glorious inheritance that God's sons will enjoy is nothing less than the new creation (vv. 18–25). The old order in which they still live is pregnant with the new. The convulsions now observed in the created order are compared to the pains of a woman in labor. The creation's groans are "a symphony of sighs"[19] shared by the sons of God (v. 23), and even by the

17. The Greek word used here is υἱοθεσία and means "appointment or acceptance as a son, adoption." "The Spirit received by the believers . . . allows them to experience the new father-son relationship" (*EDNT* 3:381).

18. According to Williams, *Paul's Metaphors*, 65, in this verse "he still has the metaphor of adoption in mind. The *mancipatio* was carried out in the presence of witnesses, to ensure that the legality of the adoption could be established beyond doubt by reference to one or more of the witnesses."

19. *Cf.* Ridderbos, *Paul*, 490: "He (Paul) hears in the whole creation a groaning for

Spirit himself (v. 26). As the sons still share in the futility of the creation the Spirit helps them in their weakness and joins in their sighs. These are not the sighs of desperation but of hope (v. 24). The object of this hope is variously described as "the revelation of the sons of God" (v. 19), "the glorious freedom of the children of God" (v. 21), and "our adoption as sons, the redemption of our bodies" (v. 23).

From v. 23 in particular it is clear that the adoption of believers as children of God is intimately related to the resurrection of their bodies on the last day. It is then that they will be perfectly conformed to the likeness of the Son of God, who through the process of adoption has become their elder brother (v. 29). This process began when God sent "his own Son in the likeness of sinful man to be a sin offering" (v. 3; *cf.* v. 32). The process is complete with the glorification of the children of God (v. 30), when finally the adopted sons will resemble the natural Son (v. 29), and will share in his inheritance (v. 17). All of this is the work of the Spirit who transforms them into the likeness of Christ through sanctification in this life, and who will perfect that transformation through the resurrection on the last day (v. 11). It is therefore not surprising that in this chapter all the references to God's sons and children (vv. 15, 16, 17, 19, 21) and to their adoption (vv. 15, 23) are "embraced" by the references to his Son that precede and follow (vv. 3, 29, 32). God's gift of his Son as a sin offering is the basis for their adoption,[20] while their conformity into his likeness is its goal.

The new way of the Spirit is the subject of the chapter in which our passage stands. He is the Spirit of adoption who transforms the sons of God into the image of the Son of God. This transformation does not happen immediately, but the Spirit brings it about progressively through the process of sanctification. He will finally bring his work to completion through the resurrection of the body on the last day. What he has begun in sanctification he will complete in glorification. This is the assurance which our passage so eloquently celebrates. Nothing will come between God and his children. The work which he has begun he will most certainly

redemption, which has the character of an eager longing of the creature subjected to death and perishableness, of being already in travail, reaching out in pain toward a new birth."

20. *Cf. TDNT* 8:399: "Institution by God is set forth as the only ground of sonship . . . It is the all-transforming act of the Son that changes bondage into sonship. Eph 1:5 backs this with a reference to God's foreordination which rules out all the boasting of man with his natural or acquired qualities."

bring to completion. Come what may, those who are his children now can rest assured that they will be his children forever.

It is against this background that Paul asks his four defiant questions:

Question 1: If God is for us, who can be against us? (v. 31)

If the question that precedes this question ("What, then, shall we say in response to this?") refers back to all that Paul has been saying up to this point, then it can be said that God is "for us" in the grandest possible way. Cranfield is surely correct when he claims that the words "God is for us" are "a concise summary of the gospel."[21] This said, however, the immediate context highlights three specific ways in which it can be said that "God is for us":

a) God is for us in the way he providentially arranges the circumstances of our lives. The way things turn out for us shows that God is for us. Even difficult circumstances that are beyond our control demonstrate this. Paul makes this clear in v. 28: "And we know that in all things God works for the good of those who love him, who have been called according to his purpose." This claim is little short of astounding. In the lives of the children of God everything works out for their ultimate good. As John Murray has pointed out:

> "All things" may not be restricted, though undoubtedly the things contemplated are particularly those that fall within the compass of believers' experience, especially suffering and adversity. . . . Many of the things comprised are evil in themselves and it is the marvel of God's wisdom and grace that they, when taken in concert with the whole, are made to work for good.[22]

b) God is for us in his eternal purpose. Paul spells this out in vv. 29–30: "For those God foreknew he also predestined to be conformed to the image of his Son that he might be the firstborn among many brothers. And those he predestined he also called, and those he called he also justified, and those he justified he also glorified." This

21. Cranfield, *Critical and Exegetical Commentary on the Epistle to the Romans*, 1: 435. The preposition ὑπέρ with the genitive case, which is used here, is a construction found throughout Romans to convey some key gospel truths: Christ died *for us* (5:6–8; *cf.* 14:15), Christ and the Spirit intercede *for us* (8:26–27, 34), and God gave up his Son *for us all* (8:32).

22. Murray, *Epistle to the Romans*, 1:314.

is the golden chain of God's purpose that runs from eternity to eternity. In this chain there are no weak links. It is not broken by cancer or pain, nor even by death. Nothing in all the world—not "trouble or hardship or persecution or famine or nakedness or danger or sword" (v. 35)—can thwart the eternal purpose that God has for his children.

c) God is for us in his timely providence and in his eternal purpose, but Paul marshals one more piece of evidence to show beyond the shadow of a doubt that God is on our side. He gave us his Son. "He who did not spare his own Son, but gave him up for us all—how will he not also, along with him, graciously give us all things?" (v. 32). Clearly God "gave up" his Son in the sense of v. 3, "by sending his own Son in the likeness of sinful man to be a sin offering." This is a remarkable choice of language. The verb "give up" (παραδίδωμι) was precisely the word commonly used in the Gospels for the betrayal, arrest and crucifixion of Jesus, both in his passion predictions and in the passion account itself (*e.g.* Mark 9:31; 10:33; 14:10–11; 15:1, 10, 15).[23] But behind all the plots and intrigues of men Paul sees the mighty hand of God. At this point John Murray quotes the memorable words of Octavius Winslow: "Who delivered up Jesus to die? Not Judas, for money; not Pilate, for fear; not the Jews, for envy; but the Father, for love!"[24] God "did not spare his own Son" is an echo of Genesis 22:16 (LXX). Abraham did not spare Isaac, and yet the lad's life was saved. At Calvary God went farther than Abraham ever had to go. He "gave up" his Son to death. The nature of that death was clearly a vicarious death—"for us all." He died on our behalf and in our place (*cf.* 5:6–8; 14:15).

If God is for us in his timely providence, his eternal purpose and the gift of his Son, then—asks Paul—"who can be against us?" Although the expected answer to this rhetorical question should be a strong negative,

23. Perhaps this was not the only reason for Paul's choice of this verb. As Dunn, *Romans*, 1:500–01, observes: "The active form of the verb differs from the passive in 4:25, and though the active is the more regular Christian formulation, at this point it serves to answer the triple παρέδωκεν of 1:24, 26, 28, thus strengthening the impression that 8:31–39 is intended to round off the whole argument thus far . . . : God's handing over his Son in grace answers his handing over his creatures in wrath."

24. Murray, *Romans*, 1:324.

the immediate context would suggest that all kinds of hostile forces could rise up and oppose us (vv. 35–39). Paul is not denying that even the most violent and even deadly adversaries could be against us. He is fully aware of the realities of this present evil age, but the context in which he asks his defiant questions is heavily eschatological and forensic in character. Therefore it is clear that he is thinking of Judgment Day. When God is for us, then ultimately no adversary will be of any account. On the Day when it matters most, there will be no one to oppose us. This same eschatological thrust is present in Paul's next defiant question:

Question 2: Who will bring any charge against those whom God has chosen?[25] *(v. 33)*

The chosen or the elect are the sons/children of God who were introduced in vv. 14–17. They are also those who have been foreknown, predestined, called, justified and glorified (vv. 29–30). Paul again asks his rhetorical question in demonstrably legal terms.[26] From a purely earthly point of view it could again be said that all kinds of charges might be leveled against God's elect. Paul himself was probably the prime example. Time after time he is arraigned before magistrates and other legal officials. Accusations were made against him by both Jews and Gentiles. In fact, the verb that is used here is found again in the New Testament only in Acts (19:38; 23:28–29; 26:2, 7), and in every case Paul is the one against whom the charges are leveled. So he of all people should have known that the elect can have charges brought against them! This background information throws Paul's point into bold relief. He is again thinking eschatologically. Once more he has Judgment Day in mind. Schreiner has summarized Paul's meaning well:

> The main point of the verse is clear. Believers can face the day of judgement with confidence, for those whom God has chosen as his own will certainly not be accused on the day of judgement. God has declared them to be right in his sight, and thus those who would accuse believers will not successfully establish their case.[27]

25. The tone of Paul's question is accurately captured by Dunn's comment in *Romans*, 1:510: "Like a court officer seeking out witnesses for the prosecution, Paul challenges the whole galaxy of created beings of all ages." A similar question is found in Isaiah 50:8–9.

26. The legal meaning of the verb ἐγκαλέω is beyond doubt. It means "accuse, bring charges against someone" (*BDAG*) or "accuse, blame" (*EDNT*).

27. Schreiner, *Romans*, 462.

The reason for this happy outcome for the believer is clearly stated in the second half of the verse: "It is God who justifies." Here Paul is harking back to his earlier discussion, particularly in chapters 3–5, where he has so painstakingly established the doctrine of justification by faith. In those chapters the verb "justify" occurs eleven times. The key conclusion that Paul reaches in this context is that "since we have been justified through faith, we have peace with God through our Lord Jesus Christ" (5:1). Clearly this is a blessing that believers in Christ already enjoy. Already they have been justified. Already they have peace with God. This is an eschatological blessing come early. Hence Paul can later argue that those whom God justified, he also glorified (8:30). This means that those whom God has already justified will also receive a "not guilty" verdict at the final judgment. There is an unbreakable link between justification and glorification.

This being the case, we need to view with some caution the claim by Sanday and Headlam that the called or the elect are "not those who are destined for final salvation, but those who are 'summoned' or 'selected' for the privilege of serving God and carrying out His will."[28] Paul is not telling his readers—so the argument runs—that their glory is assured. Rather his use of the term *elect* "only shows that they are in the right way to reach it. At least no external power can bar them from it; if they lose it they will do so by their own fault."[29] This claim vividly articulates the crux of the matter. If, as the context suggests, the *elect* are indeed the children of God (vv.14–17) in whom God's eternal purpose comes to personal realization (vv. 29–30), then it needs to be said that Sanday and Headlam's definition of the *elect* is deficient. They have indeed been chosen "for the privilege of serving God and carrying out His will," but the point is that they have been chosen to far higher privileges as well. These privileges will reach their pinnacle with the acquittal and vindication of the elect on Judgment Day. Not only are they "in the right way" to reach glory, they are *destined* to reach it. Nothing will deter them, not even "their own fault." Those who have been justified by faith have peace with God (5:1) precisely because their eternal destiny is secure. This security has a firm anchorage—"it is God who justifies." The conclusion reached by Charles Hodge is therefore to be preferred over that of Sanday and Headlam:

28. Sanday and Headlam, *Critical and Exegetical Commentary on the Epistle to the Romans*, 220.

29. Ibid., 221.

> This passage . . . proves that those who are elect, and whose election has become recognised,[30] are in a state in which they are free from condemnation. No one can lay anything to their charge. The demands of justice as regards them have been satisfied. This is not true of those who have been chosen merely to church privileges. There is an election, therefore, unto grace and salvation. The elect are safe. This is the grand theme of this jubilant chapter.[31]

The eternal security of the believer is thus intimately bound up with the doctrine of justification by faith. Those who have been justified by faith will most certainly be acquitted on the Last Day. In the words, "it is God who justifies," Paul sums up much of what he has been saying throughout the epistle. In his earlier argument he has been laying the foundation for this assertion. The basis for the believer's assurance is ultimately to be found precisely at this point. God justifies. As the supreme judge, he declares the claims of justice satisfied. He makes this declaration because of the atoning sacrifice of Jesus Christ (3:25). Because the demands of divine justice have been satisfied, God is both "just and the one who justifies those who have faith in Jesus" (3:26). Once justified, always justified. The declaration made on the basis of the propitiatory work of Christ stands forever. Christ's propitiation (which removes God's wrath, *cf.* 1:18) is the legal grounds for our justification. With this as its anchorage our eternal destiny could not be more secure.

Question 3: Who is he that condemns? (v. 34)

This is another rhetorical—and at the same time defiant—question. Again the question is not asked in a vacuum, but comes at the end of a well-developed argument. Because of the sin of our forefather Adam, and because of the imputation of that sin to his descendants, all of humanity is *under condemnation* (5:16–18). God, however, dealt with that sin. By sending his own Son in the likeness of sinful flesh, he *condemned* sin in the flesh (8:3). Therefore, "just as the result of one trespass was *condemnation* for all men, so the result of one act of righteousness was justification that brings life for all men" (5:18). This being the case, Paul can begin chapter 8 on the highest and most triumphant of notes: "Therefore, there is now *no condemnation* for those who are in Christ Jesus" (8:1). Now to-

30. Their election has become recognized through their sanctified lives, or their life in the Spirit, which has been Paul's focus particularly in 8:1–17.

31. Hodge, *Romans*, 289.

wards the end of that same chapter he is able to ask equally triumphantly: "Who is he that *condemns*?"

The remainder of v. 34 does not answer the question, but states the reason for its triumphant tone: "Christ Jesus, who died—more than that, who was raised to life—is at the right hand of God and is also interceding for us."[32] Paul's confidence in asking the question as he does lies in what Christ has done and continues to do for us. This is not a baseless triumphalism, but is securely founded on four redemptive facts. The first two facts that Paul selects indicate that he is briefly recapitulating his earlier argument at this point:

d) *Jesus died*: Paul has already portrayed the death of Jesus as an atoning sacrifice for our sins (3:25; 4:25; 5:6–8, 10). This has far-reaching legal implications. As Charles Hodge explains: "By his death, as an atonement for our sins, all ground of condemnation is removed. The death of Christ could not be a proof that the believer cannot be condemned, unless his death removed the ground of condemnation; and it could not remove the ground of condemnation, unless it satisfied the demands of justice."[33]

e) *Jesus was raised to life:* If Jesus' death was an atoning sacrifice that paid for our sins, his resurrection shows that God accepted that payment. As John Stott observes: "It is not just that he rose, although this is affirmed in the New Testament, but that he was raised by the Father, who thus demonstrated his acceptance of the sacrifice of his Son as the only satisfactory basis for our justification."[34] In linking Jesus' death and resurrection with the justification of believers, Paul is echoing his summary of an earlier argument: "He was delivered over to death for our sins and was raised to life for our justification" (4:25).

f) *Jesus is at the right hand of God:* Because of his death and resurrection he has been exalted to a position of supreme power, and he holds sway over heaven and earth. Although this thought does not

32. In some English translations this statement is treated as a question; *i.e.* "Is it Christ Jesus, who died . . . ?" (thus JB, LB, RSV). While this is possible grammatically, it hardly seems to be Paul's intention. He is providing the basis for his confidence rather than asking further questions.

33. Hodge, *Romans*, 289.

34. Stott, *Message of Romans*, 256–57.

receive much emphasis in Paul (occurring again only in Eph 1:20 and Col 3:1), there is a clear allusion to Psalm 110:1, which is one of the most frequently quoted verses in the New Testament. Jesus' session at the right hand of the Father is stressed repeatedly in the early chapters of Acts (2:25, 33–34; 5:31; 7:55–56). Because Jesus is at the Father's right hand in his capacity as the crucified and risen one, humanity is represented in the highest place, at the very throne of God. Our (legal) representative could not be in a more exalted position.

g) *Jesus intercedes for us*: With legal representation in the highest places we can also rest assured that Jesus is pleading our case. Once again the terminology is heavily legal in character.[35] Christ is the intercessor who appears for the believer at the heavenly court. As such his activity appears to complement that of the Spirit who intercedes for us in our hearts (vv. 26–27). With the references to Jesus' death and resurrection Paul has recapitulated highlights of his earlier argument, but now when he refers to Jesus' intercession at the right hand of God he is introducing a genuinely new element. The connection between the two references would, however, appear to be clear enough. Paul is connecting Jesus' past redemptive activity (his death and resurrection) and his present activity (his intercession at the right hand of God). The former provides the basis for the latter (*cf.* Heb. 7:23–25). Hence Jesus is pictured as pleading our case before God (*cf.* 1 John 2:1–2). He is our Advocate before the Judge. He pleads our case on the basis of his death and resurrection. This is a truth calculated to inspire believers with the highest sense of security and confidence.

While the terminology in vv. 31–34 has been consistently legal in nature, in v. 35 the language of law makes way for the language of love. We have already explored the background for this shift and found this to be a

35. The verb ἐντυγχάνω, which is here generally translated "intercede," is used in Acts 25:24 in a strictly legal sense. There Festus tells Agrippa about Paul: "The whole Jewish community has *petitioned* me about him." H. Balz further explains that this word "belongs primarily to the conceptual world of the ruler's court . . . where accusations against another and where requests on behalf of another are made with the hope of receiving a hearing (see also Bauernfeind, 243). The narrower theological usage of the verbs in Romans 8 and Hebrews 7 take on their meaning from this background" (*EDNT* 1:461).

natural transition in the light of adoption practices that were common in Paul's day. Once the legal requirements had been met, the adoptive father could lavish all his love on his adopted children. It is to this boundless love of God that Paul now gives his attention in the remaining verses.

Question 4: Who[36] shall separate us from the love of Christ[37]? (v. 35).

In this transition from the language of law to the language of love, we detect Paul's conviction that "Christ's role in heaven is not merely as representative of his people on earth before the eternal Judge. He is also able to reach out and sustain his people still on earth. His love enfolds them as a power which hostile and untoward circumstances cannot disrupt or prevent."[38] When Paul enlarges the above question it is clear that he is speaking from personal experience: "Shall trouble or hardship or persecution or famine or nakedness or danger or sword?" From Paul's earlier letters there is ample evidence to suggest that he is speaking autobiographically (see especially 2 Cor 6:4; 11:23–27; 12:10). The only affliction in this list that he had not experienced was the sword!

If Paul is indeed speaking from his own experience, he hastens to add that his experience is not unique. He quotes from Psalm 44:22 to show that such suffering has strong scriptural precedent: "For your sake we face death all day long; we are considered as sheep to be slaughtered."[39] This is a typical "righteous sufferer" Psalm where the Psalmists are not suffering because they had broken the covenant by forgetting Yahweh or turning to other gods (vv. 17–22). Instead, they were suffering for the Lord's sake and because of their loyalty to him.[40] Paul's verbatim quote from this Psalm therefore demonstrates to his readers that the adversities

36. In view of the list that follows it seems a little curious that Paul asks *who?* rather than *what?* Morris, *Romans*, 338, suggests that "perhaps this is no more than a recognition of the fact that the nouns he lists are all masculine or feminine; there are no neuters."

37. Some ancient manuscripts read "the love of God (in Christ)," but this is clearly a scribal accommodation to v. 39 and is not adopted by any major English translation.

38. Dunn, *Romans*, 1:511.

39. Apart from a minor stylistic variation (from ἕνεκα το ἕνεκεν), this quotation is in agreement with the LXX, which in turn accords with the Hebrew of the Masoretic text. Somewhat surprisingly Moo refers to this quotation as "something of an interruption in the flow of thought" (*Romans,* 543). This misses the point of the citation, which is to support the claim implied in the last question, namely that affliction by the ungodly has often been the experience of God's children. Paul, being a wise pastor, seems to think that this assumption needs scriptural backing.

40. Thus Stott, *Romans*, 257.

of which he had spoken in the previous verse had always been the lot of God's people.[41] Should such affliction come his readers' way, "it is not as though something strange or absurd is happening to them. It is *as it is written*."[42]

At such times, "the affliction can become so sustained and all-oppressive that there seems no end to it ('all the day') and death an everyday commonplace ('as sheep for slaughter')."[43] This was precisely the kind of tribulation that would befall Paul's Roman readers within a decade of their receiving this epistle. Many of the troubles that Paul listed in v. 35 came upon them during Nero's murderous pogrom that followed the great fire of Rome in the summer of AD 64. The Roman historian Tacitus writes that Nero made local Christians the scapegoats for the fire and punished them with "the utmost refinements of cruelty." He then spells out these punishments in some detail. Even though Tacitus loathed Christians, he cannot conceal his pity for their cruel fate:

> First, then, the confessed members of the sect were arrested; next, on their disclosures, vast numbers were convicted, not so much on the count of arson as for hatred of the human race. And derision accompanied their end: they were covered with wild beasts' skins and torn to death by dogs; or they were fastened on crosses, and, when daylight failed were burned to serve as lamps by night. Nero had offered his Gardens for the spectacle, and gave an exhibition in his Circus, mixing with the crowd in the habit of a charioteer or mounted on his car. Hence in spite of a guilt which had earned the most exemplary punishment, there arose a sentiment of pity, due to the impression that they were being sacrificed not for the welfare of the state but to the ferocity of a single man.[44]

In the face of such atrocities, to which he himself eventually also fell victim, Paul can confidently declare that "in all these things we are more than conquerors through him who loved us" (v. 37). Because these events fall within the mysterious providence of God (v. 28) they are more than conquered. For not only are they endured, they also work together for

41. See Murray, *Romans*, 1:331; *cf.* Cranfield, *Romans*, 1:440.

42. Ridderbos, *Commentaar op het Nieuwe Testament: Aan de Romeinen*, 201 [author's translation].

43. Dunn, *Romans*, 1:512.

44. Tacitus, *Annals*, 15.44, in John Jackson, trans., *The Annals* (Loeb Classical Library; London: Heinemann, 1962), 283, 285.

our good. Hence "they swell the glory of our victory."[45] This triumph is not ascribed to the will or strength of the believers but to the love of Christ.[46] In the case of the Romans their noble victory in the face of state-sanctioned terrorism has been celebrated in early Christian literature. Writing towards the end of the first century, Clement of Rome recorded their victory for posterity:

> To these men who lived holy lives [*i.e.* the apostles Peter and Paul] there was joined a vast multitude of the elect who, having suffered many torments and tortures, set an illustrious example among us. Because of jealousy women were persecuted as Danaids and Dircae, suffering in this way terrible and unholy tortures, but they safely reached the goal in the race of faith, and received a noble reward, their physical weakness notwithstanding.[47]

Clement has left us a ringing testimony to the truth of Paul's assertion that even in the most trying circumstances Christians can be super-victorious through the love of Christ. Although it is unlikely that when Paul penned these words in AD 57 he was intending to be prophetic, nevertheless his words providentially foretold the kinds of trials that the Christians in Rome could expect. There is little doubt that they derived immense fortitude from his message. Even the worst tortures that Nero could inflict did not separate them from the love of Christ. The veracity of Paul's claims was soon to be proven by his own readers in the most dramatic possible way.

In vv. 38–39 Paul raises the stakes even higher. He goes beyond such external circumstances and physical extremities as trouble, hardship, persecution, famine, nakedness, danger and sword. He now transcends the kinds of sufferings that he and the Old Testament saints had already experienced and also the sufferings that his readers were soon to experience. In expressing his settled conviction about the love of God he brings chapter 8, and with it his whole argument up to this point, to a crowning crescendo: "For I am convinced that neither death nor life, neither angels

45. Hodge, *Romans*, 291.

46. Thus Schreiner, *Romans*, 464.

47. 1 Clement 6:1–2, in Holmes, *Apostolic Fathers*, 35. In a footnote Holmes explains the reference to Danaids and Dircae: "[I]n ancient mythology the daughters of Danaus were given as prizes to the winners of a race; thus it is likely that this is a reference to Christian women being raped prior to being martyred. Dirce was tied to the horns of a bull and then dragged to death."

nor demons, neither the present nor the future, nor any powers, neither height nor depth, nor anything else in all creation, will be able to separate us from the love of God that is in Christ Jesus our Lord."

Paul ends on a note of the deepest personal conviction.[48] His opening words express utmost certainty. For Paul this is no passing whim, but an assured fact that does not allow even the shadow of a doubt. Dunn's comment on these verses is superb: "The sweep of his faith is truly majestic. No longer simply situations of stress and suffering within life, but the boundary situations of life and beyond life, the powers that determine eternal destiny, all fall under his gaze, with no different result: *nothing* can loose the embrace of God's love in Christ."[49]

For the most part Paul neatly pairs these mammoth forces that might be opposed to us. Not the greatest existential realities ("neither death nor life"), not the most powerful supernatural forces ("neither angels nor demons"), nothing in the realms of time ("neither the present nor the future") or space ("neither height nor depth") can come between the believer and the love of God. The only items in the sequence that are not paired are "powers" and "anything else in all creation." By these terms Paul clearly intends to cover every possible eventuality. Nothing natural or supernatural can stand between us and the love of God. This list far surpasses that of v. 35, perhaps identifying the cosmic forces that lie behind our earthly troubles. Be that as it may, Paul's list is so comprehensive that no possible exception can be mounted against the conviction that he articulates so eloquently. Nothing, but nothing, can separate us from the love of God.

Paul's assertion is even more emphatic when it is seen as the close of the inclusio commenced in v. 35. There he had asked, "Who shall separate us from *the love of Christ*?" Here he states that nothing in all creation "will be able to separate us from *the love of God* that is in Christ Jesus our Lord." He therefore begins with the love of Christ and ends with the love of God. Is this significant? Is there a difference? The only earlier references to the love of God in Romans are in chapter 5, where "God has poured out his love into our hearts by the Holy Spirit, whom he has given us" (v. 5) and where, moreover, "God demonstrates his own love for us in this: While we

48. "I am convinced" translates πέπεισμαι, the perfect tense conveying the notion of a settled conviction. It carries the connotation, "I have become and I remain convinced" (Stott, *Romans*, 258).

49. Dunn, *Romans*, 1:512–13.

were still sinners, Christ died for us" (v. 8). The only other specific reference to the love of Christ in Romans is within the inclusio formed by vv. 35–39. With a probable reference to Christ's death Paul declares that "in all these things we are more than conquerors *through him who loved us*" (v. 37). Divine love in Romans therefore comes to its most focused expression in the gift of the Spirit and in the death of Christ. This makes Paul's logic all the more compelling. How could God abandon those in whom he has made such a huge investment? How could he withhold his love from those to whom he has given his Spirit and for whom Christ died? This is "the love of God that is in Christ Jesus our Lord." Not only can God's children not be separated from this love, these loves cannot be separated from one another. Essentially the love of God and the love of Christ are one. The love of the Father is preeminently the love that gave the Son, and the love of Christ is preeminently that he gave himself.[50] In such love the believer is eternally secure.

CONCLUSION

In all the writings of Paul the verses we have been considering stand unsurpassed in their beauty and majesty. They are also unmatched in the powerful conviction that they so vigorously express. Charles Hodge has crisply summed up their central message:

> How wonderful, how glorious, how secure is the gospel! Those who are in Christ Jesus are as secure as the love of God, the merit, power, and intercession of Christ can make them. They are hedged around with mercy. They are enclosed in the arms of everlasting love.[51]

These verses leave us with the blessed assurance that those who are God's adopted children now will be his children forever. Those who have been justified by faith in Christ will also be acquitted at the final judgment. The chain of God's purpose, which extends from his foreknowledge to our glorification, is ultimately unbreakable. It is a chain that not even the child of God can break. Those whom the Father has adopted and loved through the death of his Son and the gift of his Spirit will be his own for all eternity. As Schreiner has pointed out:

50. Thus Murray, *Romans*, 1:334.

51. Hodge, *Romans*, 293.

> Some scholars have argued that although nothing in creation can separate one from the love of God, people can themselves choose to depart from God and thereby fall outside the scope of the saving love of God. This interpretation should be rejected. As we have seen, Rom 8:28–30 constitutes an unbreakable process. All those who are foreknown end up being glorified. No possibility is extended that some of those who are justified may not be glorified. The category of the justified is inseparable from the category of the glorified. . . . Those whom God has chosen before history began will surely persevere and attain to glorification.[52]

In closing, we return to Paul's ringing rhetorical questions that resound throughout this passage. With them he has defied every creature in time and space, whether natural or supernatural, benevolent or malevolent:

- "If God is for us, who can be against us?"
- "Who will bring a charge against those whom God has chosen?"
- "Who is he that condemns?"
- "Who shall separate us from the love of Christ?"

There is only one rousing answer to all of these questions: *Nothing and nobody!* Paul allows for no exceptions. In the saving love of God every true believer in Christ is eternally secure.

Soli Deo gloria!

52. Schreiner, *Romans*, 466.

6

Making Your Calling and Election Sure

An Analysis of 2 Peter 1:8–11

VERLYN D. VERBRUGGE

I WAS RAISED IN a Reformed community, where God's election of his people was stressed. I distinctly remember the first time I read 2 Peter 1, and verse 10 especially jarred my Calvinistic mind. Surely Peter couldn't be saying what that text seemed to be saying, could he? "Therefore, my brothers, be all the more eager to make your calling and election sure." If my salvation is totally in the hands of a sovereign God, how could I do anything to make sure that I am among the elect? In this article I will visit this puzzling text and seek to uncover what Peter means by it.

PETER'S SOCIO-RELIGIOUS WORLD

Commentators on 2 Peter usually begin with an introduction, in which they discuss issues such as the disputed authorship of this letter, its likely date of writing, its destination, its literary style and genre, and its relationship to Jude. Such issues need not concern us in this article. Suffice it to say that I accept the Petrine authorship of the book, which means I date it prior to AD 68.

Commentators also discuss the nature of the opponents, whose infiltration into the church had much to do why the letter was written. Traditionally these opponents have been viewed as Gnostics or proto-Gnostics,[1] though that hypothesis is generally not accepted today. More

1. See, *e.g.*, Green, *2 Peter and Jude*, 37–40; Schreiner summarizes the proposed arguments in *1, 2 Peter, Jude*, 278–79.

recently some scholars have argued that these "false teachers" (2:1) had philosophical links with the Epicureans, primarily because Epicureans denied the notion of a coming judgment and advocated for complete human freedom (which could lead to an immoral lifestyle, the sort of lifestyle describe in ch. 2).[2]

The issue of identifying the opponents is also one that does not need to be settled here; with Schreiner, it is probably best merely to describe their characteristics and not attempt to identify exactly who they are; the limited information we have in these three chapters does not allow for such precision.[3] But what is more important for our purposes is to examine the socio-religious world that Peter assumes in his letter. We need to grasp the structure of this world in order to understand the flow of his argument in chapter 1.

Peter essentially divides up the world of his audience into two groups. The first group is the believers (I will call them Group 1), who have been called and chosen by God, who have received faith as a gift of his grace, and who now have life and godliness (see the discussion below); they are Christians. The other group (Group 2) is that of the "false teachers," who teach "heresies of destruction" and "deny" (ἀρνέομαι) the only Master who sacrificed his life for them as a payment for sin (2:1). Those who belong to this group are headed for condemnation (κρίμα, 2:3), for destruction (απώλεια, 2:3), for the "darkness of darkness" (ὁ ζόφος τοῦ σκότους, 2:17)—which is a euphemism for hell. They are not Christians.

It does seem clear that those who belong to Group 2 have had in the past some affiliation with the church (with those in Group 1). They had the hope of escaping the corruption of the world through a relationship with Jesus Christ as Savior. That is, Group 2 people are not pagans who have never had any appreciation for the teachings of the apostles. The fact that they are trying to promote their teachings within the church (2:1) suggests that have had some relationship with the church. Perhaps they still view themselves as followers of Jesus.

But the most important observation about members of Group 2 is that they have become entangled again in the world and have succumbed to its evil devices (2:20).[4] They at one time knew the way of righteousness

2. See Neyrey, *2 Peter, Jude*, 122–28; Schreiner critiques this view in *1, 2 Peter, Jude*, 279–80.

3. Schreiner, *1, 2 Peter, Jude*, 280.

4. 2 Peter 2:20 is a first class condition of reality, in which the εἰ-clause focuses not on what these people could have been (expressed by the participle ἀποφυγόντες) but on

(*i.e.*, the way of becoming right with God), but they have turned their backs on it (2:21). Thus, Peter compares them to the angels who sinned and were sent to hell (Tartarus, ταρταρόω, 2:4), to the wicked world that was destroyed in the flood (2:5), and to the condemned sinners who were burned in the fire of Sodom and Gomorrah (2:6). Though Peter does not specifically say so, he would agree with the apostle John in 1 John 2:19: "They went out from us, but they did not really belong to us. For if they had belonged to us, they would have remained with us; but their going showed that none of them belonged to us."[5]

Now in Peter's socio-religious world, some might argue that there is a third group. The false teachers are attempting to influence members of the Group 1 to shift their allegiance to them, to follow them in their teachings and in their wicked lifestyle (2:2). This might appear to be a separate group of people "in transition," gradually sliding from Group 1 into Group 2. Now in terms of Peter's analysis in this letter (as we will see), such a group does not exist, and he is writing this letter to make sure that no one slides into Group 2. Nevertheless, I believe it is plain that the whole tenor of Peter's writing suggests that if it were to happen, any who might transfer their allegiance to the false teachers would only be demonstrating that they had not truly received the grace of God. They would have the characteristics, as outlined above, of Group 2 and never been true members of Group 1.

With this socio-religious world in mind, let us now turn our attention to 2 Peter 1.

CONTEXT OF 2 PETER 1:1–7

Context is one of the most important hermeneutical principles that determine the meaning of a passage. Thus, while much of the focus in the article will be on verses 8–11, I would be amiss if I did not first of all

what they now are—entangled in the world and its pursuits; as a result, their latter stage is worse than the first. As Jesus himself suggested in the parable of Luke 12:47–48, those who know the way of the Lord and refuse to follow it are worse off than who do not know his will in the first place.

5. While Peter does not dwell in this letter on those who never had a relationship with the church, he would undoubtedly class such people also in Group 2. That is, there is no Group 3; there are only believers and unbelievers. The apostle John does deal with those who have never been believers with his use of the Greek word κοσμός ("the world"; see, *e.g.*, 1 John 2:15–17; 5:19).

set this passage in the context of the theology that Peter advances in the preceding verses. In verse 1, Peter addresses this letter "to those who . . . have received a faith as precious as ours." Note that Peter does not speak here about those who have received salvation; rather, he refers to those who have received "faith," which is the instrument by which salvation is communicated to an individual (*cf.* Eph 2:8). Peter clearly intimates here that while "faith" is something that a person must exercise, even faith itself is a gift that one receives from God.

Moreover, the verb translated "received" is the verb λαγχάνω, a verb that occurs four times in the New Testament. In the other three instances in which this verb occurs, it is linked in a context of the casting of lots. The priest Zechariah, father of John the Baptist, was "chosen by lot" to serve in the temple ministry (Luke 1:9). The soldiers "decided by lot" which one would get the seamless garment of Jesus (John 19:24). As the early apostles were discussing a replacement of Judas between the time of Jesus' ascension and the outpouring of the Holy Spirit on Pentecost, Peter refers to the betrayer as someone who was numbered among them and (lit.) "received the lot of this service" (Acts 1:17).[6] The apostles then went on to cast lots and chose Matthias as Judas' replacement.

The important point in the casting of lots, according to the Old Testament, is that the one viewed as responsible for the outcome of the lot is the Lord God: "The lot is cast into the lap, but its every decision is from the Lord" (Prov 16:33; *cf.* also 1 Sam 14:41). In addition, most scholars consider the Urim and Thummim as a sort of casting of lots, through which the will of the Lord was determined.[7] Thus, the emphasis in 2 Peter 1:1 on the source of our faith, whereby we receive the righteousness of our God and Savior Jesus Christ, is that it comes from the Lord; it is a gift of God.

In verses 3–4, the grammar is admittedly difficult to follow.[8] But at least two elements stand out. First, Peter twice uses the perfect form of

6. This use of λαγχάνω suggests that Judas, like the other disciples, was called and chosen by Jesus as a disciple (*cf.* Mark 3:16–19; Luke 6:12–15); what is especially significant is that here this verb is linked directly with the noun κλῆρος ("lot"). The disciples did not choose Jesus; rather, Jesus chose them (*cf.* John 15:16).

7. See Tenney and Douglas, "Urim and Thummim," 1044–45.

8. See this discussion of the grammar in Schreiner, *1, 2 Peter*, 289–90. See also the article by Callan, "The Syntax of 2 Peter 1:1–7," 632–40. Callan points out the three options for verses 3–4: a concluding clause to the opening blessing (vv. 1–2), an anacolouthon, or an introductory clause (which he calls a protasis of a condition) to verses 5–7. While I

the verb δωρέομαι, a verb that means "to bestow, give." This is a middle deponent verb, so that it has an active thrust in meaning. In verse 3, δεδωρημένης stands in a genitive absolute construction with τῆς θείας δυνάμεως, which then translates: God's "divine power has bestowed on us everything we need for life and godliness." In verse 4, the subject of δωρέομαι is presumably God, and what he has given us are his "very great and precious promises,"[9] through which we become sharers in "the divine nature." Through both occurrences of this verb, in other words, Peter emphasizes that we are recipients of God's gifts; we do not earn them, nor do we bestow them on ourselves.

The second significant element in verses 3–4 is Peter's emphasis that the means whereby we become aware of these divine gifts is "the knowledge of him who called us by his own glory and goodness" (v. 3). Note especially the phrase "who called us." I cannot go into a full discussion of the notion of calling here; suffice it to say that the calling here is that of an "effectual call" given by Christ. When Christ calls believers to himself, along with that calling comes the gift of being able to respond to that call. "When God calls or speaks, it is so. . . . The call of Christ, then, is effective and performative."[10] This call enables us to escape the corruption (either moral or physical—or both) that is related to this sinful world (*cf.* Eph 4:22; 1 John 2:17; note also the notion of escape from this world into God's eternal kingdom in 2 Pet 1:11).[11]

In the next three verses (2 Pet 1:5–7), Peter instructs believers, based on the power and calling they have received from God (*cf.* καὶ αὐτὸ τοῦτο δὲ at the beginning of v. 5, which can translate "and with this especially in mind"), to grow in their Christian faith by developing and increasing in their lives eight Christian virtues: faith, goodness, knowledge,

agree with Callan that verses 3–4 must be linked to verses 5–7, I see verses 3–4 as a causal clause begun with ὡς rather than some form of a conditional sentence with a προτασίς and ἀποδοσίς.

9. *BDAG* gives an active emphasis in 2 Peter 1 to both of these middle deponent verbs; s.v. δωρέομαι (p. 266).

10. Schreiner, *1, 2 Peter, Jude*, 290.

11. Note that the words that Peter uses here are almost identical to those used in 2:20, where he indicates that the members of Group 2 were hoping to escape (ἀποφεύγω) the corruption (φθορά in 1:4; μιάσματα in 2:20) of the world (τοῦ κοσμοῦ). While φθορά can denote a variety of types of corruption and destruction (*e.g.*, physical, moral, religious, eternal), μιάσματα is more limited to moral corruption (see *BDAG*, s.v. μιάσμα, 650; φθορά, 1054–55).

self-control, perseverance, godliness, brotherly kindness, and love. It is true that Peter introduces this list in verse 5 with a second person imperative verb ἐπιχορηγήσατε ("furnish, provide"). This use of the imperative emphasizes that we are not passive in living out the Christian life. But the eight Christian qualities listed here would be impossible for us to develop in our lives without the substratum of God's sovereign gifts and call that Peter has laid out so powerfully in verses 1–4.

To summarize the context, then, Peter is concerned that believers escape the corruption of the world around them and grow in Christian graces, but they are able to do so only because they have received faith and salvation as a gift from God, and because God has bestowed on them everything they need in order to live a life of holiness and godliness; equally important, he has placed his divine nature within them, which serves as the basis for Christian living.

THE EXPECTED RESULTS OF 2 PETER 1:8–9

The connective γάρ joins verses 8–11 with verses 5–7; Peter is now able to move on to the next point of his argument.[12] The Greek word ταῦτα ("these things")—which summarizes the eight qualities just mentioned in verses 5–7—functions as the subject of the verb καθίστησιν, and it has two participles that expand its scope. These two participles (ὑπάρχοντα and πλεονάζοντα) are circumstantial participles that carry the adverbial nuance of either condition or means. We can translate verse 8 something like this, then: "These things, if they belong to you and if they are increasing" (or, "these things, by means of their existence and of their abundance in your life"), "will not cause you to be useless and fruitless in the knowledge of our Lord Jesus Christ."

The emphasis in verse 8 is essentially a double negative; otherwise put, *not* to cause someone to be *useless* and *fruitless* denotes, *mutatis mutanda*, causing someone to be useful and fruitful. In other words, Peter stresses here that if the eight qualities mentioned in verses 5–7 become an integral part of our lives and are actually increasing in abundance, they

12. The Greek connective γάρ does not always carry a causal nuance, "for, because." As *BDAG* points out, γάρ sometimes simply expresses continuation or clarification, similar to δέ (s.v. "γάρ," 189); I argued this in an unpublished paper presented at Midwest Regional SBL Conference at Calvin College, Spring 2003, "Driving Your γάρ with Caution."

will enable us to grow in the knowledge of the Lord Jesus Christ and in the practice of living useful and fruitful lives that serve and honor him.

In other words, Peter is encouraging these believers to remain in Group 1 (as outlined above) and not to slide into Group 2 by following the false teachers into their destructive heresies. He feels confident that if the believers to whom he is writing follow the lifestyle recommended in verses 5–7, they will grow "in the knowledge" (εἰς τὴν . . . ἐπίγνωσιν) of the Lord Jesus Christ. The word ἐπίγνωσις is an important term in 2 Peter; this is the third time he has used it (see 1:2, 3). Bultmann defines this word as a "decisive knowledge of God which is implied in conversion to the Christian religion";[13] Bauckham calls it "that fundamental saving knowledge on which the whole of the Christian life is based."[14] Because such ἐπίγνωσις is so critical to salvation, Peter affirms that it is from this knowledge that the false teachers have fled (2:20). Thus, the more we become fully aware of the fullness of who Christ is and what he has done for us, the less likely we are to slide into the false teachings and immoral behavior of the heretics.

In verse 9, Peter offers the converse of verse 8. Regarding someone in whom these eight qualities described in verses 5–7 do not exist and are not flourishing and who does not have a growing ἐπίγνωσις of Christ, he or she is "blind, short-sighted, and forgetful of the cleansing of his past sins." The verb μυωπάζω ("to be shortsighted, nearsighted") is a *hapax legomenon* in the New Testament and occurs only in later Christian writings. When coupled with τυφλός, it bears the meaning "he is so shortsighted that he is blind;"[15] he cannot see where he is headed.

Moreover, the people described in verse 9 have forgotten about their "cleansing from . . . sin." Cleansing (καθαρισμός) from sin, a common New Testament metaphor used to depict what happens in salvation (see Acts 22:16; Titus 2:14; Heb 9:14; 1 John 1:7, 9), is a process that is wrought only by Christ (see Heb 1:3). This metaphor is based on the purification imagery of the Old Testament law (see, *e.g.*, Lev 16:15–16, 19, 30; Ps 51:7; Isa 1:16).

But how does the πάλαι ("long ago, in the past") figure in? Even though this adverb is connected most closely with ἁμαρτιῶν ("sins"), I

13. Bultmann, "γινώσκω," *TDNT*, 1:707.

14. Bauckham, *Jude, 2 Peter* (WBC; Waco, TX: Word, 1983), 170.

15. *BDAG*, s.v. μυωπάζω (532).

hold that it refers not to past sins (as if only sins done long ago are covered by the cleansing of Christ), but that it refers to what the people referred to in this verse heard at some time "in the past" with respect to Christ's cleansing from sin. It is precisely this cleansing that is not, and never truly has been, a part of their lives; in spite of whatever moral virtues they may have been manifesting for a period of time, they are now once again wallowing in their former sinful life—just as a dog returns to its vomit or a pig to its mire (2:22). These people are, in other words (if we use the suggested scheme of Peter's socio-religious world), members of Group 2. As Moo write on this verse, "spurious Christians, false teachers, were about. Surely Peter has these people—whom he will describe in greater detail in chapter 2—in mind when he warns about the kind of person who 'does not have them [*i.e.*, the virtues of vv. 5–7].' "[16]

Thus, even before Peter enters fully into the world of the false teachers, he already describes them here. Verse 8 describes the Christian lifestyle and behavior of Group 1, and verse 9 offers a key characteristic of Group 2. A Christian cannot remain static in the Christian faith. "Instead, we are either continuing to grow or we have begun to slip backwards."[17] The problem for the Christian who does not increase in his or her knowledge (ἐπίγνωσις) of Jesus Christ, does not appreciate God's saving grace and gift of faith, and does not continue to develop a fruitful life of service to him and to others—such a person ends up in Group 2. It is not that this person has switched groups; rather, it becomes apparent that he or she never truly was in Group 1.

THE ENCOURAGED EFFORT OF 2 PETER 1:10–11

With this in mind, Peter now moves to verse 10, which he begins with διό. Because God expects his people to add to their faith the various qualities mentioned in verses 5–7 so that they may abound in the faith and live fruitful lives, he exhorts them to "put forth every effort [σπουδάζω] to make [ποιέω, in the infinitive form ποιεῖσθαι] your calling [κλῆσις] and election [ἐκλογή] sure [βέβαιος]." Each of the Greek words noted here is significant.

16. See Douglas Moo, *2 Peter, Jude*, 48.

17. Zane Hodges, "Making Your Calling and Election Sure: An Exposition of 2 Peter 1:5–11," *Journal of the Grace Evangelical Society* 11 (Spring 1998), <http://www.faithalone.org/journal/1998/Hodges.html>, accessed 23 February 2007.

The verb σπουδάζω reflects back on the word σπουδήν in verse 5, where Peter instructs believers to put forth effort to develop the eight qualities of verses 5–7 in their lives. This is a word group that denotes the putting forth of human effort. The verb σπουδάζω occurs eleven times in the New Testament,[18] and in each case it refers to something that human beings are being encouraged to do. It is used twice more in this letter. In 1:15, Peter indicates the effort he is expending in his writing so that after he dies, those whom he has led to the Lord will be able to recall what he has taught them about Jesus.[19] In 3:14, he exhorts the recipients of this letter themselves to put forth every effort to remain spotless and blameless until the return of the Lord. Thus, in 1:10, as long as we are living on this earth, we must put forth effort to grow in the Christian faith and way of life, through the help of the Holy Spirit (though Peter does not mention the third person of the Trinity here). Peter does not hesitate to say that living a Christian life requires effort on our part.

The infinitive ποιεῖσθαι is a present infinitive of the common verb ποιέω, which completes the thought of σπουδάζω. As a present infinitive, it emphasizes ongoing effort. In other words, putting forth effort to grow in the faith and Christian graces is a lifelong proposition. There is never to be a moment in our lives when we can relax and say regarding Christian maturity, "I have arrived."

We have briefly discussed the notion of calling in our comments on verse 3. The verb used in the phrase "who called us" (καλέω) in verse 3 is related to the word "calling" (κλῆσις) in verse 10. As noted in our comments on verse 3, this calling refers an "effectual call" given by Christ; it is inner call through which Christ also gives us the necessary grace to respond. This is the reason why it is linked so closely with ἐκλογή ("election"). The two together form what is technically called a hendiadys, where two words are so closely associated together they that they form a single idea—that of "elective call."[20]

18. In addition to this verse, the verb occurs in Gal 2:10; Eph 4:3; 1 Thess 2:17; 2 Tim 2:15; 4:9, 21; Titus 3:12; 2 Pet 1:15; 3:14.

19. It is worth noting here that Mayor (*The Epistle of St. Jude and the Second Epistle of St. Peter*, 102–3) sees an allusion here to the Gospel of Mark, which (according to church tradition) was written by Mark under the supervision of Peter.

20. This is the way that Schreiner (*1, 2 Peter, Jude*, 304) translates these two words. Bauckham (*Jude, 2 Peter*) points out "the author's predilection for nearly synonymous word" in 2 Peter 1 (190). Other examples are "life and obedience" (v. 3), "glory and goodness" (v. 3), "useless and fruitless" (v. 8), and "shortsighted and blind" (v. 9). Similarly here, then, "calling and election" are synonyms.

The word ἐκλογή occurs seven times in the New Testament, and in each instance it denotes something God does. In Acts 9:15, God says to Ananias, when Ananias shows reluctance to visit Saul immediately after the latter's call from heaven on the way to Damascus, "This man is a vessel of election for me," that is, "this man is my chosen instrument." In Romans 9:11, Paul writes about how God had chosen the younger son, Jacob, over the older son, Esau, even before they were born to be the one who would carry on the family promises. As Paul continues to struggle with doctrine of God's election and the role of the Jews in that election, he uses ἐκλογή three times in Romans 11: "a remnant according to the election of grace" (11:5), the elect received God's promises (11:7), and the people of Israel are still "beloved by virtue of their election" (by God). Finally, in 1 Thessalonians 1:4, Paul calls the Thessalonians believers those who are beloved by God, and for that reason the apostle writes that he is confident of "your election."

In other words, when all is said and done, believers are the *recipients* of God's calling and election. In no way can we force God's hand to become the "called" and the "elect"; it is a work of his grace. This is, of course, in keeping with the context as noted above, that everything we need for our redemption and salvation, including faith, we have received as a gift from God.

There is one final word to discuss in this crucial verse 10: the adjective βέβαιος ("firm, sure"). This is the critical word to study in the verse, since with ποιεῖσθαι it suggests the notion that we can do something to "make sure" (or "make firm") that we are among the elect. One of the most important elements to note about the βέβαιος word group is that it roots out of a legal framework. "The promises of God, the word of God, and the gospel will be fulfilled with absolute certainty because they have been legally confirmed by God, and so form the foundations of the faith."[21] Because of this firm foundation, the believer receives assurance of salvation. "The certainty of the believer's hope is inextricably rooted in the legal validity of God's word."[22]

The verb βεβαιόω ("to confirm, make firm, establish") sets the tone for this word group in the New Testament. It occurs eight times (includ-

21. See Schönweiss, "βέβαιος," *NIDNTT*, 1:658.

22. Ibid., 660. Schieder, "βέβαιος," *TDNT*, 1:600–03, also directs the reader's attention to this "technical legal sense" (603).

ing the textually suspect Mark 16:20). Four of these are in the active voice. In Mark 16:20, God "confirms" his word by signs. In Romans 15:8, Paul writes that Christ became a servant of the Jews (lit., "the circumcision") in order to "confirm" the promises made to the patriarchs. In 1 Corinthians 1:8, Paul writes that Christ "will make us firm" to the end in order that we may appear blameless on the day of the Lord. In 2 Corinthians 1:21, the apostle emphasizes that God is the one who "makes us stand firm" in Christ and anoints us. In all four of these occurrences, the one who does the confirming is either God or Christ.

The other four uses of βεβαιόω are in the passive voice. In 1 Corinthians 1:6, Paul writes that his witness about Christ "was confirmed" among the Corinthians by the way they were given God's grace and were enriched in him with word and knowledge (1:4–6 contains three passives). Colossians 2:7 likewise contains three passive voice parallel participles, that the Colossian Christians were rooted and built up in Christ and "were made firm" in their faith. In Hebrews 2:3 the author notes how salvation, which was first spoken by the Lord, "was confirmed" in believers by those who heard. And finally, Hebrews 13:9 stresses how good it is for the heart to "be made firm" by grace, not by special (ceremonial) foods. These uses of the passive (with the possible exception of Hebrews 2:3, since an agent is expressed by a ὑπό + genitive construction) are what New Testament scholars call "the divine passive"—the use of the passive voice with the implication that God is the agent, sometimes expressed in the text but often only implied.[23]

In other words, in the New Testament, the work of strengthening the hearts of believers and confirming their faith is the work of God. This same emphasis becomes apparent in a brief study of the two uses of the noun in this word group, βεβαίωσις. In Philippians 1:7, Paul writes that the Philippians are sharers with him in God's grace, whether he is in chains or is out working for the defense and "confirmation" of the gospel. While Paul does not elaborate here how he defends and confirms the gospel, others passages of the New Testament suggest that he defends it by his preaching and his legal testimony before rulers and governors (note the legal context) and confirms it by his exercise of the gifts that the Spirit

23. See the discussion of the divine passive in Wallace, *Greek Grammar beyond the Basics*, 437–38. Note especially this statement: "That God is behind the scenes is self-evidently part of the worldview of the NT writers. The nature of this book demands that we see him even when he is not mentioned" (438).

has given him (Rom 15:18–19; 2 Cor 12:12; *cf.* Mark 16:17; Acts 5:12; 19:11–12; see also Heb 2:4, in the context of the use of βέβαιος in 2:2). In Hebrews 6:16, the author uses βεβαίωσις to refer to an oath that confirms a promise, and he specifically relates it to God's oath that confirmed his promise to Abraham that he would have a son. In both uses of βεβαίωσις in the New Testament, the one doing the confirming is God, even if a human being is involved.

The third word in the βέβαιος word group is the adjective βέβαιος, which, like the verb, occurs eight times in the New Testament. In four of these, clearly the one behind what is considered firm and secure is the Lord God. In Romans 4:16, Paul refers to God's promise of salvation by grace through faith that is "firm" and secure for all of Abraham's true descendants, both Jew and Gentile. In Hebrews 2:2, the author emphasizes how the word spoken by angels was "firm," because it was God's word that they spoke (reflecting the tradition that Moses received God's law through angels as mediators; *cf.* Gal 3:19). Later in Hebrews (6:19) is a reference to the Christian experience of hope, which God offers to us as a "firm" and secure anchor for our souls (*cf.* also Rom 5:5 on the believer's hope). And in 2 Peter 1:19, Peter writes how God's word spoken by the prophets is more "firm" and secure to us because such words originated in God.

As to the other four uses of βέβαιος, one of them simply points out the obvious legal maxim that a human will does not go into effect (that is, is not confirmed) until that person dies (Heb 9:17). The other two uses of βέβαιος (omitting for the time being our text, 2 Pet 1:10) do speak of a human confidence. In 2 Corinthians 1:7 Paul feels confident about the Corinthians (*i.e.*, he has a "firm" hope) that just as they have shared in his sufferings, so they will share in his comfort. And in one of the warning passages of Hebrews, the author encourages the believers to hold "firm" to the end of their lives the conviction of their faith that they first experienced (Heb 3:14)—and let us recall that what will enable them to do so is the hope God has given them (Heb 6:19).

Let us sum up, then, our study of the βέβαιος word group in the New Testament. In the vast majority of its usages, God is at work as the one who initiates and confirms the faith of Christians. Our calling, our election, and our faith are not things that originate with us; they are gifts of God. "It is God himself who establishes, makes firm, the believer in Christ, and seals him with the Holy Spirit. . . . He is secure because he looks away from all efforts of his own and stands entirely on what lies outside himself."[24] And throughout our lives, the things that happen to us and the way we live out our faith, both of which confirm in our hearts that God is at work in our lives, are divinely appointed.

Thus, when Peter instructs the Christians to whom he is writing to "make their elective call βέβαιος," he is not suddenly shifting to a works righteousness theology, as if the way a Christian lives establishes his or her calling and election. After all, as Zane Hodges reminds us, "'the gifts and the calling of God are irrevocable (Rom. 11:29).' Thus, in no way are we to conclude that βέβαιος . . . ποιεῖσθαι means 'to confirm the call; i.e., so that it does not lapse.'"[25] Rather, Peter is saying that as believers live their Christian lives in the power of God's Spirit and as they grow in the eight Christian graces through the strength and power that come from God, they will begin to feel ever more firmly in their hearts that God indeed has called them and chosen them as his people.[26]

This is the emphasis in the last part of verse 10: "for by doing these things you will not at all, ever, stumble." The participle used here (ποιοῦντες), like the two participles in verse 8 (see above), has the adverbial nuance of either means or condition ("for if you do these things," or "by doing these things"). Writing this letter in a context of those who are in Group 2, Peter does not want his readers to follow along with them in their "destructive heresies" that deny "the Sovereign who bought them" (2:1). He knows that as long as they are living the Christian life to which they have been called and are feeling the power of God's Spirit moving in their hearts and lives, they will never stumble; that is, "they will not forsake God, abandon him, and commit apostasy."[27] Rather, they will be confirming in their hearts and by their lives their calling and their election. Make no mistake: Peter here is stressing the importance of putting for consistent effort to live a Christian lifestyle. But a Christian does not

24. Schönweiss, "βέβαιος," 660.

25. Hodges, "Making Your Calling and Election Sure," online version.

26. I should note here that Hodges, ibid., interprets βέβαιος . . . ποιεῖσθαι not in terms of personal assurance, as I do, but as "producing valid evidence *for others* to observe that God has indeed 'called' and 'chosen' him" (italics added). He derives this from the legal connotations of word in classical and Hellenistic Greek. But as my study of the βέβαιος word group has demonstrated, this legal framework is secondary to the confirming power of God's grace, which secures our salvation.

27. Schreiner, *2 Peter, Jude*, 305.

that in order to earn divine grace; rather, it is to "show evidence of this reality by means of virtuous living."[28]

The end result of remaining firm and steadfast in the Christian faith until the very end is expressed in the last verse: "For in this way an entrance will be richly provided for you into the eternal kingdom of our Lord and Savior Jesus Christ" (2 Pet 1:11). Note once again here the use of a divine passive verb in "will be provided" (ἐπιχορηγηθήσεται). Peter does not say that believers will earn an entrance into the eternal kingdom as a result of living the Christian life of the eight Christian graces, for no one earn a place in heaven. Rather, God will provide believers an entrance into that eternal kingdom as a result of his calling and election by his rich grace. The adverb πλουσίως, which modifies the verb ἐπιχορηγηθήσεται, emphasizes how rich and glorious indeed is the heavenly inheritance that God has in store for us.[29]

CONCLUSION

In summary, then, after his opening greeting in verses 1–2, Peter begins this section with the exaltation of God's grace in verses 3–4, and he ends in verse 11 with a concluding statement that "makes it clear that final salvation is not man's achievement but the gift of God's lavish generosity!"[30] These verses form the bookends or an inclusio through which this entire passage must be read. We received God's salvation by his grace through the work done by Christ, and as we tap into that power and "divine nature" (v. 4), we receive confirmation in our hearts that we truly are the elect of God and called to his service for his glory.

28. Charles, "2 Peter," *EBC*, 13:391.

29. In two of the other three instances of this adverb in the New Testament, the emphasis is on what God has richly provided for us through his Son, Jesus Christ (1 Tim 6:17 [a full life]; Titus 3:6 [the Holy Spirit]).

30. Bauckham, *Jude, 2 Peter*, 193.

7

The Adoption Metaphor and the Security of the Believer

Francis Lyall

INTRODUCTION

The New Testament uses many similes, metaphors, and other figures of speech.[1] These are ways of thinking of profound truths, and are given to us so that we can both comprehend and appreciate certain matters. They are not to be taken as precisely accurate technical explanations, but draw on known ideas so as to allow an understanding and a grasp of theological truth. They are "as if" statements.[2] For example, in Hebrews 12:1 we are exhorted to run the race setting aside everything that would hinder us—compare athletic meetings every summer—but how many of us strip off and run? "Adoption" is one such figure of speech, and is a very clear legal analogue communicating valuable truths. It has produced sundry theological musings,[3] and appears compactly in some Reformation confessions of faith, but these conceal something rather strange. Adoption was not known to the civil law at the time or place the Reformation confessions were formulated.

1. Copyright © F. Lyall, 2008. Emeritus Professor of Public Law, University of Aberdeen, Scotland, U.K. Of course there are figures of speech also in the Old Testament, as well as the "acted parables" of the prophets which serve a similar function.

2. Derrett, *Jesus's Audience*, 101–6.

3. I am reluctant to cite since too many anachronistically apply concepts from modern law, although I would not quarrel with the reassurance they intend to provide.

THE CONFESSIONS[4]

The Seventeenth Chapter of the *Thirty–Nine Articles of Religion of the Church of England* of 1571 states that among the benefits of predestination is that Christians are made sons of God by adoption. Article Seven of the *Canons of Dordt* of 1618, "On Election," states *inter alia* that God predestined those "whom he adopted as his children through Jesus Christ." The fullest treatment, however, is in Chapter Twelve of the *Westminster Confession of Faith* of 1647 which states "Of Adoption":

> All those that are justified, God vouchsafeth, in and for his only Son Jesus Christ, to make partakers of the grace of adoption: by which they are taken into the number, and enjoy the liberties and privileges of the children of God; have his name put upon them; receive the Spirit of adoption; have access to the throne of grace with boldness; are enabled to cry, Abba, Father; are pitied, protected, provided for, and chastened by him as by a father; yet never cast off, but sealed to the day of redemption, and inherit the promises, as heirs of everlasting salvation.[5]

THE SOURCE

There are many places in the New Testament where an author uses the language of law to put across the message.[6] Slavery, freedmen, citizenship, earnest (ἀρρηα), marriage, and inheritance all provide images: adoption is one among many. The strangeness of the Reformation confessions is that, as noted above, at the time that they were drafted not only was there no contemporary law of adoption to provide meaning for the concept they referred to, but there had not been such a concept in law for centuries.[7] What was relied on was the use of the word in the New Testament,

4. Conveniently available at the website of the Center for Reformed Theology and Apologetics: <http://www.reformed.org/documents/index.html>, accessed May 19, 2008.

5. See also Question 74 of the *Larger Catechism*, and Question 34 of the *Shorter Catechism*, both adopted by the Westminster Assembly.

6. See Lyall, *Slaves, Citizens, Sons: Legal Metaphors in the Epistles*.

7. The first British law on the matter was the Adoption Act of 1930. In the British Empire the first was the New Zealand Adoption of Children Act of 1881. In the United States the Massachusetts Adoption of Children Act of 1851 takes precedence. In Europe adoption fell into oblivion as a legal process with the fall of the Roman Empire. It reappears in the French *Code Civile* of 1793: see Carbonnier, *Droit civil, 2/ La Famille*, 18th ed., 1997, 479–98, in *Themis: Droit Prive*, ed. C. Labrusse-Riou (Paris: Presses Universitaires

as that was understood by the drafters of the Reformed confessions. We do not know what that understanding was,[8] but later theologians have written about "adoption" using ideas of their own times, not always illuminatingly.

That is not good enough. Any attempt to read modern ideas into the concept of adoption hides the depths of the truth the analogy contains. Modern adoption is not adoption as known in New Testament times. Properly to appreciate what was being said, we need to understand the legal notion drawn upon by the writer. We have also to consider the likelihood that the New Testament author knew both what he was talking about and how the recipients of his letters would understand the concept.

To take the latter point first: "adoption" is a term employed only by Paul among the New Testament writers. He uses it five times: three times in Romans (8:15, 23; 9:4) and once each in Ephesians (1:5) and in Galatians (4:5). In Romans 8:15, Ephesians 1:5, and Galatians 4:5, the adoption metaphor points to the selection of believers as members of God's family and their living under the guidance and authority of the Father. In Romans 9:4 the place of the Jews as the chosen people is underlined. Last, the allusion in Romans 8:23 to waiting for the adoption refers to the final transformation, when we will totally pass from our former state into something wholly new.

In terms of Paul's audience, those in Rome would certainly have known Roman law. It was the law ruling in their community. There is reason also to believe that those in Ephesus, a major city in Asia Minor, though not itself a Roman colony, would have sufficient knowledge to decode the imagery. The churches in Galatia, if they were Derbe and Lystra, would also have known the idea, and if Galatians was written to churches in North Galatia, these were even more Romanized. Apart from some sort of personal knowledge, adoption was the way in which the Imperial family was perpetuating itself and so would have been known to non-Romans throughout the Empire.[9] As for the writer, Paul himself was born a Roman citizen (Acts 22:28), and therefore both a subject of and able to use Roman law. That was the basis of his appeal to Caesar (Acts 25:10–12). He was also

de France, 1997); and H. and Mazeaud, et al, *Lecons de Droit Civil*, 443–45.

8. Calvin's *Institutes* makes frequent reference to adoption, but without elaborating its legal basis. See Calvin, *Institutes of the Christian Religion*, 1:555 n. 25. Calvin trained as a lawyer before entering the Church and his studies would have included Roman law.

9. See Lyall, n. 6, Appendix 4, "The Epistles," 223–38.

legally trained—a lawyer—and therefore his knowledge of law (whether Jewish or Roman) and use of its terms would have been more informed and accurate than that of an ordinary person.[10] In short, on these grounds alone it seems most likely that one should look to Roman law to round out the concept of "adoption" in the New Testament.

But what of other possibilities? Was Jewish law, Greek law, or any other a contender for the origin of Paul's words? Within the Roman Empire there were many laws, not just Roman Law. One was subject to the law of one's province or nationality, or even of one's home city. Whether within any given community one could rely on these laws for protection depended on whether that law was recognized and permitted its own system of enforcement.[11] Roman Law was the superior law. It would take precedence for those entitled to its protection, and was therefore highly valued by its citizens and an object of envy to others.[12] But, as said, other laws existed within the Empire and might be thought to provide some basis for Paul's language. However, for adoption, the long and the short of the matter is that Jewish Law did not have a concept of adoption.[13] In the Greek law of which we have knowledge, adoption was not common. Where we know of it, it functioned as a testamentary device—one "adopted" by will the person whom one wanted to inherit one's estate.[14] In the Near East, Babylonian law used adoption as a way to place a son for apprenticeship purposes, he returning to his original family when he had served his time and learned his trade.[15] None of these provide as satisfactory or as full a meaning for "adoption" as does Roman law.

10. I assert this through my own experience. Whatever one's original basic legal training, one picks up all sorts of knowledge about how this and that legal system do certain things differently from one's original legal "home." Paul was trained as a Jewish lawyer, but as a citizen he would have known the law of his citizenship. See Lyall, n. 6, Appendix 5, "Paul," 239–49.

11. This could happen where there was a sufficient community of the particular "nationality," and the local ruling authority was agreeable. *Cf.* the application of Christian, Hindu, or Sharia law in different communities in India and elsewhere in the present century.

12. *Cf.* the changed attitude of the Roman centurion and others to Paul in Acts 22:29 after learning that he was a Roman citizen, and the similar reaction of the authorities in Philippi (Acts 16:37–39).

13. Lyall, n. 6, 70–81.

14. *Cf.* MacDowell, *Law in Classical Athens*, 99–108. Of course, other Greek cities might have had different adoption laws and practices, but nothing is known of these.

15. See Lyall, n. 6, ch. 4, "Adoption," 67–99, with Notes at 259–63.

Accordingly I refer "adoption" as used by Paul to Roman law as its origin and therefore explore its meaning within that context.

THE MEANING

In all the legal systems that have the concept, adoption involves a change of formal legal relationship between people.[16] As a matter of law someone leaves his or her family and becomes part of another family—in law one can only be part of one family at a time. Adoption is therefore an element of Family Law, and involves fundamental personal relationships. It also is a matter of status.[17]

In Roman law, assuming that one was a citizen and not a slave, there were different possibilities as to family status.[18] One could be *sui iuris*, that is independent and not controlled as a matter of law by another. As such one might be single, but if one was married or had lawful children one was oneself a head of a family—a *paterfamilias*[19]—with others subservient to one's authority. On the other hand, if one was under the family authority—under the *potestas* (power/authority)—of a *paterfamilias*, one was *alieni iuris* (sc. under the law/authority of another). Different adoption procedures applied in the two cases; *adrogatio* of someone *sui iuris*, and *adoptio* of someone *alieni iuris*. Over the centuries both procedures mutated. Important for our purposes is what they and their effects were in New Testament times.[20]

16. Islam does not have the formal concept of adoption although it recognizes a form of words giving an indication that someone is treated as "family." However, there is no formal legal process, the relationship with the old family remains, and there is no legal relationship as son or daughter with the new family: see *Qur'ān* 33:4–5.

17. In law "status" involves rights and duties, privileges and immunities, abilities and disabilities that cannot be altered by negotiation or agreement.

18. Generally: Buckland, *Textbook of Roman Law*, 101–41; Jolowicz, *Historical Introduction*, 242–68. The *Institutes of Gaius* I.97–107, 134–135a, deals with adoption. Gaius, who had a historical bent, wrote *c.* AD 161. See F. de Zulueta, trans. and ed., *The Institutes of Gaius*, 2 vols. (Oxford: Oxford University Press, 1946) (text and translation in vol. 1; commentary on adoption in vol. 2, 33–34, 42–44) which uses the most up-to-date text, or J. Muirhead, trans. and ed.. *The Institutes of Gaius and Rules of Ulpian* (Edinburgh: T&T Clark, 1880) (commentary in footnotes).

19. As '*pater*' = '*father*' implies, only males could be heads of families. Women could be *sui iuris*, but if married were under the *manus* (hand = power) of the husband and so were *alieni iuris*.

20. Both Buckland and Jolowicz (n. 18) outline and discuss adoption law as at different times from Republican times, through classical law, the Dominate and down to

In a way *adrogatio* was of greater significance in the social structure of the community. For Romans the *paterfamilias* was extremely important. As the head of the family, he was responsible for the family cult, performing the ritual worship of the family gods, and in particular of the *genius* or tutelary spirit of the family. The adoption of the *paterfamilias* of another family therefore involved the termination of his family cult. This was obviously a serious step involving religion and therefore originally there was a preliminary inquiry by the pontiffs (priests) into the motives and desirability of the adoption. If they approved, the matter went to an official body of citizens[21] in a procedure chaired by the *Pontifex Maximus*.[22] If the assembly approved, the adoptee denounced his family cult—the *detestatio sacrorum*. The adoptee and any of whom he was formerly the *paterfamilias* were then placed under the authority of the new *paterfamilias*. By analogy, becoming a Christian can be thought of as being called by one's new "Father" to deny and depart from the gods that one previously worshiped and become part of a new family.[23]

Adoptio was the adoption of someone who was part of, but was not the head of, another family—someone who was *alieni iuris*. Here only the person being adopted was involved, not his children or wife, if any. What happened was that the new "Father" asserted his right as a *paterfamilias*, the adoptee having gone through a fictitious sale procedure by his former *paterfamilias*.[24] The analogy of one's being "bought by the blood of Christ" is obvious.

Justinian. Roman legal history develops over some 1,000 years, from the Twelve Tables of 450 BC to Justinian's codifications and revisions of *c.* AD 560.

21. Originally this was the *Comitia Curiata*, but they seem to have been replaced by thirty lictors (*lictores curiati*) by the time of Cicero.

22. The Pontifex Maximus was the High Priest of the College of Pontiffs in Rome. Until relatively recently the title was used by the Pope.

23. Obviously as the *adrogatio* procedure involved officials in Rome, originally it could take place only there. Under the Empire *adrogatio* was allowed by imperial rescript, and therefore could take place anywhere.

24. Buckland, n. 18, at 121, outlines the procedure. This derived from an old rule by which if a father sold a son three times (as he could), the son was free from his *potestas*. The intention is that X, son of A should be adopted by C. A, the father, sold X, the son, to B, who "freed" him, but that returned X to A's *potestas*. A second sale from A to B then occurred, and again B "freed" X. Then A sold X to B a third time. This time, however, B did not free X. C, the real adopter, then brought an action to recover "his" son from B. B did not defend the action, and X was adjudged to belong to the *potestas* of C who claimed status as *paterfamilias* and therefore all family rights over X. As this procedure

In both *adrogatio* and *adoptio* all the adoptee's legal ties with his former family were terminated, and he was placed under the full authority of his new Father. Adoption therefore has significance for us, perhaps not in its exact procedural detail, but in the notion of someone originally not part of particular family leaving his or her former family, becoming part of a new family and being brought under the authority of a new *paterfamilias*. The authority of the *pater* was absolute in private law.[25] The *pater* had powers of discipline, even up to death. The *paterfamilias* owned the "property" of all members of his family, and so on. Although the *pater* could give monies to a son or daughter to trade with, it was he who ultimately benefited or lost by their transactions. He could arrange their marriages, and even require their divorces. On the other hand, he had duties to look after all those in his family, supporting them financially and otherwise. Indeed in the matter of responsibility, things went further. For example, if a son injured another person, it was the *pater* that was responsible in damages.

All these elements contribute to the assurance that the Christian can have in appreciating his salvation as having become one of the sons or daughters of the Father, making one able to call him "Abba, Father" (Rom 8:15[26]).

But some may query whether in all this there is not the threat that an adopted child,[27] under the *potestas* of the heavenly Father, could have that status revoked or lost either by the Father freeing that son, making him *sui iuris*, by his allowing his adoption by another, or even by selling him as a slave? Later Roman law did restrict what an adopter might do—usually in relation to matters of succession—but in New Testament times that had not happened. It must be agreed, however, that the analogy of adoption is not cast-iron in terms of modern theology. My personal response to this

only required a magistrate, and not a ceremony in Rome, it could occur anywhere where there was a Roman magistrate available. See also for an almost contemporary account *Gaius* cited above n. 18.

25. As a matter of public law the paternal authority was limited, for example, were a son to become a magistrate.

26. Actually Rom 8:15 speaks of going from slavery into sonship—an even starker transformation but one which was legally possible.

27. I use the word "child," but the Roman adoption procedures could occur at any age. I have also been using male language. *Adoptio* of a female was possible. Until classical times, however, *adrogatio* of a female would not happen, as a female could not be the priest of a family cult—though priestesses of various public gods certainly existed.

point is that it is always an error to push analogies too far. Analogies are given to allow us to grasp and believe truth, not to provide blueprints. There is no biblical evidence that God does cast off his children. "Abba, Father" may be difficult for those whose relationship with their human father has been imperfect. My father was killed in the Second World War when I was only one year old, and I only began to see what the fatherhood of God really meant when I became a father myself. So, for those troubled I would say, hold on to your "adoption." It will mean more as time goes on. You may lack the referents fully to appreciate what this metaphor implies. Indeed, I suppose some may never do so. Nonetheless, grapple with it. Extraordinarily, for I do not believe that the Westminster divines knew Roman law, their summation of the biblical teaching is an accurate reflection of the Roman law of New Testament times. It indicates ways to grasp how, in Christ, having been one of a different family, we become one of the family which has God as its *paterfamilias.* Whether one likes to think of oneself prior to conversion as independent (*sui iuris*) or under the authority of another (*alieni iuris* to Satan), adoption indicates the security inherent through adoption and now having God as our Father. To him we owe obedience, and from him we gain everlasting privileges. But, of course, it all goes further than that bald statement: in the very best sense, by adoption we become sons and daughters of God, joint-heirs with Christ (Rom 8:17). Families are societies, not groups of individuals bound together only by rights, duties and rules.

PART TWO

Historical and Philosophical Studies

8

First Clement and Jewish Hellenism

Historiography and "Grace" in Light of Surviving Second Temple Motifs and First Century Christianity

Brandon G. Withrow

In his book *Orthodoxy*, G. K. Chesterton tells of a story he had once considered writing about an English yachtsman who, due to a slight miscalculation, believes he has found an undiscovered island in the South Seas. The confused but patriotic man arrives armed for a fight and ready to plant the British flag "on that barbaric temple which turned out to be the Pavilion at Brighton."[1] While many would take this Don Quixote figure as a fool for such an error, Chesterton puts a spin on his bumbling: "What could be more glorious than to brace one's self up to discover New South Wales and then realize, with a gush of happy tears, that it was really old South Wales?"[2]

THE PROBLEM OF 1 CLEMENT

For the last two centuries the scholarly consensus has argued that the early Christian letter of 1 Clement (written around 96 CE) is New South Wales. These historians and theologians believe that Clement presents something other than orthodox Christianity, something tangential and foreign to the Pauline gospel of grace. According to this view, Clement's gospel is skewed by Jewish moralism and Stoic concepts of God and the

1. Chesterton, *Orthodoxy*, 9.
2. Ibid., 10.

world. As to the first, Jewish moralism is said to find its roots in the system of the law. By emphasizing eternity as a reward for a moral life or law-based obedience, one would not—this position assumes—hold to a gospel of grace.

As to the second, Stoicism (from *Stoa* or porch, named for the school with a painted porch where Zeno of Citium taught philosophy in Athens around 300 BCE) conflates nature, rationality, and God. The universe is one and the same with God, and its order is evidence of his existence. Unrighteousness is a form of disorder, so Clement appeals to the order of the universe as a model for spiritual order and righteousness. These two factors—Clement's emphasis on living a moral life and his terminology reflecting order in creation—form the basis for the belief in Clement's alleged heterodox theology.

The greatest proponent of this view that early Christianity was almost immediately the result of a "fusion of Jewish and Greek elements" was the prolific liberal Protestant Adolf von Harnack (1851–1930), who was influenced by F. C. Baur (1792–1860) and the Tübingen school.[3] This school of thought may no longer dominate the university, but its conclusions and concerns remain effective in scholarship and are often assumed.[4] While some of these historians have attempted to place Clement within his cultural context, they begin with a premise that finds its origins strictly within the conventional language of the Protestant Reformation, especially in its response to Rome. Similarly, conservative Evangelical responses to Roman Catholicism have also been dismissive of Clement's theology, ruling out a true orthodoxy based strictly on a Protestant lens.

In the last twenty years, more moderate Evangelical scholars have responded with different conclusions, conscripting Clement and other church fathers for contemporary ecumenical purposes. This is particularly clear in circles where theologians have sought to recapture the great tradition and to find common ground for inter-religious dialogue with their Catholic counterparts; Clement's presentation of the Christian gospel became a handy tool for this discussion. This newer and more pragmatic perspective also diminishes the important historical and cultural elements required for accurately understanding this early Christian figure.

3. Harnack, *History of Dogma*, 57; Baird, *History of New Testament Research*, 2:123.

4. See for example, Maurice Wiles, "Church Fathers," in *Encyclopedia of Christianity*, ed. James Bowden (New York: Oxford University Press, 2005), 245–46.

Representing this thought, Thomas C. Oden, a leading figure in the Evangelicals and Catholics Together dialogue of the end of the last century, appeals to Clement in his *The Justification Reader* (2002). In this volume, Oden notes that both Evangelicals and non-Evangelicals alike have largely misunderstood the church fathers as rejecting a Pauline understanding of the Christian gospel. "Key texts from the West by Clement of Rome, Augustine, Prosper, Fulgentius," writes Oden, "demonstrate patristic anticipations of Reformation teaching on justification."[5] Rather than seeing Clement as one who decidedly rejected Paul's gospel in favor of another system of salvation, Oden argues that as the "earliest of Paul's interpreters . . . his Letter to the Corinthians (32:4, 33:1), clearly struck to the root of justification teaching."[6]

One should not ask if Clement was a Lutheran or Calvinist Reformation hero in order to determine if he was truly Pauline. The current state of biblical studies alone, notably the ever-controversial New Perspective on Paul and its many variants, would challenge the Reformation understanding(s) of Paul altogether.[7] Even to speak of Clement as *anticipating* the Reformation falls into the trap of gauging Clement's choice of language by a discussion centuries later. Clement, like all of us, expresses his religion in the context of his culture. He uses phrases that are part of his personality, society, and religion; but the mere use of these phrases does not constitute his total failure to be an orthodox Christian of his day. Examples of synergistic thought in early Christianity exist, but, as will be seen, this particularly early letter is not a prime example of such an approach. Rather, it follows a biblical trajectory that comes from the New Testament writers themselves, and misreadings of Clement have more to do with an extremely large generation gap.

In light of the theme of this book, *eternal security,* the primary purpose of this chapter is to determine what Clement understood as the Christian gospel of grace in light of the historical-cultural and theological trajectories that informed his thinking. In doing this, I do not intend to

5. Oden, *Justification Reader*, 45; Righteousness in Clement usually refers to the fruit of faith in sanctification. Clement uses phrases such as "reckoned or accounted" (10:6) which are quoted from Genesis 15:6 (LXX), but no further explanation is given.

6. Ibid.

7. For example, NPP's insistence that the works of the law were not ultimately about *earning* salvation, but about *showing* one to be part of the covenant people could be offered as an important context for Clement's emphasis on righteous living.

argue for a Reformation Clement or a Catholic Clement; rather, I intend to offer a different approach historiographically, looking at the place of this letter within first-century Christianity and what this means for Clement's understanding of grace in his day.[8]

WHO IS CLEMENT?

As to who is Clement of Rome, we know "next to nothing," as Johannes Quasten writes, and no one knows for certain who wrote the epistle that bears his name.[9] It is assumed that the author holds some sort of high ecclesiastical office, as it is said to be written from Rome. Other ancient Christian writers have identified the author as Clement, the third bishop of Rome. Eusebius, Irenaeus, Clement of Alexandria, Origen, Cyril of Jerusalem, and Basil of Caesarea attest to this conclusion.[10] All the Greek manuscripts attribute it to him and no substantive historical reasons for rejecting this tradition exist.[11]

One famous theory promoted by Dio Cassius is that Clement of Rome was the famous Titus Flavius Clemens, a member of the imperial Flavian family who was executed on the charge of "atheism"—that is, one who rejects the Roman gods, not necessarily all gods.[12] A spin on this theory is that Clement was a freedman belonging to the family of his namesake.[13] There is nothing impossible about this last theory, but it cannot be confirmed. In addition, Eusebius and Origen identify him with the Clement of Philippians 4:3.[14] Other early testimonies place him as the second or third bishop of Rome, following the idea of apostolic succession.[15]

8. My work on Clement began some years ago when working on my masters. A rushed version of that work was published online; what is accomplished in this chapter, while maintaining the spirit of that earlier work, is admittedly significantly different (and hopefully more accurate!).

9. Quasten, *Patrology*, 1:42.

10. Eusebius, *Ecclesiastical History* 3.16; 3.4; Irenaeus, *Against Heresies*, 3.3.3; Clement of Alexandria, *Stromata*, 1.7.38; 4.17–19; Origen, *On First Principles*, 2.3.6; Cyril of Jerusalem, *Cat.* 8.8; Basil of Caesarea, *De Spirit Sact.*, 29.

11. Cyril Richardson, *Early Christian Fathers*, 1:36.

12. Dio Cassius, *Hist. Rom.*, 67, 14.

13. Richardson, *Early Christian Fathers*, 37.

14. Eusebius, *Ecclesiastical History*, 3.4.15; Origen, *Commentary on John*, 6:36.

15. Tertullian, *Prescription Against Heretics*, 32; Irenaeus, *Against Heresies*, 3.3.1.

The book of 1 Clement consists of three sections: a salutation and introduction; the problem facing the church and its solution; and a summation. The epistle is written to the divided and troubled Corinthian church. Given the assumed authority Clement wields in his text, that is, as an outsider writing with ecclesiastical and pastoral exhortation to a church in another city, he is clearly a person of some regard. The church appears to have suffered a coup, and is divided into various groups vying for power. This was not entirely unlike the days of Paul, in which the Corinthians organized their respective numbers according to who followed Paul and who followed Apollos (1 Cor 1:12–13; 3:4). As an epistle, it is, as Quaesten remarks, "of great consequence"; it is an important window into the theological and ecclesiastical world of early Christianity.[16] For this reason, what Clement tells us about faith, grace, and works, is useful for gauging the temperature change of theological development or change in early Christianity. Many historians have hoped to divine, at the very least, Clement's ethnicity from the letter's content. Few have refused to guess, and in this way he has been understood as either a Hellenistic Gentile, a Jew with a moralistic tradition, or some combination of the two. The latter is most often believed to be the case and has played a significant role in determining just how Pauline or Reformational Clement really is.

CLEMENT'S RECEPTION AND THE JEWISH HELLENISTIC BACKGROUND

Several factors have led to the conclusion that Clement has a Jewish background and likely one that emphasizes moralism. A quick survey of Clement's letter provides a glimpse into his primary use of the biblical text. A large portion of his biblical support comes from the Septuagint, used widely by both Jews and Christians, particularly New Testament writers. His citation of the New Testament, though not as frequent as the Old, is often from the teachings of Jesus or the apostle Paul. These citations are often close to the originals but not exact, as they are not always taken directly from copies of the New Testament books. As Bart D. Ehrman notes, Clement at his early time

> does not yet have anything like a canon of "New Testament" Scripture, and yet . . . is beginning to ascribe authority to the words of Jesus and the writings of the apostles. . . . He quotes

16. Quaesten, *Patrology*, 1:44.

> Jesus' words on several occasions (see chs. 13 and 46), evidently as he knows them from oral traditions rather than as written Gospels, since the quotations do not match any of our surviving texts. In addition he refers explicitly to Paul's first letter to the Corinthians (ch. 47) and alludes on numerous occasions to other writings that later came to form part of the New Testament canon (for example, Hebrews; see ch. 36). That is to say, we can see here the very beginning of the process in which Christian authorities (Jesus and his apostles) are assigned authority comparable to that of Jewish Scriptures, the beginnings, in other words, of the formation of the Christian canon.[17]

Therefore, it is not absolutely possible to determine strictly from his citation of the Old Testament text whether Clement was Jewish or Gentile.

Other evidence seems to indicate that, if he was not Jewish, he was, at least, well-versed in a Jewish tradition. In writing about Clement's liturgical prayer in 59:3—61:3, historian L. W. Barnard finds parallels with Jewish liturgy. He points out that:

> Bishop Lightfoot long ago in his famous commentary gave many highly suggestive parallels between the prayer and the Jewish *Shemoneth 'Esreh*, the "Eighteen Benedictions." The Talmud states that the "Men of the Great Synagogue" instituted certain benedictions and prayers and the "eighteen" were arranged by Simeon ha-Pakoli in the time of Gamaliel II (AD 80–120). . . . There is sufficient similarity between Benedictions 1, 2, 17 and 18 and 1 Clement to make it highly probable that in his liturgical prayer Clement was drawing on certain of the daily blessings known and used in the Hellenistic synagogues of the diaspora of his day.[18]

Early assessments have noted an intense emphasis on Clement's exhortation to live the moral and righteous life as a sign that he had a Jewish background and maintained a Jewish moralism. T. F. Torrance argues for

17. Ehrman, *Apostolic Fathers,* 1:26; on Clement's use of the Apocrypha, see also Barnard, "The Early Roman Church, Judaism, and Jewish Christianity," 373–76. Barnard is relying largely on Karlmann Beyschlag's work *Clemens Romanus und der Frukatholizismus: Untersuchungen zu 1 Clemens 1–7.* Barnard also finds Jewish Christianity in Clement's uses of terms such as "schism, sedition, persecution, and martyrdom" (374).

18. Barnard, "Early Roman Church," 378; for more information see Lightfoot, *Apostolic Fathers,* 1:392–96. Despite this Jewish history, Barnard comments, "It is unnecessary, however, to postulate that the Jewish-Christian traditions which it held were violently opposed to the Pauline theology, as apparently Beyschlag believes" (375).

this position in his classic book, *The Doctrine of Grace in the Apostolic Fathers*, writing disparagingly that Clement "may use the language of election and justification, but the essentially Greek ideas of the unqualified freedom of choice is a natural axiom in his thoughts, and entails a doctrine of 'works,' as Paul would have said." Later Torrance concludes that Clement "like the whole mass of Judaistic writers . . . thinks of God's mercy as directed only towards the pious."[19] Along the same lines, Johannes Weiss analyzes Clement's Stoic doctrine of faith in God and came to the conclusion that "there is little which is peculiarly Christian which is to be discerned in the epistle's faith in God. The mode of expression is upon the whole a beautiful coinage of Jewish Hellenism; 'diaspora Judaism plus the Cross,' which has undergone a strong Greek influence."[20] This conclusion is derived primarily from some key passages in which a strong pietistic moralism is emphasized as apparently necessary for one's salvation, such as 30:3 where he tells the Corinthians to "be justified by deeds, not by words."[21] Likewise, in 10:7 we find passages that correlate the "faith and hospitality" of Abraham as a means of acceptance before God. In 11:1 it was because of "hospitality and piety" that Lot was "saved out of Sodom." In 12:1 Rahab was saved by her "faith and hospitality." Weiss concludes from such passages that "repentance, perfected in obedience and humility, must be used to obtain forgiveness."[22]

Adding to the evidence, Clement's use of humility is also interpreted as a means by which a person may obtain salvation. One incriminating passage is found in 30:2–3, where Clement (quoting James 4:6) writes: "'God' . . . [resists] the proud but giveth grace to the humble. Let us then join ourselves to those to whom is given grace from God; let us put on concord in meekness of spirit and continence, keeping ourselves far from all gossip and evil speaking and be justified by deeds, and not by words." Based on these words, Torrance argues, "Clement substitutes for the New Testament doctrine of sonship, the bare idea of subjection before God."[23]

19. Torrance, *Doctrine of Grace In The Apostolic Fathers*, 54–55.

20. Weiss, *History of Primitive Christianity*, 2:855.

21. Kirsopp Lake, trans., *Loeb Classical Library: The Apostolic Fathers*, Vol. 1, *1 Clement* (Cambridge, MA: Harvard University Press, 1985). All references will follow the chapter and verse format.

22. Weiss, *Primitive Christianity*, 862.

23. Torrance, *Doctrine of Grace*, 48.

Who can blame Torrance *et al.*, for such a conclusion? When Clement speaks about "the humility and obedient submission of so many men of such great fame" in 19:1, it does sound as much to modern Protestant ears. "Faith," writes Torrance of Clement, "can only bring justification when by its very exercise it manifests this quality of abasement before God."[24] Similarly, Clement says:

> Let us observe that all the righteous have been adorned with good works; and the Lord himself adorned himself with good works and rejoiced. Having therefore this pattern let us follow his will without delay, let us work the work of righteousness with all our strength (33:7–8).

Hence Torrance remarks that working out salvation by following Christ's example "is for Clement justification by faith . . . the very essence of his religion."[25]

In a similar argument, Johannes Weiss argues of Clement's letter that a "*strong moralism* runs through all its expressions from the first page to the last," and that Clement's use of Pauline terminology "is only a borrowed one."[26]

> There stand, in other passages of the letter, two which are completely different; one of which, closely akin to the passage just quoted [32:4], says, 'to be justified by deeds and not by words' (30:3). The other stands in an earlier connection: Abraham, St. Paul's great example of faith received grace 'on account of his faith and hospitality' (10:7). Lot was saved because of his hospitality and piety (11:1); Rahab, again like Abraham, on account of her faith and hospitality (12:1). It immediately becomes clear from these formulae how little understanding there was in this age of Paul's great struggle for justification by faith.[27]

Weiss concurs with Torrance that according to Clement, "one must only be obedient and submissive to his will and do good works."[28]

24. Ibid., 49.
25. Ibid.
26. Weiss, *Primitive Christianity*, 853, 861.
27. Ibid., 861.
28. Ibid., 862.

In a milder approach, what Weiss calls "strong moralism," Cyril Richardson dismisses as a mere "strain."[29] Richardson finds that this "links him on the one hand with Hellenistic Judaism and the other with Stoicism."[30] And with barely a handful of evidence he concludes that "these instances must suffice to indicate the extent to which Clement has moved away from the Pauline gospel into an atmosphere more concerned with the moral life."[31] But Richardson graciously adds that, "this does not, however, exclude both acquaintance with, and some grasp of Pauline gospel. The cleavage is not so sharp as is sometimes made out."[32] Charles Nielsen rejects some of this interpretation, but replaces it with the concept of a bishop who either knowingly or unknowingly contradicts himself. Nielsen says Clement wavers "back and forth between the idea of gift and the idea of works."[33] Clement is "aware of at least one contradiction in his thought. It is significant that he lets the contradiction stand."[34] Nielsen argues that Clement is ultimately a theologian of contradiction, not harmonization.

As with the general emphasis on living a righteous and moral life, other terminology plays into the Stoic interpretation of Clement's letter. Examples from pagan mythology, and more importantly, Clement's focus on the realm of nature and its order, have driven many historians to conclude that Clement, mixing Stoic philosophy into his theology, reads Paul through the Greek lens of order and nature. Why is this important to his understanding of grace? In order to encourage fellow Christians to godly living and to promote order in the Church, Clement—according to this interpretation of him—appeals to universal and natural order, rather than Christ. For example, in 20:1–2, he writes, "The heavens moving at his appointment are subject to him in peace; day and night follow the course allotted by him without hindering each other." But, as will be seen, merely appealing to natural order and creation does not necessitate a Christianity of unfettered Stoicism. There is a better approach to understanding Clement.

29. Richardson, *Early Christian Fathers*, 38, 39.

30. Ibid., 38.

31. Ibid., 38.

32. Ibid., 39.

33. Nielsen, "Clement of Rome," 139.

34. Ibid., 148.

CLEMENT'S HISTORICAL CONTEXT

What should be made of these elements in Clement's thought? Several approaches could be taken. One could outright attempt to harmonize every passage Clement puts forward to give his text a reading that is fashionably acceptable to whatever system of theology is desired. In so doing, all problems easily could be wrapped up in a tight package, posing no threat to the text. 1 Clement, however, is an epistle and not an early systematic theology, though some like J. B. Lightfoot have attempted make it so by arguing for Clement's midrashic "comprehensiveness."[35] Clement's vast knowledge of both testaments does allow him to pull passages from many parts of Scripture to make a point, but Charles Nielsen rightly concludes that "proper exegesis is not always concerned with an either/or, yet too many commentators seem to want to make Clement more consistent than either life or Clement really is."[36]

A second option is simply to react to Clement's comments as if he has betrayed the faith, rejecting Paul's understanding of grace in favor of other systems. This disparity between the Christian tradition and Clement's letter could be amplified through constant appeals to troubling texts, as seen above.

There is, however, a third option. In this approach, one need not harmonize his text perfectly, or claim that Clement has forsaken his Christian faith for mere Hellenistic Judaism. From this point of view, one is not even asked to choose between a Clement who is knowingly or unknowingly contradictory. Each of these points are lovely conventions of modern thought that miss the target altogether. Understanding Clement's text is not about forcing it solidly within these decontextualized frameworks. Rather one might be able to get closer to the mind of the letter's composer historically by examining: the letter's "situatedness" in light of its appeal to the biblical text; the "survival" of Second Temple "motifs" (to use the words of James Kugel) in Clement's text as well as how he relates and understands these motifs in light of Scripture; and, lastly, Clement's textual "diversity." In looking at these three factors, one will find that Clement's

35. Lightfoot, *Apostolic Fathers*, 1:95. Clement does call for the Corinthians to look "into the depths of the divine knowledge" (40:1), to study the "Holy Scriptures, which are true" (45:2), to "take up the epistle of the blessed Paul the Apostle" (40:1). Clement commends "a good understanding of the sacred Scriptures" and notices when the Corinthians have "studied the oracles of God" (53:1; 62:3).

36. Nielsen, "Clement," 131.

text is not simply a crow decked in the feathers of another bird (as Jerome once described Ambrose)—or to put it another way, a Hellenistic-Jewish text masquerading as a Christian text; rather it is a text firmly in line with the New Testament's cultural trajectory.[37]

Applying these categories in biblical studies has proven to be controversial at some Evangelical colleges, universities, and seminaries.[38] "Situatedness," for example, examines the biblical text within its surrounding cultural context. When parallels are found between the biblical text and its historical context, some Evangelicals have wondered whether this takes away from the uniqueness of the Bible or whether this calls into question its inspiration or inerrancy. What happens when, for example, the Bible apparently appropriates a regional "myth"? Evangelicals in conservative institutions have hoped to utilize this connection by downplaying myth. As a one-time professor of Moody Bible Institute once carefully wrote on the Near Eastern connections to the book of Genesis: "while the Genesis account is, to be sure, nonmythical, it is difficult to demonstrate that it is decisively antimythical."[39]

In recent times, similar attention has been given to Peter Enns's book, *Inspiration and Incarnation: Evangelicals and the Problem of the Old Testament*. Enns maintains the inspiration of the biblical text by appealing to the analogy of the incarnation. "The starting point for our discussion is the following," writes Enns, "*as Christ is both God and human, so is the Bible.*"[40] Other Evangelicals have insisted that these factors, though a part of the biblical text, are still under the guidance of the Holy Spirit, so that, what the Bible appropriates may come from its context, but its verity is assured by the controlling inspiration of the Spirit. In other words, Jude quotes 1 Enoch by the Spirit because that which is quoted is ultimately true. Fortunately, in dealing with a work like Clement's epistle to the Romans, the question is not ultimately about a particular doctrine or the exact purity of Clement's text. However one approaches these points doctrinally, they are very relevant for setting up the world of 1 Clement.

37. Rufinus, *Apology Against Jerome*, 2.25.

38. For a discussion on Evangelicals and inerrancy, see Bovell, *Inerrancy and the Spiritual Formation of Younger Evangelicals*.

39. Walton, *Ancient Israelite Literature*, 38.

40. Peter Enns, *Inspiration and Incarnation*, 17.

Situatedness

"Situatedness" looks at the position of the Old Testament or New Testament as it relates to the world of its composition. "Why does the Bible in places look a lot like the literature of Israel's ancient neighbors?" asks Enns.[41] If the Bible is divine, is there not a danger in implying that its writers understand and write using a mythological, or, at best, an incomplete and humanly flawed understanding of the universe? Drawing straight lines between the biblical text and the literature and traditions of other cultures has not always proven easy. The connections between the Babylonian creation story, *Enuma Elish*, and Genesis, for example, while once considered strong—as Hermann Gunkel (1862–1932), a pioneer of form criticism, once argued—are now understood to contain significant resemblances rather than an exact genealogy. On the other hand, the similarities between flood stories like the Gilgamesh Epic and the Genesis flood appear to be more than mere resemblances.[42]

How is "situatedness" seen in the Old Testament? Enns points to the well-studied parallels between the Code of Hammurabi, which was discovered in 1901–02 and the Mosaic Law. For example:

> Code of Hammurabi, 209—"If a man strike a man's daughter and bring about a miscarriage, he shall pay ten shekels of silver for her miscarriage."[43]
>
> Exodus 21:22—When people who are fighting injure a pregnant woman so that there is a miscarriage, and yet no further harm follows, the one responsible shall be fined what the woman's husband demands, paying as much as the judges determine (NRSV).

If Moses merely obtained the law from God without some connection to his context, what should we do about these similarities, especially when Hammurabi's law code was drafted centuries earlier than the biblical account? Discoveries like these have pushed biblical scholarship to uncover the surrounding context of the biblical world.[44] Similarly, in the New Testament, the reliance on non-canonical but culturally prominent

41. Enns, *Inspiration and Incarnation*, 15.

42. For a recent look at Israelite literature and religion in its context and in relation to the history of biblical studies, see Hess, *Israelite Religions*.

43. Harper, *Code of Hammurabi, King of Babylon About 2250* BC, 77.

44. Enns, *Inspiration and Incarnation*, 31–32.

texts can be seen in examples like Jude 14–15 in which 1 Enoch 1:9 is cited authoritatively, or John's use of the Greek term *logos* in John 1:1.

The so-called "Stoic" passages of 1 Clement are also an example of this situatedness, but this situatedness is not a bare substitution of Stoic ideas for biblical ones. While Clement is not considered a canonical book by Christians today and therefore is not believed to be preserved by divine inspiration, the impression the surrounding culture left on Clement's text does not demand its absolute defection from the Christian gospel. As a matter of fact, Clement's thought, as it is connected to the world around him, is not without a justification based on the biblical text itself. The biblical text and the Christian worldview set the trajectory for the writer of 1 Clement. For example, while Robert M. Grant and Holt H. Graham are drawn to the conclusion that Stoicism did have an influence on Clement, they also note that the primary chapters of his letter that are said to rely on Stoic ideas (20–27) have parallels with the Old Testament as well. Chapters 20:1–2 and 24:3, for example, while sounding Stoic, also reflect Psalm 19:1–2.

> Clement's use of 'abyss' (20:5) recalls the Old Testament ('abyss in Job 38:16, a passage to which he is turning) [20:7], while 'basin' of the sea recalls Psalm 64:8 (Sinaiticus), and 'gathering together' is from Genesis 1:9. The 'bounds' placed around the sea (20:6) are from Job 38:10, and Clement quotes the next verse in Job [38:11] immediately.[45]

Other so-called Stoic passages could be understood in this same vein. When discussing the resurrection and its parallels in the natural world, it is likely that while Stoicism may have had some import for Clement as a thinker, he is clearly not stepping entirely out of a biblical and Pauline framework; examples from the natural world prove to be helpful to Paul in 1 Corinthians 15. And given that Clement is writing to the Corinthian church and appeals to the Corinthian letter of Paul, his choice of language makes perfect sense.

A commentary on Genesis written for today's student, for example, would likely address issues and use language pertinent for current discussion, while simultaneously (depending upon the author) drawing conclusions that appeal to a Christian or Jewish tradition. When it comes to Clement's text, for example, the resurrection is proved by saying:

45. Grant and Graham, *Apostolic Fathers*, 2:44.

> Let us look, beloved, at the resurrection which is taking place at its proper season. Day and night show us a resurrection. The night sleeps, the day arises: the day departs, the night comes on. (24:2–3)

While these orderly descriptions may reflect the language of Stoicism in vogue at the time, they are also similar to Paul's choice of language in 1 Corinthians 15. In verses 40–41 Paul also draws an analogy from the stars, sun, and moon to show that heavenly bodies are not all the same. Similarly, Clement finds an example of the resurrection from seeds planted in the ground, showing that they eventually bring about fruit by first dying. Grant and Graham believe that this has Stoic roots, yet a parallel example is used by Paul in 1 Corinthians 15:36–38: "Fool! What you sow does not come to life unless it dies. And as for what you sow, you do not sow the body that is to be, but a bare seed, perhaps of wheat or of some other grain. But God gives it a body as he has chosen, and to each kind of seed its own body."[46] And finally, both Clement and Paul call Christ the "first-fruit" of the resurrection (1 Clem 24:1; 1 Cor 15:20). It may be that where Clement differs from Paul, even when using similar language, is a result of Stoic influences, but the analogies used in 1 Corinthians clearly set the agenda.

1 Clement 20 is most often discussed as the prime example of Stoicism in this epistle.[47] In verses 1–2 he writes, "The heavens moving at his appointment are subject to him in peace; day and night follow the course allotted by him without hindering each other." Stoic philosophy argued that one can conclude God's existence from observing order, and it is argued that Clement is showing this Stoic "influence" in this passage.[48] However, despite the similarities, it seems that the natural order has a different function in Clement's argument. W. C. Van Unnik, contrasting Stoic philosophy and Clement's theology in his article "Is 1 Clement 20 Purely Stoic?" argues that:

> Among the Stoics the order [of the universe] seems more or less established in itself and makes men thinking . . . that there must be behind it an organizing power, and that it is from the order

46. Ibid., 50; Clement also seems to be mixing the Gospel of Mark with Paul (Mark 4:3).

47. See, for example, Daniélou, *Theology of Jewish Christianity*, 1:43–44.

48. Hatch, *Influence of Greek Ideas*, 171. Hatch is still required reading in some schools.

> of nature that this divine power can be known; in 1 Clement the order is established by the command of the Creator and reveals the will of God, the keynote of the passage being not so much the order in nature as the command of God.[49]

For Stoicism, nature proves God's existence, but for Clement it proves the "will of God." As Nielsen observes, "Certainly when one reads 1 Clement one gets the overwhelming impression of the power of God's will."[50] It is not so much that order in the universe proves God's existence, but that order in the universe demonstrates that God's will is for order to exist in the churches.[51] It is very possible that the Stoicism popular in the intellectual centers of his day does in some sense lie behind these passages, but it does not appear to be without significant modification based upon the larger body of the biblical text. Clement was, after all, fully justified in interacting with the intellectual world around him; it was the example of Scripture and therefore nothing foreign to Christians in this day. Like John using the loaded term *logos* and Paul quoting from Greek poets (Acts 17:28), Clement does not transcend his culture. And while there is no doctrinal reason to argue for a form of Clementine infallibility or for complete purity in his text, there is clear evidence that his thought is still well within, and guided by, his first-century Christian tradition.

Second Temple Motifs and Diversity

The survival of Second Temple motifs and diversity must be taken into consideration next. By handling these together, it will be shown that Clement's apparent contradiction of his own words on grace and works is due in part to his received traditions, what he learns from them, and the lack of urgency one in his day would feel to harmonize their apparent discrepancies.

It is during the Second Temple period (*c.* 587/6 BCE—70 CE) that we find the composition of the Apocrypha, the Pseudepigrapha, and the Dead Sea Scrolls, and the biblical authors demonstrate their familiarity with these texts. Paul's reference to Jannes and Jambres is a popular example

49. Van Unnik, "Is 1 Clement 20 Purely Stoic?" 184.

50. Nielsen, "Clement," 133; see also Wong, "Natural and Divine Order in 1 Clement," 81–87.

51. Taking his usual moderate stand, J. N. D. Kelly calls these "echoes" of later Stoicism (*Early Christian Doctrines*, 83).

of this scenario. The two magicians of Pharaoh are not named in Exodus or anywhere else in the Old Testament, so when Paul calls them by name in 2 Timothy 3:8, scholars cannot help but take notice. This is largely because the names do appear to be in circulation during Paul's day and, as Enns notes, come "from the Second Temple interpretive world of which Paul was a part."[52] The writer of Hebrews also demonstrates this connection; when speaking of prophets being "sawn in two" (11:37), the author is probably referring to the pseudepigraphal *Ascension of Isaiah* (1:1—3:12; 5:1b–14), which began as a Jewish text and was finished by Christians. As F. F. Bruce notes, the account of Isaiah's martyrdom is most likely of earlier Jewish origins and is connected with Qumran texts.[53] Likewise, Jude 9 mentions the dispute between Michael and Satan over the body of Moses, a point also not in the biblical text, but which—as other early church fathers have claimed—is believed to be from the *Assumption of Moses*. The extant Latin copy of this text is believed to be from the Greek, which in turn is from an Hebrew or Aramaic original, and was likely written early in the first century following an oral tradition.[54]

Jude's citation of 1 Enoch, mentioned above, is also an example of this interpretative trajectory. Enoch is a minor figure of Genesis 5:22–24, but what is said about him causes nothing less than centuries of musings, legend, and fanciful speculation. The text reads:

> Enoch walked with God after the birth of Methuselah three hundred years, and had other sons and daughters. Thus all the days of Enoch were three hundred sixty-five years. Enoch walked with God; then he was no more, because God took him.

The story of Enoch being simply "taken" by God inspired subsequent generations to speculate on what eventually happened to him, which, in turn, evolved into a written Enoch tradition. "Having—according to many interpreters—entered into heaven alive," writes James Kugel in *The Bible as it Was,* "Enoch was naturally assumed to have continued living there, and, in the process, to have acquired unique knowledge of 'heavenly things'—not only the ways of God and angels, but also of natural

52. Enns, *Inspiration and Incarnation*, 143; it appears in the Qumran scroll *Covenant of Damascus* (5:17–19) and in the *Targum Pseudo-Jonathan* on Exodus 1:15. For a more complete discussion of this tradition, see Kugel, *Bible as it Was*, 290–91.

53. Bruce, *Epistle to the Hebrews*, 327–28.

54. Enns, *Inspiration and Incarnation*, 144–45; Kugel, *Bible as it Was*, 571–72.

phenomena on earth as observed from above." Enoch's privileged position proved too tempting to ignore for many writers. "It is in part upon this (very old) assumption," continues Kugel, "that there arose an early body of writings attributed to Enoch."[55]

By the time of the writing of the book of Jude, this continually-growing text was a well accepted source of knowledge and Enoch was considered a true prophet. Therefore, he is not only quoted in Jude, but listed in Hebrews 11:5, right before Noah, as a hero of faith ("By faith Enoch was taken so that he did not experience death; and 'he was not found, because God had taken him.' For it was attested before he was taken away that 'he had pleased God'"). 1 Clement 9:2 follows the pattern of Hebrews 11, also placing him right before Noah ("We should consider Enoch, who was transported to another place because he was found to be righteous in his obedience; and his death was never found").

If the late first-century dating of this text is accurate, and if Clement was born within the late Second Temple period and perhaps even knew some of the Apostles themselves (as tradition seems to indicate), then his world is not far from theirs. Like it did for the Apostles, the Septuagint remained his primary source for Old Testament Scripture, and Clement's perception of the Old Testament appears to be not all that different from the New Testament writers. Donald Alfred Hagner notes that Clement's citations of the Old Testament (not including allusions) number around seventy and some of these are of significant length. His letter contains more citations of the Old Testament than any New Testament epistle, with Romans trailing not far behind. "It may be said that in his quotation of the OT Clement stands quite manifestly in the mainstream of first and early second century Christianity," writes Hagner, "with the writers of the NT before him, and the select company of the Apostolic Fathers after him."[56]

It is likely that this Judeo-Christian background heavily informs even the most pagan section of his letter, namely, the famous Phoenix chapter (25). Here Clement uses the Phoenix mythology as an example of resurrection from the ashes of death. Despite the pagan history of this myth, this was not an unusual story for a Christian to believe at this time. As Clement's translator Kirsopp Lake writes, "this story was supposed by Christians to be sanctioned by the Septuagint version of [Psalm 92:12],

55. Kugel, *Bible as it Was*, 102.

56. Hagner, *Use of the Old and New Testaments*, 22, 35.

where there is a confusion between *phoinix* = phoenix, and *phoinix* = palm tree."[57] It would be reasonable for Clement to use this as an example if he believed that Psalm 92:12 read, "The righteous shall flourish like the phoenix" rather than "like the palm tree." Clement's inclusion of this myth is not without Scriptural support, therefore, even if that support is misunderstood.

With Clement inheriting the vestigal Second Temple interpretive tradition, especially given that there is no formal Christian canon as of yet, it is no surprise to find apocryphal books like *Judith* being cited in chapters 55 and 59 of his letter to the Corinthians, alongside Esther.[58] As a church leader, the majority of Clement's citations are to what are now considered by Protestants canonical Scripture, but these other books are also conversation partners, if not also authoritative for him. Along these lines, Clement appeals to God's compassion and mercy by citing in 60:1 phrases that are likely from Sirach 2:11. And in chapter 23, he cites authoritatively as "Scripture" a passage whose origins are unknown.

Kugel has demonstrated that Clement and other Christians of the first century are following this Second Temple interpretive tradition. When Lot's wife is turned into a pillar of salt in Genesis 19:26, for example, subsequent interpreters wondered if there might be another purpose beyond simple punishment. In Wisdom 10:7–8, she is understood to be a memorial to the "unbelieving soul"—a view that is proliferated by Philo (*Abraham* 141), and is found in 2 Peter 2:6 and Jude 7 as well as others, including 1 Clement 11:1–2, which reads:

> For of this a sign was given when his wife went with him, but changed her mind and did not remain in agreement with him, so that she became a pillar of salt unto this day, to make known to all, that those who are double-minded and have doubts concerning

57. Lake, *1 Clement*, 53 n. 1. A similar situation occurs in another biblical book cited often by Clement. In Job 29:18, the word *phoinikos* appears in the Septuagint. Some translations go with "palm tree." The NRSV reads "phoenix" ("Then I thought, 'I shall die in my nest, and I shall multiply my days like the phoenix'). Either "phoenix" or "palm tree" are possible. As to the former, phoenix best parallels the mention of a "nest" in verse 18, but in the case of the latter, the discussion of a "root," "water," and "dew" in verse 19 ("my roots spread out to the waters, with the dew all night on my branches") could imply palm tree. For an abbreviated history of this text, see Hartley, *The Book of Job*, 392. For a discussion on the phoenix tradition in Christianity as it relates to Clement, see Himuro, "The Phoenix in The First Epistle of Clement to the Corinthians," 523–44.

58. *Cf.* 1 Clement 55:4–6 with Judith 8–9 and Esther 7.

> the power of God incur judgment and become a warning to all generations.[59]

Unless Clement is understood as working out of this trajectory, one is destined to miss his point and fall into the perilous trap of reductionism.

This background is also important for understanding Clement's emphasis on living righteously. When it comes to his presentation of salvation to the troubled Corinthian church, Clement is concerned with two important but true points: true Christians live godly lives and therefore do good deeds; *and* no one is saved by those deeds. When writing to a church that is intent on division, pride, strife, and sin (3:1–3), it is not unexpected for Clement to emphasize the need for unity or order under the presbyter, as well as humility and piety. There are numerous passages, therefore, that speak of humility and obedience. But do works of humility and obedience add up to a rejection of grace? Morality and the virtues of Christianity were "removed" from Corinth (3:4). Clement believes he is writing to Christians (62:3), so the priority in his mind is to exhort them to good works, not salvation. Amidst their daily challenges he wants to "remind" them of righteousness (62:3). More importantly, his existing Christian tradition and the surviving Second Temple motifs encourage this dual emphasis on piety and grace.

In paraphrasing James 4:6, Clement writes, "'God' . . . [resists] the proud but giveth grace to the humble. Let us then join ourselves to those to whom is given grace from God; let us put on concord in meekness of spirit and continence, keeping ourselves far from all gossip and evil speaking and be justified by deeds, and not by words" (30:2). Likewise, in 30:3, Clement writes "*ergois dikaioumenoi*" ("be justified by works"), which recalls James 2:21, "*ergon edikaiothe*" ("justified by works"). More than merely reflecting on James or falling into the common James versus Paul problem, Clement's appeal to James reveals the significance of these surviving Second Temple motifs. This can be seen in 1 Clement 10–12, where both Abraham and Rahab are used as examples of "faith and hospitality."

Kugel argues that when it came to Abraham, early Jewish commentators often wondered why the patriarch was seen as righteous before the eyes of God. In the biblical text, he just appears and is instantly given a blessing, though no real back story is given as to why. This disturbed

59. Kugel, *Bible as it Was,* 192–93. See also 174–75 on Isaac as a willing victim.

many early interpreters and they looked for examples in the text of Abraham's moral superiority. One of the most obvious examples comes from Abraham's obedient willingness to sacrifice his son. Clement recognizes this in 10:7 and this is noted in James (2:21–22) as well: "Was not our ancestor Abraham justified by works when he offered his son Isaac on the altar? You see that faith was active along with his works, and faith was brought to completion by the works."

Another area that became particularly evident of Abraham's moral superiority came from his hospitality. When Abraham comes into contact with God's angels, the first thing he sets out to do is prepare a pleasant and hospitable environment for them. Genesis 18:1–8 lays out in some detail how he prepared a hospitable place for these messengers. "The whole lesson of this lengthy passage," explains Kugel, "seemed to be [to its early Jewish interpreters] that hospitality and generosity to strangers are a great virtue."[60] This set Abraham in contrast to the type of reception the messengers from God received in Sodom. More importantly, it eventually rubbed off onto Lot. Lot welcomed the strangers when they arrived, unlike the residents of Sodom. From this it was concluded that Lot's righteousness was demonstrated through his hospitality.[61] Clement reflects this tradition: "For his hospitality and piety Lot was saved out of Sodom when the whole countryside was judged by fire and brimstone" (11:1).

This appeal to hospitality is not pure Jewish moralism; rather, it is yet another example of following the biblical interpretive tradition which he was given.[62] Clement says that Rahab was saved because of her "faith and

60. Ibid., 189.

61. Ibid., 191; *cf.* Josephus, *Jewish Antiquities*, 1:200.

62. Torrance also sees Clement as positing Christ as a mere moral example. "The death of Christ is brought in as an example," writes Torrance of Clement, "that having His death before our eyes we may have an insatiable desire to do good, and to be humble before God . . . In the last resort therefore Clement is unable to ascribe saving significance to Christ himself" (*Doctrine of Grace*, 47). In other words, Christ is not the substitutionary atoner of our sin. It is true that Clement presents Christ as our example, but Christ presents himself in such a way when he washes his disciples' feet (John 13). It is natural for Clement to find in Christ's sacrifice both an atonement and example, which is not a contradiction, but just two ways of looking at Christ. That Clement argues for more than an example is clear when he says, "In love did the Master receive us; for the sake of love which he had toward us did Jesus Christ our Lord give his blood by the will of God for us, and his flesh for our flesh, and his soul for our souls" (49:6). One could also note his words in 7:4, "Let us fix our gaze on the Blood of Christ, and let us know that it is precious to his Father, because it was poured out for our salvation." In 12:7 Clement finds a type

hospitality," which no doubt refers to the way she harbored the spies sent into Jericho, a point made in James 2:25: "In the same way, was not even Rahab the prostitute considered righteous for what she did when she gave lodging to the spies and sent them off in a different direction?" James—as also the writer of Hebrews (11:31)—relates her hospitality to the spies as evidence of her faith, giving Clement the precedent to use it in his epistle as well. Clement's emphasis on living righteously is not only a part of his interpretative tradition, but also sanctioned by Scripture, which shares in that tradition, even if it is protected supernaturally.

But what about Paul's doctrine of grace? Clement carefully—and, one could possibly argue, consciously (though he never states it explicitly or explains the logic of his thinking)—directs his readers to grace. To correct sin, one must emphasize morality; to correct self-righteousness, one must emphasize grace. Clement spends thirty-one chapters on works of righteousness, but when he reaches 32:3–4, he quickly changes directions and reminds the Corinthians of the Pauline doctrine of grace:

> All of them [Abraham, Jacob, etc.] therefore were all renowned and magnified, not through themselves or their own works or the righteous actions which they had wrought, but through his will; And therefore we who by his will have been called in Christ Jesus, are not made righteous by ourselves, or by our wisdom or understanding or piety or the deeds which we have wrought in holiness of heart, but through faith, by which the Almighty God has justified all men from the beginning of the world: to him be glory for ever and ever. Amen.

The "all of them," in this passage is a clear and conscious connection between the "fathers" who righteously persevered (Enoch, Abraham, Rahab, Jacob, and others) and Paul's doctrine of justification by faith alone.

of Christ in Rahab's scarlet thread. He says, "And they proceeded to give her a sign, that she should hang out a scarlet thread from her house, foreshadowing that all who believe and hope on God shall have redemption through the blood of the Lord." And again in 21:6 he says, "Let us reverence the Lord Jesus Christ, whose blood was given for us." In these instances there is a clear reliance on the blood of Christ for redemption. Contrary to Torrance's view, Clement finds salvation in the sacrifice of Christ. Christ's death both saves human beings and gives them an example to live by, yet this high priest (36:1), through his "sufferings," was the real "provision" for salvation (2:1–2). Like Torrance, A. C. McGiffert says that Clement "agreed with other Christians of his day that salvation is to be had only by obeying God and doing his will" (*A History of Christian Thought,* 1:85).

Grace appears in other places as well. Clement urges Christians not to brag about their humility because "we have everything from him" (38:4) and so even "humility" is "given" (56:1). Works of righteousness are not ours and we are "adorned" by God with "good works" (33:7). In the same passage in which Clement speaks of being "justified by deeds," he clearly sees these deeds (including humility) as a blessing (30:8).[63] As Robert Grant and Holt Graham explain, "Justification is by faith alone (32:3–4), but Clement, like Paul, cannot believe that it excludes the practice of 'the works of love' (*cf.* especially Rom 6:1). Idleness is no virtue; readiness for 'every good work' (Titus 3:1; 2 Tim 2:21; 3:17; 2 Cor 9:8) is indispensable."[64] So what can be done about Clement's apparent disparity? Charles Nielsen writes, "I can only conclude, then, that Clement meant what he said in ch. 32, meant it so strongly, in fact, that he let it stand knowing full well that it flatly contradicted the major emphasis of the letter."[65]

This is where the idea of "diversity" can help. Diversity, as a concept touching on the biblical text, also has not been well received by Evangelicals; in some forms, it is tantamount to the idea of contradiction (thus Nielsen's conclusion of Clement). Writing of diversity in biblical literature, Peter Enns notes that by *diversity* is meant "the Old Testament's different perspectives or points of view on the same topic." Are there contradictions or different perspectives within the biblical text? Many Evangelicals respond negatively to these questions by arguing that the admission of diversity disrupts the unity of Scripture—after all, could not the Holy Spirit from the vantage point of eternity maintain the unity of the temporal text? Enns hopes to clarify these issues not by ignoring them, but by employing the incarnational analogy, something crucial for understanding the nature of a divine book within an historical context.[66] As Christ is the God-man, that is, fully divine and fully

63. It is passages like these that are used as prooftexts by Torrance to demonstrate that Clement understands justification by righteous acts such as humility, but then fails to take seriously Clement's important clarifications.

64. Grant and Graham, *First and Second Clement,* 59.

65. Nielsen, "Clement," 134; J. B. Lightfoot said on this passage that "we have seen Clement combining the teaching of S. Paul and S. James. . . . So here, after declaring emphatically that men are not justified by their own works but by faith . . . he hastens to balance this statement by urging the importance of good works" (Lightfoot, *Apostolic Fathers,* 2:100).

66. Enns, *Incarnation and Inspiration,* 73.

human without diminishing his perfection, so also Scripture is both a divine and human book.

There is an example of diversity from the book of Proverbs that helps modern readers enter into Clement's mind. Proverbs, which is often used as a one-quotation-fits-all manual for living, offers wisdom in decidedly conflicting terms. For example:

> Do not answer fools according to their folly,
> or you will be a fool yourself.
> Answer fools according to their folly,
> or they will be wise in their own eyes. (26:4–5)

Commenting on this passage, Enns notes the "complexity involved in handling Proverbs. *Both* of these sayings are wise, even though—to state the obvious—they say the opposite." The point of the text, Enns notes, is to tell the reader that one needs to think about each principle and consider the appropriate application of one versus the other in any given situation. The writer of Proverbs, however, does not apparently feel the need to clarify that point.[67]

In terms of Clement's understanding of grace, diversity—of the kind seen in Proverbs 26, above—is crucial. While the epistle is meant to reflect the mind of one person, it utilizes various literary methods. Appeals to biblical texts, historical events, and mythological creatures are followed up with liturgical prayers, wisdom literature, and poetry. Likewise, Clement's appeal to righteous living is well within his inherited Christian tradition, specifically as he sees both James and Hebrews, and, by extension, the Second Temple world. He is also familiar with Paul. His position in Rome probably gave him access to Paul's letter to the Roman church, and his letter to the Corinthians clearly demonstrates his familiarity with other letters written by Paul, specifically those written to the Corinthians. Both James and Paul carried with them apostolic authority. To appeal to both of them does not require Clement's intentional harmonization of them. Much like the diversity found in Proverbs, it is simply enough to state two true things, especially when these two things are written by apostles. It is purely a function of modern scholarship—one entirely exhumed from the first century world and its surviving Second Temple motifs—to find a problem here. Whether Paul and James were compatible or whether their diversity required reconciliation is a problem for sixteenth-century

67. Ibid., 74.

Reformation theologians in dialogue or debate with their Catholic counterparts, but not for a first-century Christian clergyman—who has inherited a tradition closer to the apostolic tradition than any theologian today—whose modern interlocutors have different concerns.

OLD SOUTH WALES

Modern examinations of the epistle of 1 Clement can fall into one of several traps, and readers may simply cast it off as an early example of Christian corruption. For the Evangelical, Clement could be understood as presenting something contrary to Paul, perhaps even proto-Catholic. To others, Clement may simply be another example of the immediate defection of the early fathers from Paul's doctrine of grace due to the sway of Hellenistic Judaism. Another approach would be to imagine a Clement of Rome who anticipated Luther centuries in advance; Clement's epistle, from this perspective, foreshadows the Protestant Reformation and in so doing reflects Paul. But an alternative is to re-examine Clement not as Chesterton's New South Wales, but as Old South Wales; that is, to understand that Clement's presentation of his doctrine of grace and its relationship to works exists firmly within the Christian tradition to which he belongs. Clement is, in this way, even closer to the Apostles than his modern counterparts who find fault in him.

Given this alternative, Clement does seem to emphasize ideas common to certain groups of his day, but not outside of the literary and theological context he inherited from the biblical writers of his own period. He is no idiot, bumbling in contradiction; rather, he is simply working out of his given historical trajectory, comfortable with it because he knows nothing else. Theologically, Clement is presenting an argument that is pointed for the audience of his day. After Paul, the Corinthian church continued to struggle with unrighteous living; their reputation as "ready unto every good work" (1 Clem 2:7; *cf.* Titus 3:1) was being surpassed by sin, strife, jealousy, and disorder (1 Clem 3:2). "Righteousness and peace" were far removed from them (3:4). To encourage perseverance in righteousness, Clement calls them to piety, hospitality, humility, and godliness—and James becomes a suitable source. But to stave off pride, he reminds the Corinthians that salvation is by faith only and he appeals to Paul's doctrine of grace.

Today's Evangelical theologian might fear any encouragement toward living righteously out of fear that it places too much value on the necessity of human participation for one's eternal security in Christ. However, this type of detail is beyond Clement's world, in which the Christian is called to live a godly life and persevere, as well as to remember that one's position as righteous before God is strictly a matter of grace through faith. Clement—whoever the writer really was—is content, though he does not necessarily realize it, to live neighborly with this tension in the land of Old South Wales.

9

Predestination and Salvific Assurance in Early Modern Thought and Life

Kirk R. MacGregor

Although frequently vilified by non-Calvinists as a repugnant doctrine, few even within the Reformed tradition are aware that Calvin's doctrine of predestination was originally intended as a doctrine of comfort. Thus the import of predestination for the citizens of Geneva during Calvin's oversight and for the Huguenots suffering persecution in France proved far different than its import in seventeenth-century Protestant Scholasticism, especially following the 1618–19 Synod of Dort where it amounted to a rejection of Arminianism and a test of Calvinist orthodoxy. It is my position that Calvin's original intent for predestination must be reclaimed in order to remain historically faithful both to Calvin and to the New Testament documents from which the doctrine springs. Significantly, this reclamation is open to all Christians who believe the Bible teaches sovereign individual predestination, regardless of whether they hold compatibilist or libertarian views with regard to human free will. In other words, the assurance of eternal salvation which logically stems from sovereign individual predestination is logically independent of the doctrine of total depravity and its claim that hereditary corruption extends to every facet of human nature, including free will. Thus the findings of this article are ecumenical in scope and can be profitably maintained by Reformed Christians, who are compatibilists, as well as adherents of the anthropologies maintained by radical evangelical theologian Balthasar Hubmaier (1480–1528) and neo-Scholastic Jesuit Luis de Molina

(1535–1600), libertarians who, contra Jacob Arminius (1560–1609), also affirmed sovereign individual predestination.[1] The method we shall take is complementary in nature, weaving together the interdependent strands of theological development and social history into a complete and unified account. Thus we shall first demonstrate from Calvin's *Institutes of the Christian Religion* and other related documents the inextricable logical ties between sovereign individual predestination and an unimpeachable salvific assurance supplied by the Holy Spirit. We shall then explore how this theory reached concrete application by translating into an unshakable certitude of future glorification among Genevan and French Protestants amidst their sixteenth-century historical circumstances.

CALVIN AND THE ROLE OF PREDESTINATION IN PRACTICAL THEOLOGY

Certainly the point on which Calvin has been most frequently maligned from the sixteenth century onward is his doctrine of predestination, an unfair criticism because, as chapter 7 indicates, this doctrine received formulation neither in whole nor in part by Calvin but rather eleven centuries earlier by the late-Augustine. Nonetheless, the reason why Calvin, unlike Aquinas, Luther, Zwingli, and other previous exponents of predestination, has suffered blame is because he both spelled out the logical implications of the doctrine and insisted that the laity understand those logical implications. While Aquinas, Luther, and Zwingli recognized that late-Augustinian predestination logically demanded that if God has selected certain persons to be saved, then God has in the same way selected certain persons to be damned, this proved a conclusion too emotionally devastating for such doctors of the church to draw. Thus, pre-Calvinist adherents of late-Augustinian predestination gladly declared that God unconditionally elected some, they drew back from its logical equivalent that God unconditionally damned some. Instead, they appealed to divine ineffability (*i.e.* the view that God is fundamentally beyond rational categories and thus beyond words), arguing that the non-election of the damned comprised a mystery wherein human understanding of God proved futile. But due precisely to his honesty and logical integrity, Calvin refused to "punt" to ineffability; realizing that God is the supremely rational mind

1. For the particulars see MacGregor, "Hubmaier's Concord of Predestination with Free Will," 279–99; *A Molinist-Anabaptist Systematic Theology*, 64–86.

in whose essence are housed the laws of logic, Calvin maintained that God cannot transcend the laws of logic without violating his own nature. Hence Calvin demanded that, whether people like it or not, we must not shrink back from asserting that God has unconditionally selected certain persons to be damned. Interestingly enough, many of Calvin's Reformed colleagues agreed with this tenet in principle but not in practice, insisting that predestination must only be preached to those who could handle this "solid food" but withheld from "babes in Christ." In other words, the full scope of predestination should be revealed to the *illuminati* or "luminaries of erudition" (*i.e.* theologians and pastors) but hidden from "ordinary Christians," who were bound to misunderstand it. Calvin rejected this solution as dissimulation on two grounds, the second of which the Genevan reformer ranked as more important than the first. First, owing to the doctrine of the priesthood of all believers, Calvin exclaimed that the idea of a doctrine appropriately preached only to the sophisticated but not to the unsophisticated was a violation of the nature of the Gospel. Rather, all persons must know predestination alongside its logical implications, let the proverbial chips fall where they may. Indeed, where the chips fell themselves furnished indirect identification of the elect and the reprobate. As Calvin explains in his commentary on 2 Corinthians 2:14–16, the full disclosure of predestination is "a fragrance from life to life" to "those who are being saved" but "a fragrance from death to death" to "those who are perishing." Consequently, persons who took offense to the predestinary "aroma of Christ to God" marked themselves out as reprobate, while those who received it gladly showed themselves to be elect.

Second and more importantly, Calvin demanded that the doctrine of predestination be preached to all because of its profound practical use. At this juncture it must be emphasized that the practical use of predestination constitutes the underlying subtext which constantly resurfaces throughout all Calvin's writings on this topic. Had predestination seemed to Calvin a speculative abstraction, he would have cared less about its discussion in seminaries (the Reformed Academies), much less in churches. But since predestination, for Calvin, was the aroma of Christ—the birthright of all adopted children of God—how dare the pastor, whose job it is to stir up this aroma, deprive his flock this life-giving nourishment? For Calvin, the Pauline aroma of Christ metaphorically depicted a full disclosure of predestination since it, first and foremost, was the doctrine of comfort *par excellence* for the individual believer.

> Besides, in the very darkness that frightens them not only is the usefulness of this doctrine made known but also its very sweet fruit. We shall never be clearly persuaded, as we ought to be, that our salvation flows from the wellspring of God's free mercy until we come to know his eternal election, which illumines God's grace by this contrast: that he does not indiscriminately adopt all into the hope of salvation but gives to some what he denies to others.[2]

From these remarks it follows that if predestination is false, then salvation is ultimately not dependent upon God but upon individual believers. This deduction is quite agonizing, for relying on ourselves for final glorification amounts, in Luther's axiom, to relying on a "broken reed," and does not allow anyone to repose confidence in their salvation.[3] For all who subscribe to sovereign individual predestination, regardless of the ground of predestination (*e.g.* the divine creative decree, *scientia media*, and so forth) or the ground of human freedom (*e.g.* compatibilist or libertarian), it is philosophically evident that Calvin is correct. This is because, putting aside anthropological debates over why the following occurs, individualized divine grace is illustrated by the fact that God could have created each elect person in situations where, instead of choosing to appropriate salvation, the person would choose to reject it. Likewise, for each reprobate person, God could have created that person in situations where, instead of choosing to reject salvation, they choose to appropriate it. Furthermore, no other reason can be gleaned for these predestinary choices except for God's sovereignty—that is to say, if God chooses to create a world at all, then it is logically necessary for him to make such choices. Therefore, those who gainsay God's predestinary choices cut off the branch on which their survival depends, since their dislike of God's choices entails their wish that the world, and derivatively they themselves, would not exist. Through a skillful exegesis of the Greek text, Calvin makes this point very well while commenting on Romans 9:18–21. Here Calvin notes the often overlooked syntactical point that in the rhetorical question, "Or has not the potter the right over the clay, out of the same lump to make *on the one hand this* (ὃ μὲν) vessel for honor and *on the other hand that* (ὃ δὲ) for dishonor," the pairing of ὃ μὲν and ὃ δὲ constitute, in the terms of contemporary grammarians, a correlative clause. Since the two clauses are logically tied, Calvin reads Paul as asserting that if the lump of clay is used

2. Calvin, *Institutes*, 3.21.1.

3. Luther, "Letter to Elector John: Wittenberg, June 16, 1531," 50:46.

at all, it is by the nature of the case impossible for either all the vessels to be used for honor or for all the vessels to be used for dishonor. Instead, any usage of the lump (*i.e.* creating of any actual world) logically entails the production of some noble vessels and some common vessels. Thus for Calvin, a predestination-free world is not a world. Accordingly, all human criticism of God's predestinary choices unwittingly gainsays the potter's doing anything with the lump of clay.

COROLLARIES FOR DAILY LIFE

Calvin's result carries with it a number of ramifications directly affecting the day-to-day psychology and lifestyle of all believers. To begin, the wellspring of biblical humility lies in the recognition that none of us could save ourselves; if we think we could, then we are full of ourselves and guilty of *hubris*. In philosophical terms, humility dictates that transworld salvation, the notion that some individuals are so virtuous that they would have been saved in any world God could have chosen to create, is a contradiction in terms; on biblical grounds, Calvin also opposed transworld damnation, the notion that some individuals are so duplicitous that they would have been lost in any world God could have chosen to create. Believers will never be so indebted to, or reliant upon, God until they realize that God could have chosen multiple worlds in which they go to hell, and that God could have chosen multiple worlds in which persons lost in the actual world would be saved.

> If—to make it clear that our salvation comes about solely from God's mere generosity—we must be called back to the course of election, those who wish to get rid of all this are obscuring as maliciously as they can what ought to have been gloriously and vociferously proclaimed, and they tear humility up by the very roots. Paul clearly testifies that, when the salvation of a remnant of the people is ascribed to the election of grace, then only it is acknowledged that God of his mere good pleasure preserves whom he will. . . . They who shut the gates that no one may dare seek a taste of this doctrine wrong men no less than God. For neither will anything else suffice to make us humble as we ought to be nor shall we otherwise sincerely feel how much we are obliged to God.[4]

4. Calvin, *Institutes*, 3.21.1.

Once individuals realize that they are genuinely saved at some point in time, it follows that they are among God's elect, which furnishes them with complete and supreme salvific assurance.

But, we may ask, how do individuals glean this knowledge of genuine salvation? Calvin supplies two answers: one intangible and one tangible. The intangible way is through the *sensus divinitatis*, the self-authenticating (or, in modern philosophical parlance, properly basic) witness of the Holy Spirit, who resides within the soul of the elect and confirms the elect's predestinary status. According to Calvin's commentary on John 14:16–26, it is the indwelling Spirit who affords believers certainty that they are forever united with Christ, in whom they were predestined before the foundation of the world (*cf.* Eph 1:11). The tangible way of acquiring salvific certainty, as Robert M. Kingdon, Raymond A. Mentzer, and the present author have elsewhere argued, comes through an antithetical relationship between the Eucharist and church discipline.[5] In this relationship, reception of the Eucharist supplied the recipient with unshakable certainty of election.

> Godly souls can gather great assurance and delight from this Sacrament; in it they have a witness of our growth into one body with Christ such that whatever is his may be called ours. As a consequence, we may dare assure ourselves that eternal life, of which he is the heir, is ours; and that the Kingdom of Heaven, into which he has already entered, can no more be cut off from us than from him; again, that we cannot be condemned for our sins, from whose guilt he has absolved us, since he willed to take them upon himself as if they were his own. This is the wonderful exchange which, out of his measureless benevolence, he has made with us; that, becoming Son of man with us, he has made us sons of God with him.[6]

The philosophy behind this system, institutionalized in Geneva and elsewhere as the Consistory, was to admit to the Lord's Table those whose lives were filled with the fruit of the Spirit, and to deny admission to those whose lives were not. The Genevan Consistory, made up of all the elders and city pastors with one syndic (who was also an elder) as its presiding officer, acted as a morals court which met every Thursday. At this time the twelve elders, each representing one of the city's twelve districts, would report to the consistory names of residents who did not behave prop-

5. Kingdon, "Control of Morals in Calvin's Geneva," 3–16; Mentzer, *Sin and the Calvinists*, vii–ix, 97–128; MacGregor, *Central European Synthesis*, 212–22.

6. Calvin, *Institutes*, 4.17.2.

erly, a high percentage of which misbehavior entailed domestic quarrels and sexual promiscuity. The consistory analyzed each case. On the one hand, if the sin was minor and the miscreant contrite, she or he might be dismissed with a scolding. On the other hand, if the sin was major and the miscreant unrepentant, she or he could be barred from the Lord's Supper. Once barred, measures were taken by the Consistory to ensure that, before readmission to the Eucharist, the miscreants had remedied their relevant faults to an adequate degree. Although surprising to us, the Genevan faithful viewed this system as a heartening thing, for the Eucharist comprised the visible mark of the saints by which they could recognize each other and find objective assurance that they themselves were among the redeemed. Exegetically, Calvin indissolubly tied eternal security to the Lord's Supper via John 6:48–58, which he, unlike Luther, perceived as pregnant with Eucharistic meaning. Since Jesus claimed straightforwardly that "I am the living bread which came down from heaven; if anyone eats of this bread, he *will* (not "might") live forever" (v. 51) and that "whoever feeds on my flesh and drinks my blood *has* (not "will have") eternal life, and I *will* (not "might") raise him up on the last day" (v. 54), Calvin emphasized that the aim of the Supper is to confirm Christ's promise of salvation for the faithful:

> [T]he very powerful and almost entire force of the Sacrament . . . [is] to seal and confirm that promise by which he testifies that his flesh is food indeed and his blood is drink, which feed us unto eternal life. By this he declares himself to be the bread of life, of which he who eats will live forever. And to do this, the Sacrament sends us to the cross of Christ, where that promise was indeed performed and in all respects fulfilled.[7]

Another key function of predestination is to relieve believers of the anxiety to be good enough to keep the salvation they currently possess. Thus, predestination ensures not only that one has been forgiven of all past sin, but also that one's final beatitude is providentially protected by God despite any future shortcomings. Alister E. McGrath explains this point quite well:

> One of the central functions of the doctrine is to emphasize the graciousness of God. For Luther, God's graciousness is reflected in the fact that he justifies sinners, men and women who are totally

7. Ibid., 4.17.3–4.

> unworthy of such a privilege. For Calvin, God's graciousness is demonstrated in his decision to redeem individuals irrespective of their merits: the decision to redeem an individual is made without reference to how that individual might be. For Luther, God's graciousness is demonstrated in that he saves sinners *despite* their demerits; for Calvin, that graciousness is demonstrated in that he saves individuals *irrespective* of their merits.[8]

According to Calvin, this fact sustains believers during times of weakness. The Genevan reformer was certainly not so naïve as to think that the elect will be "good-doing machines" throughout the course of their lives; rather, all believers personally struggle with sin and need to know, at the very most in those moments, that their final salvation stands secure no matter what. Contra the "boisterous," "tyrannical," and "high-minded" view of Calvin echoing down the centuries since popularized by Catholic controversialist Albert Pighius (1490–1542), no one was more aware of these struggles than Calvin himself. Writing quite poignantly about his own periods of moral and spiritual weakness, Calvin forthrightly admits:

> Thus I see myself perpetually tossed about, so that there is not a moment when I do not seem to be sinking. Nevertheless, as God sustains His elect to prevent them drowning, I am confident of standing against these innumerable storms. If Pighius asks how I know I am elect, I answer that Christ is more than a thousand testimonies to me. For when we find ourselves in His body, our salvation rests in a secure and tranquil place, as though already located in heaven.[9]

Employing the Pauline analogy of the salvific race, predestination guarantees the unconditional presence of God's *gratia cooperans*, or cooperating grace, necessary for crossing the finish line. Thus, all the elect may rest assured that God has bequeathed them unlimited access to his infinite storehouse of grace, whose treasures will never be withheld or exhausted because of previous mistakes. Owing to their possession of the mind of Christ on this score (1 Cor 2:12–16), believers need never fear scenarios such as the following: "I know I possessed salvation at past time t_1, but during the following time period t_2 I didn't make good use of the cooperating grace I was given. May God, so to speak, lay me to waste at current time t_3 by refusing to give me the grace I need to reach beatitude?" This

8. McGrath, *Reformation Thought*, 137.
9. Calvin, *Concerning the Eternal Predestination of God*, 130.

is because a necessary attribute of *gratia cooperans*, regardless of whether it cooperates with compatibilist or libertarian free will, is its indefatigable character, such that although persons can defy it temporarily, they cannot defy it permanently (with the "cannot" here taken *in sensu diviso* on compatibilism and *in sensu composito* on libertarianism).[10] For this doctrine of grace Calvin cites Philippians 2:13 as his *locus classicus*:

> [W]e must not suppose that subsequent grace is paid to him as a reward, as though by using the earlier well he has merited it. . . . And [I say] that God unceasingly so accomplishes his work in them that whatever he bestows on them right to the end is freely given. . . . All of this, if I have any understanding, is comprehended by Paul in a single statement when he teaches that there is one God who effects in us both to will and to do according to his good pleasure. He speaks not of a single day, but of a continuing course of action, whose sole cause he defines as God's good pleasure, that is, his gracious kindness which pays no attention to any merit.[11]

Consequently, the grace, and not its recipient, keeps working until it achieves its desired effect.

When challenged by Pighius that such an understanding of grace could not be biblically tied to eternal security, Calvin was not content to merely proof-text explicit passages like John 10:26–29[12] and Ephesians 1:13–14,[13] but argues that the invincible power of *gratia cooperans* to bring believers to salvation constitutes the implicit logic of Romans 8:

> But when [Pighius] dares to allege that it is not to be found in Scripture, this is a gross falsehood easily disproved. For Paul teaches that those who were elected are called and justified, so as

10. This distinction is expounded in MacGregor, *Systematic Theology*, 40–41, 79.

11. Calvin, *Bondage and Liberation of the Will*, 175.

12. Calvin, *Institutes*, 3.21.1: "And as Christ teaches, here is our only ground for firmness and confidence: in order to free us of all fear and render us victorious amid so many dangers, snares, and mortal struggles, he promises that whatever the Father has entrusted into his keeping will be safe [John 10:28–29]. From this we infer that all those who do not know that they are God's own will be miserable through constant fear."

13. Calvin, *Bondage and Liberation*, 243: "Perseverance [is] also God's gift, not given according to our merits . . . whatever grace is bestowed on us to the very end of our lives is freely bestowed on us, not repaid for our gratitude, as though by using earlier favours well we merit this of ourselves. . . . I have shown quite clearly that the grace to begin and to persevere to the end is not given according to our merits, but is granted according to his own most secret and at the same time most just, most kind, and most wise will, since those whom he has predestined he also has called."

> to attain at length to the bliss of immortality; and then, as if fortified on all sides by a powerful defence, he triumphantly exults: Who shall stand against the elect of God? . . . he applies it for the use of each believer. I am persuaded, he says, that neither death nor life, nor angels nor principalities, nor things present or future will separate us from the love of God which is in Christ. So the confidence of eternal salvation, which Pighius wants to break up into single moments, Paul extends to future time beyond the limits of this present life, and shows that it emanates from nowhere but the election of God, while Pighius represents it so that a conflict between the two results.[14]

Drawing together the exegetical threads of the past (election), present (justification), and future (sanctification) salvific assurance afforded by predestination, Calvin summarizes:

> Paul is witness that none are led by that Spirit except the sons of God, whom he also pronounces to be heirs of eternal life (Rom 8:14). Otherwise what he writes elsewhere would not stand: We have the Spirit from heaven, so that we know what things are given us by God, and thus have the mind of Christ (1 Cor 2:12, 16); and in vain would he also call that Spirit with which the faithful are sealed the earnest of future redemption (Eph 1:14). But that the known election of God may strengthen the faith of perseverance, that one prayer of Christ should suffice for proof, where He commends all the elect to the Father, specifically separating them from the world, so that, even if it perish, they may remain safe and intact.[15]

In short, theological and philosophical grounds indicate that no other doctrine except sovereign individual predestination can produce the thoroughgoing and timeless eternal security held out by the New Testament as the anchor of all believers.

CASE STUDY: THE HUGUENOTS AMIDST FRENCH GOVERNMENTAL PERSECUTION (1557–1598)

In the sixteenth century, the divine assurance imparted by predestination was not an abstract theory to which believers gave intellectual assent and nothing else; rather, it was the foremost matter of practice which supplied the lifeblood for Reformed existence. Nowhere was such daily life

14. Calvin, *Predestination*, 131.

15. Ibid.

application better exemplified than among the Huguenots, or community of Reformed Christians in France, who suffered tremendously during the state-sponsored program of Protestant persecution known as the Wars of Religion (1557–1598). Due to their unicovenantal theology, wherein Hebrew Biblical and New Testament believers belonged to the same family, the Huguenots, following Calvin's lead, used the language of the Psalms to express their confidence in ultimate salvific protection. Famously in Geneva, Calvin transformed the Psalms into a veritable hallmark of the Reformed tradition, setting many of Clément Marot's French versifications of the Psalms to music and commissioning his assistant Theodore Beza to versify in French and set to music the remaining Psalms. By 1562, the Marot-Beza Psalter emerged as the most popular Reformed book in Switzerland, France, and the Netherlands.[16] Throughout his written correspondence to the Paris church in the late 1550s, Calvin continually employed direct and indirect quotations from the Psalms to fortify its members in bearing the yoke of persecution as Christ bore his cross. For example, in his March 1557 letter to the Paris church, the exhortation to find refuge "in the shadow of the wings of God" derives from Psalm 57;[17] likewise, in his letter written the following September, the assurance that God treasures the sufferings of the elect—"If God sometimes allows the blood of his faithful to be spilled, he nevertheless carefully collects their precious tears"—is substantiated via citation of Psalm 56.[18] Employing the literary technique of metalepsis (*i.e.* alluding to a Scriptural text for the purpose not simply of appropriating that particular text but also of conjuring up in the audience's minds the entire passage to which the text belongs as well as the historical context surrounding that entire passage),[19] Calvin's words recalled not only the direct reference in verse 8 ("You put my tears into your bottle; are they not in your book?") but also the following verses, wherein David articulates his confidence in divine protection, places his full trust in divine providence, and prays for strength to endure. The goal of Calvin's Psalmic references was to evoke in the Huguenots a full and uncompromising attitude of trusting acceptance both in and of

16. Diefendorf, *Beneath the Cross*, 132–33, 136–37.

17. Calvin, "A l'église de Paris," 122–26.

18. Ibid., 140–41.

19. This device is explained thoroughly by Hays, *Conversion of the Imagination*, 2–3.

God amidst suffering.[20] Calvin's utilization of the Psalter both to exhort and to comfort is also evident in his letter of February 1559 smuggled into the prisoners jailed in Paris on account of their Reformed convictions. Recollecting the verses from Psalm 119 that "the chains of the wicked have robbed me, but I have not forgotten your law," Calvin implicitly summons the many other verses of this longest psalm, thereby making it into a meditation on the way of righteousness, a prayer for strength in persecution, and a celebration of the present joy and the unimpeachable promise of future bliss possessed by persons faithful to the divine law. As a result, the Huguenots appropriated the Psalms, in the summation of Barbara B. Diefendorf, "to express their confidence in divine protection, their conviction of being a chosen people, and their sense of sin."[21] Thus Merlin de l'Espérandière described the situation of the Paris church in 1567 with the same reference to being sheltered "under the wings of God" that Calvin used in 1557 and with the same intent that a providential protection would see the church safely to final beatitude through the refiner's fire of persecution.[22] That the Psalms were so internalized by the Huguenots as to govern personal conscience is seen in the writings of Anthoine du Croy, the prince of the Porcein region, whose consciousness of wrongdoing stemmed from the Psalmic depiction (Ps 51:2–3) of "my sin and my iniquity, which are, as David says, always before me."[23]

The Huguenots interpreted the Psalms with a tripartite hermeneutic of historical, prophetic, and immediate meanings. Historically, the Psalms reflect the Hebrew Biblical context of David's own sufferings and eventual victory over his enemies. Prophetically, the Psalms reflect the sufferings and triumph of Christ. Immediately, the Psalms were viewed as reflecting the Huguenots' own current suffering and final triumph guaranteed by their election, where their contemporary significance in terms of political and social ramifications were directly set out in the prefatory caption attached to each psalm. To make the application to the current situation still more explicit, some editions of the Huguenot psalter included a list directing the reader to the most appropriate psalm for each occasion or state of mind. Psalms to use as prayers for a church that was afflicted or

20. Diefendorf, *Beneath the Cross*, 138.

21. Ibid.

22. de l'Espérandière, "To Beza, from Longueville (Paris)," 8:29.

23. du Croy, "Testament," 8:95.

enfeebled, oppressed by combat, or held captive by its foes were prominent on the list. Some editions also included a prayer after each psalm.[24] The most popular set of prayers was composed by Augustin Marlorat, briefly a minister in Paris but more closely associated with the church of Rouen, in which city he was martyred in 1562. Many of Marlorat's prayers make direct reference to the enemies that were persecuting the faithful, but they always refer at the same time to the covenant that God made with his chosen people and to his promise never to abandon them.[25] Therefore, the Psalms taught French Protestants to view persecution as a trial imposed by God and a special mark of the covenant guaranteeing their predestination before the foundation of the world. Huguenot pastors successfully used texts like Psalm 119:79, "It is good for me that I have been afflicted, that I might learn thy statutes," to urge their congregations not to flee but to accept persecution, even to the point of death.[26] In this way, the Psalms furnished a framework for reinterpreting persecution as a criterion of authenticity, such that, paradoxically, the faithful community could point to its persecution as a sign of its past election and secure future redemption. Since the Huguenots felt that all who genuinely lived the Christian life would be persecuted,[27] those so-called Christian groups facing no persecution or, even worse, engineering persecution against others were perceived as, by definition, among the reprobate and so eternally doomed to destruction.

Instances of these themes abound in Huguenot literature from the 1560s to the close of the sixteenth century. Published at Lyons in 1563, Antoine de la Roche Chandieu wrote in the preface to his *Histoire des persecutions et martyrs de l'Eglise de Paris* that "the afflictions that God has sent us are so many marks and signs of his good will toward us and his adoption."[28] Two years later at Lyons, Jean de L'Espine published his

24. Diefendorf, *Beneath the Cross*, 138–39.

25. Augustin Marlorat, in *Les pseaumes de David, mis en rime françoise. Avec une oraison à la fin d'un chacun pseaume faite par M. Augustin Marlorat*, by Clément Marot and Theodore Beza (Paris: pour Antoine Vincent, 1566), 39, 149.

26. Diefendorf, *Beneath the Cross*, 140.

27. Thus Jean de L'Espine reminded his flock that "persecutions are inevitable to all who wish dutifully to follow Jesus Christ . . . to be disciples and students of Jesus Christ, we must take his cross on our shoulders and follow him" (*Traitté consolatoire et fort utile contre toutes afflictions qui adviennent ordinairement aux fideles Chrestiens*, 6–7).

28. Antoine de la Roche Chandieu, *Histoire des persecutions et martyrs de l'eglise de Paris*, viii.

Traitté consolatoire, which used the glue of suffering to bind Calvin's New Testament foundations for eternal security with the fruits of that security poetically expressed in the Psalter. Based on the epigraph Romans 8:17, "If we are children, then we are heirs of God and joint-heirs with Christ, if indeed we share in his sufferings so that we may also share in his glory," de L'Espine admonished his audience to neither flee nor try to escape affliction.[29] But in order to lighten the yoke of these tribulations, de L'Espine charged his audience to glory in them and to remember that "our king," whom it is our honor to follow in all things, always accompanies us into battle.

> If it is an honor to a captain to abandon his life sooner to violate the faith he has pledged his prince, so is it to a Christian man to keep to the very end that [faith] that he has sworn to Jesus Christ and to die rather than to commit or to suffer anything that impairs it.[30]

Such insights were carried beyond mere duty into the realm of joy by Daniel Toussain, who expressed in a devotional on Psalm 124 that "affliction, among other uses, bring the faithful man a special zeal to trust uniquely in him, and so to experience the effects of his divine force."[31] With the certainty that although "the church since its earliest days has suffered greatly . . . nothing can destroy it," Toussain offered to God the following prayer:

> Your poor church is in this world like a lamb in the midst of wolves, like a rose among the thorns. But at the same time, O great God, we are so happy when he who created heaven and earth shows himself to be on our side. And we see that you are with us when miraculously you deliver us, when daily you uphold us.[32]

Based on his experience of the *sensus divinitatis*, Toussain conveyed his tremendous personal confidence in final salvific deliverance amidst persecution and commended this same confidence to all who apprehend the Holy Spirit in a properly basic way.

29. De L'Espine, *Traitté consolatoire*, 6–7.

30. Ibid., 10–12.

31. Toussain, *Prieres et consolations prises de plusieurs passages de l'Escriture, & des livres des anciens*, dedicatory epistle.

32. Ibid., 119.

> O, happy is the man who . . . not seeing any help in the world, looks at God and is assured of being seen by him! The mother often looks at her child with pity, because she cannot help him. But your look, Lord, is efficacious for your children; it is medicine for their ills.[33]

The Huguenot writings provide a potent counterexample to the anti-Calvinist notion that the "capricious election" of God provokes introspective anxiety in his followers, as the French Protestants displayed no trace of this fear. On the contrary, as de L'Espine boldly declared, while the elect are not all given the same measure of faith, this is irrelevant in the final analysis since "we are assured of eternal life as long as there is a single spark of faith in our heart."[34] De L'Espine beautifully encapsulated the Huguenot concept of God as a powerful Father whose degree of power is directly proportionate to his level of being "clement, mild, and full of grace [*doux, benin et gracieux*]. Do we need to fear his judgment? On the contrary, we hope to judge the world with him."[35] Founded on the solid rock of predestination, Huguenot spirituality therefore insisted that God's diverse promises all lead to the same end—to show believers the love God bears for them and the care he has for their salvation—which generated a confident, outgoing, and joyous witness to Christ despite the external pressures threatening to hamper it.

CLOSING REFLECTIONS

The theory of Calvin and the praxis of the Huguenots disclose the pluriform positive consequences of sovereign individual predestination for Christian thought and life of every era. As spiritual descendants of the Reformation, contemporary Christians would do well to lay aside rhetoric stemming from divisions over whether or not sovereign individual predestination contradicts libertarian human freedom, as solid cases can be made on both sides. For behind these secondary divisions lie primary agreements that not only initial salvation but also final salvation are dependent solely on God and constitute free gifts without regard to merit. Oftentimes believers feel that while their regeneration is a free

33. Ibid.

34. de L'Espine, *Traicté des tentations et moyens d'y resister*, 56–57.

35. de L'Espine, *Excellens discourse de J. de l'Espine, angevin, touchant le repos & contentement de L'esprit*, 632.

gift of Christ, they must work to sustain that spiritual state. But a biblical conception of predestination shows this to be profoundly not the case. On the contrary, as "good trees" (Matt 7:17–18) regenerated persons, by definition, will naturally open up their souls to God just as naturally as they breathe and so allow God's transforming love to flow through them to others, being carried along by God in the same way the biblical writers were carried along by the Holy Spirit (2 Pet 1:21). Here the words of Luther are *à propos*:

> Believers are a new creature, a new tree. Therefore all those modes of speech, which are customary in the law, do not belong here, such as, "A believer is bound to do good works," in the same way that it is not proper to say, "The sun is bound to shine," since it does this of itself, unbidden, as it is made for this. So a good tree of itself brings forth good fruits; three and seven are ten already, they are not first bound to be ten. To say of a sun that it ought to shine, or of a believer that he must do good, is ridiculous.[36]

Hence there is no need to fear that one will fail to be good enough to keep salvation. This fact yields tremendous certitude and confidence, especially in the midst of tragedy and temptation when it is so easy to act in ways contrary to one's ultimate convictions. It is a paradox of human psychology that people often place extra pressure on themselves to live out their convictions during times of trial, which pressure makes them much more likely to fail. Fortunately, salvific assurance based on predestination lifts this pressure and enables believers to live out the tenets of their faith in seasons of contentment and persecution alike. In these ways, predestination yields a happy and vibrant faith that shares in the power of Christ's resurrection by rising above all human obstacles, as it empowers believers to set their minds on things above (Col 3:1–2) and to rest assured that they will ultimately find themselves in the beatific position where their pre-promised treasure is currently stored (Matt 6:21).

36. Luther, *Works*, 22:717.

10

An Anthropological Look at Eternal Life

The Internal Changes Accompanying Salvation

Kirk R. MacGregor

One prevailing theme of the Pauline (both Proto- and Deutero-) and Johannine Epistles comprises the absolute certitude that followers of Jesus may repose in their salvation, a certitude which comes from looking within at the fundamental inclination of the soul. Ephesians 1:13–14 stands as the *locus classicus* of this theme: "In Christ you yourselves also, having heard the message of the truth—the good news of your salvation—when you believed in him (πιστεύσαντες ... ἐν ᾧ), you were sealed with the Holy Spirit of promise, who is a deposit guaranteeing our inheritance into/until (εἰς) the redemption of his possession, to the praise of his glory" (*cf.* 2 Cor 5:5). Three features of this passage deserve emphasis. First, the phrase πιστεύσαντες ... ἐν ᾧ connotes far more than *assensus* or simple subscription to various doctrines about Christ. (As James 2:19 and the Synoptic Gospels indicate, even the demons hold to a correct view of Christ, yet they tremble with fear awaiting imminent destruction.) Rather, it refers to *fiducia* or personal commitment to Christ, depicted in the New Testament and foreshadowed throughout the Hebrew Bible as a spiritual marriage between Christ and each believer. In this marriage, believers pledge their lives and love to Jesus; reciprocally, among the infinitude of benefits Jesus pledges to believers are guidance and companionship throughout the earthly life and entitlement to the beatific vision in the hereafter (Paradise followed by the new heaven-earth). Second, such an inheritance is qualified with the preposition εἰς, carrying the dual meaning that believers constitute Jesus' possession and, by virtue of their ownership by this perfect Savior, will necessarily receive full redemption of soul plus body at the general resurrection. Third, all who enter into spiritual marriage and await Christ's final deliverance presently and internally possess a guarantee of their justified status before God: the Holy Spirit, who permanently seals and lives within their souls. Once this passage is exegetically deciphered, a number of questions emerge which belong properly not to the realm of biblical but to the realm of philosophical theology. Such issues include: What exactly does the Spirit's sealing entail? In particular, what transformative effects does it produce in each believer's soul? Moreover, how do those effects manifest themselves in the course of daily living? Accordingly, the framing of biblically faithful and philosophically coherent answers to these queries will occupy the course of this chapter.

THE SPIRIT'S SEALING AND PRESENCE IN LIGHT OF NEW TESTAMENT ANTHROPOLOGY

To understand the nature of conversion wrought by the Holy Spirit, we must delineate the doctrine of human nature, or anthropology, held by the New Testament authors, especially as it pertains to the creaturely condition when alienated from, and reconciled to, God. According to the Apostle Paul, each individual estranged from God is a ψυχικός ἄνθρωπος ("soul-ish human," normally rendered "natural/carnal/fleshly human"), while each individual in right relationship with God is a πνευματικός ἄνθρωπος ("spiritual human"). Paul discloses the meaning of these terms in 1 Corinthians 2:14–15: "A ψυχικός ἄνθρωπος does not accept the things of the Spirit of God, for they are foolishness to him or her . . . but the πνευματικός discerns all things." Here we find that ψυχικός and πνευματικός represent opposite dominating principles towards which a person can be fundamentally oriented—either the person's own ψυχή ("soul") or the πνεῦμα ("Spirit") of God. These terms have nothing to do with substance or what someone is made out of—clearly a ψυχικός ἄνθρωπος is not a person made out of soul—but with orientation. Thus a ψυχικός ἄνθρωπος signifies a human primarily inclined toward the selfish desires of his or her own soul on an individual level and his or her own group, be it family, race, or nation, on a communal level. Conversely, a πνευματικός ἄνθρωπος refers to a human primarily inclined towards the desires of the Holy Spirit and is therefore God-centered rather than self-centered.[1] Transposing the most optimistic reading of New Testament anthropology into philosophical terms, every person, from the time they start freely sinning, damages their soul in such a way that only the Holy Spirit can repair and so becomes, in dominical metaphor, a "bad tree" (Matt 7:17–18) and a "slave to sin" (John 8:34).[2] In other words, each person is born with libertarian free will, having the ability to do anything on the spectrum between the two poles of (1) living ultimately for self and (2) living ultimately for God. At the outset, poles (1) and (2) are equal in desirability. But when one starts sinning, one strengthens (1) to such a degree that, even though it is possible to perform (2)-type actions, (1) becomes tremendously more desirable for the person and constitutes one's *modus operandi*. This strengthened (1) is what Paul terms σάρξ (the "flesh" or "sinful nature"). For a person in this condition, the vast majority (say 90%) of one's actions are ultimately rooted in self-centeredness, even those which on the surface appear spiritual, and those actions which are genuinely God-centered (say 10%) amount to the exception proving the fleshly rule. Hence the immaterial mind or soul is faced with the libertarian free, but unequally motivated, choice to follow (1) or (2), where the former enjoys a disproportionately strong appeal to that of the latter. Accordingly a person following σάρξ—of which any such choice is Paul's definition of ἁμαρτία (sin)—is designated as unregenerate (Rom 14:23). Although logically possible for an unregenerate person to always choose the impulses of the spirit and resist those of the flesh, God knows in his prescience that no one will actually so choose. Such persons, Jesus taught, are "once-born" and cannot enter the Kingdom of God (John 3:3). Since humans cannot perform "surgery" on their own souls, so to speak, no one can save themselves from this condition. As Bernard of Clairvaux poignantly illustrated, humans living apart from God have dug for themselves a naturally inescapable pit and then have willingly fallen into it.[3]

1. MacGregor, "1 Corinthians 15:3b–6a, 7 and the Bodily Resurrection of Jesus," 232–33.

2. Perceiving this interpretation as a drastic understatement, exponents of the late-Augustinian tradition, including Thomists, Lutherans, and Calvinists, would locate our spiritual damage at the moment of conception (*i.e.* original sin).

3. Bernard de Clairvaux, *De gratia et libero arbitrio*, in *Sämtliche Werke lateinisch/deutsch* I (Innsbruck: Tyrolia-Verlag, 1990), 208.

The only way for someone to enter the Kingdom of God is for the person to make a free decision to, through the power of God, trust in Jesus and follow his Kingdom of God message, at which point the Holy Spirit accomplishes something miraculous in the person's soul—namely, καινὴ κτίσις, the "new birth" or the "new reality" (2 Cor 5:17). Here the Holy Spirit gives the person a "soul operation" in which their spiritual condition is diametrically reversed. This operation strips (1) of its power and greatly empowers (2), so that living to carry out the desires of God becomes tremendously more desirable for the person and constitutes his or her new *modus operandi*. Reconnected to the divinely powered impulse for which it was created, this strengthened (2) is what Paul as well as Jesus termed πνεῦμα (the "spirit," lowercase "s"; Rom 8:16; 1 Cor 14:2, 14–15; 2 Cor 4:13; Gal 5:16–24; Mark 14:38; John 3:6; 4:24), and the Holy Spirit's soteriological operation in its totality is what Paul/the Pauline amanuensis, the Apostle Peter, James, and the Elder John dubbed "regeneration" (παλιγγενεσία or ἀναγεννάω; Titus 3:5; 1 Pet 1:3; 1:23; Jas 1:18) or being γεννηθῇ ἄνωθεν ("born again/from above"; John 3:3, 7). The double entendre is instructive: not only must one receive birth for a second time, now spiritual rather than physical, to enter God's Kingdom, but such birth can only be accomplished by God himself via the Third Trinitarian Person—no one can will oneself to regeneration or be good enough to regenerate oneself. Further, regeneration is how God adopts humans into his family, such that all who have received the Spirit's revivifying nourishment are adopted sons and daughters of God:

> For you did not receive a spirit of slavery to fall back into fear, but you have received a spirit of adoption, by which we cry, "Abba, Father." The Spirit himself bears witness with our spirits that we are children of God, and if children, also heirs—on the one hand, heirs of God; on the other hand, co-heirs with Christ, if indeed we suffer with him that we may also be glorified with him. (Rom 8:15–17; *cf.* John 1:13)

Notice that the end result for the believer is even better than how the person started out prior to sinning—then (1) and (2) were equal, but now (2) is tremendously more powerful such that the person is utterly changed, genuinely desiring to live for God and consistently doing so. Now this is not to say that the "born again" person never sins, but simply that sinful or (1)-type actions occur much less frequently (say 10%) and now comprise the exception that proves the rule of (2)-type or God-centered actions (say 90%) which dominate the believer's life. Since these spiritual actions are ultimately incited by the Holy Spirit, Paul calls their totality "the fruit of the Spirit" (Gal 5:22). For these reasons, the regenerate's new Spirit-empowered life is "freedom" (Gal 5:1) and "marriage to Jesus," for whom the law's condemnation has been put to death by Jesus' atoning work on the cross and the previous marriage to that condemnation consequently annulled.[4] As Jesus explained, "So if the Son sets you free, you will be free indeed" (John 8:36). In the following quotation Paul draws together all the threads of this section into a salvific narrative, where the first person represents the collective experience of the redeemed:

> Do you not know, sisters and brothers—for I am speaking to people who know the law—that the law has authority over a person only as long as she or he lives? For example, by law a married woman is bound to her husband as long as he is alive, but if her husband dies, she is released from the law of marriage. So then, if she marries another man while her husband is still alive, she is called an adulteress. But if her husband dies, she is released from that law and is not an adulteress, even though she marries another man. So, my sisters and brothers, you also died to the law through the body of Christ, so that you might belong in marriage to another, to him who was raised from the dead, in order that we might bear fruit to God. . . . Once I was alive apart from law; but when the commandment came, sin sprang to life and I died. I found that the very commandment that was intended to bring life actually brought death. . . . Therefore there is now no condemnation for those who are in Christ Jesus, because through Christ Jesus the law of the Spirit of life set me free from the law of sin and death. (Rom 7:1–4, 9–10, 8:1–2)

When facing salvific doubts, every believer is exhorted to simply perceive whether this freeing change has occurred in their lives. If they are fundamentally inclined to do the will of God, regardless of lingering sin or temptation, believers know beyond doubt that they possess the gift of eternal life, which shall never be taken away from them (John 6:37–40; 10:28–29).

Describing the grace of regeneration, the prophet Ezekiel adds that the Holy Spirit not only repairs the believer's soul but also forever takes up residence there: "I will give you a new heart, and I will put within you

4. MacGregor, *A Molinist-Anabaptist Systematic Theology*, 35–36.

a new spirit; and I will remove from your flesh the heart of stone and give you a heart of flesh. And I will put my Spirit within you, such that you will walk in my statutes and be careful to observe my ordinances" (36:26–27). The Spirit's abiding presence in all followers of God received foreshadowing by Moses, who longed that the Israelites of his day would experience this anointing despite the threatening prospect of divinely directed people to others: "The Spirit also rested upon…two men, whose names were Eldad and Medad . . . and they prophesied in the camp. . . . Joshua son of Nun, who had served as Moses' aide since youth, said, 'Moses, my lord, stop them!' But Moses rejoined, 'Are you jealous for my sake? I wish that all Yahweh's people were prophets and that Yahweh would put his Spirit on them" (Num 11:26–29). Such disquietude on the part of unbelievers (and even, as seen with Joshua, some fellow believers) stems from the fact that Spirit-directed persons are ultimately answerable to no authority but God; so the apostles told the Sanhedrin, "We must obey God rather than human beings" (Acts 5:29). Jesus explained this situation to Nicodemus, "The wind blows where it wishes and you hear its sound, but you do not know where it comes from or where it goes. So is everyone who is born of the Spirit" (John 3:8). Genuine followers of Jesus are in the Spirit, and the Spirit is in them, for no true believer lacks the indwelling presence of the Holy Spirit.[5] The indwelling of the Spirit begins at the moment of personal commitment to Christ (Gal 3:1–5), when God sends forth "the Spirit of his Son into our hearts, crying out, 'Abba, Father'" (Gal 4:6). Consequently, James D. G. Dunn points out that, according to the New Testament, people are legitimate Christians only if they have received the Holy Spirit:

> The one thing which makes a [person] a Christian is the gift of the Spirit. [Persons] can have been for a long time in Jesus' company, can have made profession of faith and been baptized in the name of the Lord Jesus, can be wholly "clean" and acceptable to God, can even be "disciples," and yet not be Christians, because they lack and until they receive the Holy Spirit. . . . This has an important consequence, for it means that the thing which determines whether a

5. Robert G. Gromacki, "The Indwelling and Filling of the Holy Spirit," in *Understanding Christian Theology*, gen. eds. Charles R. Swindoll and Roy B. Zuck (Nashville: Nelson, 2003), 498.

> [person] is a Christian is not his profession of faith in Christ but the presence of the Spirit.[6]

The unconditional and exceptionless fact that the Holy Spirit will permanently live in the souls of believers is guaranteed by the Father's affirmative response to Jesus' prayer: "And I will pray the Father, and he will give you another Counselor (ἄλλον παράκλητον),[7] in order that *he may abide with you forever*" (John 14:16; emphasis mine).

This furnishes believers with a second unmistakable evidence of their eternal security, since they can immediately apprehend the Holy Spirit's habitation in their souls, which indwelling guarantees them access to the beatific vision. Denominated the *sensus divinitatis* since Medieval Scholasticism, apprehension of the Spirit's presence is Scripturally characterized by the noun πληροφορία ("full assurance, absolute certainty, complete confidence"; 1 Thess 1:5; Col 2:2; 4:12; Rom 4:21; 14:5), thereby defining the believer's knowledge that the Spirit lives within as, in philosophical terms, properly basic. Properly basic beliefs are beliefs which arise appropriately from our experience, but which are impossible to logically prove by that experience. In the absence of any defeaters (compelling disproofs), humans are rational to hold such beliefs. To illustrate, other properly basic beliefs include belief in the external world, belief in the existence of other minds, and belief in the reality of the past, all of which are completely unprovable (*i.e.* one could be a brain in a vat stimulated with electrodes by a mad scientist to believe in the external world), but which, *sans* defeaters, persons are rational to hold. Hence followers of Jesus may know, with the same certainty as they know the external world exists, that the Spirit occupies their souls and, derivatively, that they will forever be among the redeemed: "By this we know that we abide in God and he in us, because he has given us of his Spirit" (1 John 4:13).

6. Dunn, *Baptism in the Holy Spirit*, 93, 149; emphasis his.

7. It should be emphasized, contra Jehovah's Witnesses and other groups which maintain that the Holy Spirit is God's impersonal active force rather than a divine Person, that John explicitly guarantees the personality of the Spirit by using the adjective ἄλλον rather than ἕτερον for "another." This is because ἄλλον means "another of the same kind or species," whereas ἕτερον means "another of a different kind or species." Thus Jesus affirmed that the Father would send another Counselor of the same kind or species as himself, namely, a personal one.

NECESSARY LIFESTYLE RESULTS OF REGENERATION

Jesus revealed that the Holy Spirit's "soul operation" called regeneration automatically causes the believer's soul to function much differently than the unbeliever's soul. It is not as though new believers must try to make their souls act differently than before; rather, without any effort of their own, their souls will naturally incline toward attitudes and behaviors glorifying to God. However, individuals outside the pale of spiritual marriage to Christ, including those who pretend to be believers but are not, will over any significant period of time necessarily lack such attitudes and behaviors, which simply cannot be habitually produced by the unregenerate soul. Thus Jesus summarized in the Sermon on the Mount:

> Beware of false prophets, who come to you in sheep's clothing, but within are ravenous wolves. By their fruits you will know them. Surely grapes are not gathered from thorns or figs from thistles? So every good tree produces good fruits, but the rotten tree produces bad fruit. A good tree is not able *to habitually produce* (the participle ποιεῖν is continual aspect) bad fruit, nor is a rotten tree able *to habitually produce* (ποιεῖν) good fruit. Every tree *not habitually producing* (μὴ ποιοῦν) good fruit is cut down and thrown into the fire. Therefore, by their fruits you will know them. (Matt 7:15–20; emphasis mine)

Previously intimated by the 90/10 percentiles, the continual aspect of all New Testament verbs and verbal nouns describing personal behavior stands as both a comfort for believers and a warning for unbelievers. Since Jesus employed the continual aspect "a good tree is not able to habitually produce bad fruit" instead of the finite aspect "a good tree is not able to produce bad fruit," believers need never fear that they have lost their salvation following sin. By contrast, Jesus' utilization of the continual aspect "nor is a rotten tree able to habitually produce good fruit" rather than the finite aspect "nor is a rotten tree able to produce good fruit" prevents unbelievers from thinking they possess or have earned salvation when they occasionally perform God-honoring actions, for it is precisely their occasional nature which invalidate them from earmarking salvation. Denoting the Pauline "spirit" as "God's seed," the Elder John draws together these doctrinal threads with the following statement: "Everyone having been born of God is not continually practicing sin, because God's seed remains in him, and he is not able to continually sin, because he has been born of God" (1 John 3:9).[8]

The first epistle of the Elder John coupled with Paul's letter to the Galatians proceed to list several traits, whose sum total comprise the "fruit of the Spirit" (Gal 5:22), characteristic of all possessing a revivified human spirit. When people are asked to characterize a believer's life, the adjective that comes to mind should not be "hypocrite" or "sinner," but rather something like "carrying out the Kingdom of God," where the Kingdom of God designates the philosophy of life where God is the king over all earthly affairs (*e.g.* social, political, economic, religious, and so forth) and where God rules as an other-centered servant leader instead of as a self-centered domineering tyrant. Consequently, one specific result in life is ἀγαπή, the unconditional, suffering love uniquely emanating from God which makes up the gasoline for the engine of God's Kingdom:

> Beloved ('Αγαπητοί), let us love (ἀγαπῶμεν) one another, because love (ἀγαπή) is of God, and everyone who continually loves (ἀγαπῶν) has been born of God and knows God. The one not continually loving (μὴ ἀγαπῶν) does not know God, because God is love (ἀγάπη). . . . We love (ἀγαπῶμεν) because he first loved (ἠγάπησεν) us. If anyone says, "I love ('Αγαπῶ) God," and hates one's sisters or brothers, that person is a liar, for the one not continually loving (μὴ ἀγαπῶν) one's sister or brother, whom one has seen, is not able to love (ἀγαπᾶν) God, whom one has not seen. And this command we have from him, that the one loving (ἀγαπῶν) God must also love (ἀγαπᾷ) his sister or brother. (1 John 4:7–8, 19–21)

Here note the exclusivity of the term ἀγαπή and its variants to designate the "love" marking the believer's behavior. For ἀγαπή, the highest grade of love, is distinct from lower grades of love, such as φιλία (friendship love) and ἐρος (sexual love), supplementary loves which only possess validity when conjoined with the primary love ἀγαπή. In other words, believers should have φιλία for their friends and ἐρος for their spouses in addition to, not instead of, ἀγαπή for such persons, as the latter supplies

8. Wayne Grudem furnishes helpful commentary on John's intended meaning: "Here John explains that a person who is born again has that spiritual 'seed' (that life-generating and growing power) within him, and that this keeps the person living a life free of continual sin. This does not of course mean that the person will have a perfect life, but only that the pattern of life will not be one of continuing indulgence in sin" (*Systematic Theology*, 704).

the foundation for the former. Empowered by ἀγαπή, another effect of regeneration is overcoming "the world," where the world alludes to the anti-Kingdom-of-God Kingdom philosophy of life marked by personal selfishness and "top-down" social domination and oppression according to which the world typically operates:[9] "And his commands are not burdensome, because all who have been born of God overcome the world" (1 John 5:3–4). Here the Elder John explains that the "spiritual human" possesses the innate ability to overcome the pressures and temptations of the world that may otherwise keep one from following God's paths and obeying his commands. Moreover, the "spiritual human" will actualize that innate potentiality and so overcome these pressures, rendering it joyful, not burdensome, to obey God's commands.[10] The Elder John goes on to observe that "this is the victory that overcomes the world—our faith (πίστις)" (1 John 5:4), because biblical faith, or personal commitment to God, is the appropriate response when confronted by *gratia praeveniens*, a response to which the Spirit reciprocates via regeneration of that individual.

The most famous summary of practical life-defining traits engendered by the Spirit's power comes from Paul: "Now the fruit of the Spirit is love (ἀγαπή), joy (χαρὰ), peace (εἰρήνη), longsuffering (μακροθυμία), kindness (χρηστότης), goodness (ἀγαθωσύνη), faith (πίστις—one's personal commitment to Jesus must continue throughout life; one must never seek a "spiritual divorce"), gentleness (πραΰτης), and self-control (ἐγκράτεια); there is no law against such things. Persons who belong to Christ Jesus crucified (ἐσταύρωσαν) the flesh (τὴν σάρκα) with its passions and desires" (Gal 5:22–24).[11] Seven of these nine attributes have yet to receive attention in our study. Χαρὰ alludes to deep and abiding happiness independent of this-worldly circumstances; such joy is especially complete when what was spiritually lost or immature is respectively found or grows to maturity (Luke 15:6–7, 9–10, 32; Phil 2:2). Joy is possible pre-

9. MacGregor, *Systematic Theology*, 2, 270.

10. Grudem, *Systematic Theology*, 705.

11. Expectedly, Paul contrasts the fruit of the Spirit with the works of the flesh, whose habitual presence spells eternal destruction: "But the works of the flesh (σαρκός) are manifestly obvious, which are fornication, impurity, licentiousness, idolatry, sorcery, enmities, strife, jealousy, anger, selfishness, divisions, factions, envy, drunkenness, carousing and things like this. Just as I said beforehand, so now I say again, the ones habitually practicing (πράσσοντες, continual aspect verb) such things will not inherit the Kingdom of God" (Gal 5:19–21).

cisely because of εἰρήνη, peace of mind regardless of situation springing from the well of peace with God (Rom 5:1). A corollary to the atonement, this peace is a gift from Jesus himself: "Peace (Εἰρήνην) I leave with you; my peace (εἰρήνην) I give to you; not as the world gives do I give to you. Let not your hearts be troubled, neither let them be afraid. . . . I have said this to you, that in me you may have peace (εἰρήνην). In the world you have tribulation; but be of good cheer, I have overcome the world" (John 14:27; 16:33). Such peace affords believers the supernatural ability, when anxieties enter their minds, to choose not to worry, namely, not to pay attention to those anxieties but to trust God for their resolution: "Worry about nothing, but in everything by prayer and petition with thanksgiving let your requests be made known to God. And the peace (εἰρήνη) of God, surpassing all understanding, will guard your hearts and your minds in Christ Jesus" (Phil 4:6–7). Further, εἰρήνη manifests itself in a very practical peace between all those who know God. James Montgomery Boyce spells out the various relationships which, through the Holy Spirit, should function as disclosures of εἰρήνη:

> This latter peace should be seen...in the home (1 Cor 7:12–16), between Jew and Gentile (Eph 2:14–17), within the church (Eph 4:3; Col 3:15), and indeed in the relationships of the believer with all [persons] (Heb 12:14). Moreover, Christians are to strive for it (1 Peter 3:11). The importance of this word is evident from its frequent and extensive occurrence in the NT—eighty times and in every book.[12]

This essential virtue facilitates μακροθυμία, the quality of tolerating or putting up with others, even (and especially) when one is severely tested. The importance of longsuffering is underscored by its being most often used in Scripture concerning the nature of God, as in Joel's words of assurance: "Return to Yahweh your God, for he is gracious and merciful, longsuffering, and abounding in steadfast love, and relents from sending calamity" (2:13).

The divine kindness out of which God acts toward humanity, χρηστότης is what the Bible posits of God in its repeated affirmations that "God is good." Even transcending the Golden Rule, "Do unto others *as you would have them do unto you*" (Matt 7:12; emphasis mine), believers are to show kindness by treating others *as God has treated them*. Similarly,

12. Boyce, "Galatians," 10:498.

ἀγαθωσύνη designates generosity that flows from kindness and which is often directed toward persons not meriting the action. Appealing to the Judaized version of the Greek philosophical categories under which he was trained by Gamaliel, Paul stipulates that followers of Jesus must exhibit πραΰτης, defined by Aristotle as classifying "the person who is so much in control of himself that he is always angry at the right time and never angry at the wrong time."[13] Philo remarked that Moses, praised in Torah as the gentlest or meekest among his contemporaries (Num 12:3), exemplified this virtue, whose possession is necessary for learning, dispensing discipline, receiving discipline, meeting opposition, and giving a godly witness.[14] Finally, ἐγκράτεια is the attribute that supplies victory over fleshly desires and which is thereby inextricably intertwined to chastity in both mind and conduct.[15] Against the aforementioned nine virtues there is no law, for the moral law functions to restrain evil, and these qualities do not need to be restrained. In addition, Paul suggests that it is logically impossible for the moral law to stand against such as live in this manner since, by virtue of being so led, they in principle fulfill all that the moral law requires. However, believers must never return to their pre-Christian ways of life. In a carefully nuanced Greek verse which, in itself, permits no ambiguity but which, due to translation into conceptually looser languages like Latin and English, has frequently suffered misinterpretation down through history, Paul asserts that individuals belonging to Jesus "crucified" (ἐσταύρωσαν, aorist or simple past tense), not "have crucified" (σέσταύρκᾶσιν, perfect tense), the flesh. Paul uses the simple past rather than perfect tense to convey the clear meaning that, metaphorically speaking, the flesh of believers has been nailed to the cross but is not yet dead, struggling for life until the moment of physical mortality. Much damage has been levied against Christians struggling with sin by well-meaning friends and church leaders when the latter insist that Christ has annihilated the flesh of all true believers, thereby indirectly calling the regeneration of the former into question (*i.e.* "if person *P* deals with a fleshly temptation, *P* must not be a real Christian, since Jesus has destroyed the flesh of all the redeemed). Rather, the flesh is currently condemned to an agonizing death, suffered in slow and lingering fashion, thus in the

13. Aristotle, *Nicomachean Ethics*, 4.5.1.

14. Philo, *De vita Mosis*, 2.50.279.

15. Boyce, "Galatians," 499.

process always desperately pressuring the believer to take it down from the cross and revivify it. But the believer is not to remove, or even seek to remove, from the cross what has once been nailed there.

CONCLUDING INSIGHTS: APPROPRIATING THE SPIRIT'S INTERNAL SUSTENANCE

How can individuals truly know they are children of God? By examining their own spiritual state, believers can discern in a properly basic way both that the dominating principle in their lives comprises the observance of God's will and that the Holy Spirit lives within (the *sensus divinitatis*). These two answers find encapsulation in Paul: "The Spirit himself bears witness with our spirit that we are children of God" (Rom 8:16). Accordingly, Scripture exhorts followers of Jesus to appropriate the Spirit's internal sustenance through purity, worship, and service, in the process experiencing daily spiritual growth. Concerning purity, the believer's body is literally a temple of the indwelling Spirit (1 Cor 6:18–20). Therefore, believers should treat their bodies and the bodies of others "in sanctification and honor" (1 Thess 4:4), rather than attempting to justify ethically dubious behavior with such rationalizations as "we are consenting adults," "no one gets hurt," "we love each other," and so forth. Robert G. Gromacki rightly avers that the believer "must reject this kind of nonbiblical logic for one basic reason: The Holy Spirit is hurt when a Christian violates the proper sexual usage of his body."[16] Grounded "in spirit and in truth" (John 4:24), true worship of God is relational, personal, and directed by the Holy Spirit. As a result, saved Jews and saved Gentiles, fused together as "one new humanity" in Jesus, now "both have access by one Spirit to the Father" (Eph 2:15, 18). The biblical relationship between the Spirit and the church is a symbiotic one: as the Spirit unifies the fellowship or communion of believers, simultaneously the church must vigilantly "pray in the Holy Spirit" (Jude 20)—consequently the church develops into "the dwelling place of God in the Spirit" (Eph 2:22). Emerging from the nature of the "spiritual human," believers should serve God "in the newness of the Spirit and not in the oldness of the letter" (Rom 7:6); in other words, true service is marked by ἀγαπή rather than legalistic conformity to tradition or social expectations. The hallmark of genuine service is its benevolent edification, construed here broadly to include all forms of "building up,"

16. Gromacki, "Indwelling and Filling," 500.

of both believers and non-believers, for this is how Jesus himself served. All followers of Jesus must build on this foundation, cognizant that it is the only basis whereupon they may render account of their accomplishments before the judgment seat of Christ (1 Cor 3:11–15). By cultivating the triplicate pillars of purity, worship, and service, believers grow from spiritual infancy to adulthood (2 Pet 3:18), fostering increasing awareness of their spiritual inheritance "that we might know the things that have been freely given to us by God" (1 Cor 2:12). As long as believers refuse to substitute human effort, or conformity to human-made standards, for reliance on the divine power of the Spirit, the church *in toto et personam* will mediate reconciling spiritual encounter to a lost and dying world, so reinfusing the world with foretastes of restorative power which God will consummate at the general resurrection.

11

Salvation from the Wrath to Come in the Present Epoch

Georg Plasger

THE SUBJECT OF GOD'S WRATH— THEOLOGICAL INQUIRIES

We find multiple statements in the New Testament that speak explicitly about the wrath of God. Particularly in the writings of Paul, the subject of God's wrath is not an unusual topic. Nevertheless, there is an uneasiness in Protestant theology whenever the subject of God's wrath is addressed. Aren't these biblical statements simply anthropomorphisms? Aren't we simply applying human characteristics to God? Another question arises from these, doesn't such a heated emotional view of God endanger his transcendence? Doesn't the concept of a wrathful God lead us to conclude that his anger is grounded in an emotional expression of irrationality? Or is Paul's view of God dualistic in which there are two sides of God held together in a dynamic tension? Moreover, it is clear that, according to Paul, a deliverance from God's wrath takes place in the lives of those who are justified. Doesn't this imply that God repents or changes his mind and that he did not know from the beginning where history was heading? Doesn't the love of God take priority? If not, in what can the Christian trust? Is the loving will of God clear? These are all questions that may arise from biblical teaching on these matters.

THEOLOGICAL VIEWPOINTS ON THE SUBJECT OF GOD'S WRATH

Before we look at specific biblical statements that address the topic of God's wrath and deliverance therefrom, I would like to briefly describe three differing viewpoints regarding God's wrath. These examples address, in order, the questions raised in the former paragraph.[1]

Viewpoint 1: God is love and not angry (Albrecht Ritschl)

The theologian of liberal Protestantism Albrecht Ritschl (1822–1889) severely criticized the notion that God was wrathful. The starting point for Ritschl was the love of God. Therefore, only the love of God is decisive: "[T]he concept of God's wrath has no religious value for the Christian."[2] While it is true that in the Old Testament God could respond wrathfully towards his chosen people, he was never gracious and wrathful at the same time. Ritschl held that the fluctuation between wrath and grace in the Old Testament was superceded in the New Testament, where the grace of God stands clearly in the foreground. According to Ritschl, all the statements regarding the wrath of God in the New Testament refer to a future wrath during the end times where all those who "with a raised hand" sin against God will be destroyed.[3] Displaying ambivalence toward the facticity of the New Testament authors' perceived intent, Ritschl does not indicate whether the people involved will actually be destroyed or whether all the inhabitants of the earth will be saved during the end times. At least in a metaphorical sense, wrath will remain on these stiff-necked individuals, but whether this is literally carried out at the end of time is irrelevant. In a similar vein, present-day Christians may experience testing and metaphorically interpret it as God's anger; but this perspective for Ritschl possesses no factual basis since God only acts graciously towards his children.

1. An overview of the different positions can be found in Volkmann, *Der Zorn Gottes: Studien zur Rede vom Zorn Gottes in der evangelischen Theologie* (The Wrath of God: Studies on Language of the Wrath of God in Protestant Theology). Volkmann discusses, above all, Martin Luther, Friedrich Schleiermacher, Albrecht Ritschl, Werner Elert, and Karl Barth.

2. Ritschl, *Die Christliche Lehre von Rechtfertigung und Versoehnung* (The Christian Teaching on Justification and Reconciliation), 2:154.

3. Volkmann, *Zorn Gottes*, 187.

God is love—therefore, for those whose sins have been forgiven, there is no wrath. It follows for Ritschl that the object of God's wrath cannot be understood soteriologically in the sense that the wrath of God was appeased through the death of Christ. Wrath is merely the flip side of love, the sphere in which love is absent. The wrath of God, according to Ritschl, is a logical consequence of the absence of love but not an actual personal intervention by God.

Viewpoint 2: Martin Luther's dualistic God-concept

According to Martin Luther, God's wrath is a reaction against human sin. Luther views divine wrath from two perspectives: first, from the perspective of eternity; and second, with regard to justified individuals.[4] Since Luther believes that not every individual will be saved, the wrath of God will be directed at those who will be eternally condemned. For those who are the elect and justified, God's eternal wrath is already past. Just how the wrath and love of God belong together here is not logically conceivable; rather, it remains a mystery that will be revealed in the Eschaton, at the end of time.

In the present, however, Christians can also experience the temporal wrath of God. This happens when God deals with the "old person of sin" who must be destroyed (Rom 6:6; Eph 4:22; Col 3:9), which results in the building up of the new justified person.

Luther represents a dualistic view of God in which the love of God indeed dominates over his wrath, but his wrath is also clearly seen as one of his valid reactions to the sins of humanity. Thus, according to Luther, the wrath of God belongs to a soteriological context.

Viewpoint 3: The Wrath of God as his "burning love"[5] (Karl Barth)

In contrast to Ritschl, who actually pushes the theme of God's wrath aside and accepts it merely as a theological construct, and also in contrast to Martin Luther, who understands the wrath of God in opposition to the love of God, Karl Barth (1886–1968) attempts to understand wrath as an attribute (or characteristic) of God which does not stand in tension with his love, but rather is an expression of it. This is because, Barth argues,

4. Luther speaks here from *opus alienum* and *opus proprium*—God's wrath is subordinated to his love. *Cf.* Volkmann, *Zorn Gottes*, 91–93.

5. Karl Barth, *Kirchliche Dogmatik*, 2.2.205.

the wrath of God is not directed at his creatures but rather towards the futility or evil which threatens the creation. Consequently, God's wrath is expressed for the good of his creatures and can be recognized in the event which took place on the cross at Golgotha; the wrath of God came upon the one who hung on the cross for the good of humankind. According to Barth, it is only when one considers the cross and the crucified Christ that one can speak theologically of the wrath of God. Eschatologically, the judgment which has already taken place on the cross will become revealed to the whole world. For Barth, the wrath of God is an essential part of and an implementation of his grace, and therefore does not call into question his love.

SALVATION FROM WRATH IN THE WRITINGS OF PAUL

Having previewed the aforementioned viewpoints, we will now consider the passages that Paul has written on divine wrath. In this regard, it is important to ask whether Paul falls into one of the previously mentioned models or whether he introduces entirely different ideas regarding the subject. We will not examine the entire corpus of Pauline writings regarding the wrath of God but only those passages which speak of deliverance from the wrath of God.

1 Thessalonians 1:10

In his introduction to 1 Thessalonians, Paul focuses his attention on the conduct of the church and, with few words, describes the current condition of the life of the church: The church had turned from idols to serve the true and living God (1:9).[6] After referring to their conversion (a statement concerning a past event) and their service (a statement concerning the present), Paul directs their focus towards the future: the church awaits the Second Coming of the risen Christ, "who rescues us from the wrath to come" (1:10). The time references are striking. From one perspective, the church awaits the returning Lord who will come again, and it can be added that he comes to judge the living and the dead, as later expressed in the Apostles' Creed. But the time at which final deliverance will occur cannot be determined, for the participial phrase Ἰησοῦν τὸν ῥυόμενον ἡμᾶς ἐκ τῆς ὀργῆς τῆς ἐρχομένης is linked more to the person

6. Paul accents here the "unique" or "one and only" God, not simply an abstract idea of monotheism.

doing the delivering than to its time. Jesus Christ is the deliverer, and his Second Coming will constitute the deliverance from the future wrath. The grounds for deliverance from wrath are more clearly explained in 1 Thessalonians 5:9.

In addition, the question of who belongs to the group of those delivered is not clear from the wording. At least the church in Thessalonica and Paul himself are included, because the use of the pronoun "we" links together the writer and his readers. But it is not clear whether Paul is using a somewhat exclusive "we" or whether the plural pronoun refers to all humankind or perhaps to the major part of it.

1 Thessalonians 5:9

The subject of 1 Thessalonians 5 is the Day of the Lord, who will come like a thief in the night. Paul exhorts the church to be awake and sober in their faith, to love one another, and to wait hopefully for their salvation, the same three dimensions—conversion, service, and waiting—mentioned in 1:10. It is expected that the Day of the Lord will bring salvation. This designation for salvation is then thematically explained in 5:9–10, "For God has not appointed us to wrath, but rather for attaining salvation through our Lord Jesus Christ, who died for us, so that whether we are awake or asleep, we will live together with him." Again, the exact specification of "we" can not be determined; further, there is no *genitivus auctoris* (subject of the genitive) introduced in the designation of wrath in 1:10 nor here in 5:9. This is because God predestined humanity to obtain salvation, not to suffer wrath. The deciding factor here is the personal declaration that Jesus Christ is the originator of salvation since he died for us (*pro nobis*) so as to make possible "our" life. It is those who are reconciled—exempt from God's wrath—that will live. Conversely, this means that those who are not exempt from the wrath of God will not live but are already dead. Thus, for Paul, the wrath of God corresponds to spiritual death or separation from God. The central reason that Christians will not suffer death is that Jesus "died for us." The death of Christ brings life to humanity. Those who deserve death are kept or preserved by him who did not deserve death, the one who freely took the wrath of God upon himself. Because God did not appoint believers to wrath but rather to live with and through Jesus Christ, which experience of life already exists, believers are already reconciled to God and presently live in fellowship with him.

Salvation from the Wrath to Comein the Present Epoch

Romans 5:9

In Romans 5:1–11, Paul addresses the theme of justification by faith, which he designates as reconciliation (vv. 1, 10–11). Once again the major motif concerns "the one who died." This *reconciliation* motif provides the central reason for Christ's death, the event that encompasses and influences all time. Reconciliation through the death of Christ occurred "while we were yet sinners" (v. 8) and "while we were still enemies" (v. 10); thus it precedes justification. The divine intervention in Jesus Christ takes effect in the present ("having *now* been justified"; v. 9) and has an outworking into the future ("we shall be kept from the wrath"; v. 9). The reconciliation that has taken place was not effected through the individual's acceptance of justification but rather is a present reality.[7] In addition, as is usual with Paul, the intimate connection and entwining of the death and resurrection of Jesus Christ is recognizable. Even though he only speaks of the death of Jesus Christ in verses 6, 8, 9, and 10a, in verse 10b he makes clear that the life of Jesus Christ contains eschatological promises. Christ's death and resurrection belong indivisibly together and build a complex context that gives to persons both present reconciliation and future life. Since Christ died a substitutionary death, all those who belong to him will live, being exempt from wrath and exempt from death.

Just as in 1 Thessalonians 5, here in Romans 5 the originator of wrath is not named; but from the context of the letter to the Romans it is clear that God himself is the one who will execute righteous judgment on the day of the Lord (Rom 2:5). At the end of time "we" will be kept from experiencing God's wrath and be saved through Christ's life (5:10). In his use of "we" Paul keeps, as he normally does, a tension between exclusivity and inclusiveness. On the one hand, he does not speak of a total restora-

7. In the debate over the understanding of reconciliation in 2 Corinthians 5, Otfried Hofius' view is to be preferred to that of Cilliers Breytenback: that "God has reconciled" cannot be relativized through the phrase "be reconciled to God"; rather, the latter is a condition of experiencing God's reconciliation. The relevant literature includes Hofius, "Versöhnung" (Reconciliation), 2–4; "Erwaegungen zur Gestalt und Herkunft des paulishishen Versoehnungsgedankens" (Considerations of the Form and Origin of Paul's Thoughts on Reconciliation), 186–99; "Gott hat unter uns aufgerichtet das Wort von der Versoehnung, 2 Kor 5:19" (God has Committed to us the Word of Reconciliation, 2 Cor 5:19), 3–20; "Suehne und Versoehnung. Zum paulinischen Verstaendnis des Kreuzestodes Jesu" (Atonement and Recociliation: Paul's Understanding of Christ's Death on the Cross), 25–46; Breytenbach, *Versoehnung. Eine Studie zur paulinishen Soteriologie* (Reconciliation: A Study on Pauline Soteriology).

tion (*apokatastasis panton*) since he refers to the coming wrath. On the other hand, neither does he represent the view that holds to two differing destinies of history. Finally, Paul stresses the abundance of grace when he says in Romans 11:32, "God has shut up all in disobedience, so that he may show mercy to all."

Ephesians 5:6 and Colossians 3:6

In two letters where Paul's authorship is debated, there are two similarly worded statements that refer to the wrath of God. After naming individual sins there follows the statement, "For because of these things the wrath of God comes upon the sons of disobedience (Eph 5:6; similarly Col 3:6). Experiencing God's wrath is a consequence of sin. According to Ephesians 5:6, sin manifests itself in immorality, impurity, and greed; in Colossians, passion and evil desire are included. It appears that the letter to the Ephesians has a dual view of the end of the world because the children of disobedience (Eph 2:2; 5:8) are contrasted with the children of light (5:8); the latter will receive immeasurable riches in the coming ages, the former, to whom the children of light once belonged, will experience wrath. However, Ephesians 5:6 is part of a *paraenese* (warning) directed to those who believe—even these are threatened by the wrath of God if they do not live as children of light.[8] Colossians mentions the coming wrath only in a limited way; it is wrath which threatened believers as they were still in the condition of being the "old persons," *i.e.* before they were saved. But now, since the Christians are saved, they should also live as saved individuals. Here as in Ephesians the concept of wrath is linked to a statement of warning and therefore should be understood more as a threat than a description of the last days.

8. One might wrongfully surmise that there is a logical difference between the security of believers and this *paraenese*; however, here I think one must distinguish between possessing a security grounded in one's own control and apprehending a security grounded in God. The former was witnessed in the events precipitating the Reformation: persons who bought plenary indulgences thought they could personally guarantee their own salvation. To this Luther insisted that believers have nothing in their own hands by which to personally guarantee salvation; only through the Word (a double entendre connoting the living Christ and the written Scripture) can believers find a God-centered security of faith. Accordingly, the *paraenese* admonishes Christians not to be secure in the sense that they trust in their own act of faith for salvation. For it is not faith that produces justification, but rather faith is the channel through which salvation flows from God and can be apprehended. Since God is the reconciler, believers must not be *selbstsicher* (self-sure); thus Ephesians warns believers not to look upon themselves but to God.

THE WRATH OF GOD AND JUDGMENT

Normally in the Old Testament, the wrath of God is not purely an emotional event in which God is offended and therefore desires to punish individuals. The basic line of thinking is not a divine reaction to human transgression of a command, though it includes that. Rather it is that God desires to reestablish and rebuild the fixed order in the relationship between himself and individuals.[9] In this sense, the concept of wrath is congruent with judgment and righteousness in the Old Testament in that it has to do with the reestablishment of rights and the restoration of the devastated sinner. The intended purpose of wrath is not to destroy persons but rather to save them.

Is this basic idea recognizable in Paul when he speaks of individuals being given protection from wrath and when he speaks of salvation from wrath through the death and resurrection of Jesus Christ?

Paul's argumentation develops as follows. The sinner stands under God's wrath. What form does the wrath of God take, namely, what happens to the person when s/he experiences God's wrath? The person will not live in God's presence. S/he will die; s/he will not be resurrected. Thus, protection from the wrath of God is salvation, reconciliation, justification, and freedom from death, all of which has already taken place before physical death. This is why Paul can state, "The wages of sin is death, but the gift of God is eternal life in Christ Jesus our Lord" (Rom 6:23).

The main argument detected in the verses introduced above regarding the freeing of sinners from that which threatens them, is the declaration that Jesus Christ "died for us." Paul continually emphasizes that Jesus' death was substitutionary in nature because it was a death that was actually due us but assumed by Christ. He died for us and in our place. This implies that he became the object of God's wrath. Since he bore the wrath of God in that he died for us, the reconciled are freed from the consequence of that wrath. Thus, they will not die, but live.

God himself assumes his own wrath and gives to his creation new life. So, Paul formulated fundamental Christological ideas that structurally follow or blend into Old Testament concepts. Judgment occurred to our benefit. The wrath of God does not destroy but rather saves. We are saved from death and kept from wrath because Jesus Christ himself took God's wrath upon himself.

9. Plath, *Furcht Gottes* (Fear of God), 105.

THE THEOLOGICAL MESSAGE REGARDING THE WRATH OF GOD

Therefore it is only correct to speak about God's wrath from the perspective of its close connection to the substitutionary death of Christ. It is evident that Paul is not willing to relinquish this connection. When the wrath of God or the judgment of God is viewed as unimportant, then the salvific meaning of Christ's death is diminished. Then the sin of humanity would remain unpunished, leading to the dramatic result that each individual would be left in one's sin and bound in one's separation from God.[10] But, because God rescues the individual from separation from himself and takes the consequences of sin that were due the sinner upon himself, the sinner is freed and becomes a new person. God remains faithful to his covenant, which is recognizable in the substitutionary death of Jesus and in his vicarious resurrection.

Of the later theologians whose viewpoints we summarized, Albrecht Ritschl is the farthest away from this interpretation of Paul's texts. He attempts to separate the wrath of God completely from the death of Christ. Indeed, he correctly stresses that God is not the recipient of a sacrifice. But he so strongly separates the wrath of God from his love that, in the final analysis, God's love degenerates into that which is directed towards those who do not believe. He does not consider that here a soteriological purpose should be assumed. Also, with Luther we must consider that he separates grace and righteousness far from one another. According to Luther, God would be righteous if he punished men, but since he is merciful, the sinner receives a future. Therefore, Luther reads into God a dualism that, in the final analysis, separates God and Jesus. In Jesus God shows grace, but outside of Jesus God is wrathful. Karl Barth's position is very close to Paul's when he interprets the wrath of God as burning love. Only in the Christ-event can we understand what God is really able and ready to do. He remains true to the covenant with his creation.

Therefore, it is only too understandable that Paul does not unfold the subject of God's wrath separately from the topic of God's love. Essentially, the subject appears, particularly in the selected passages, only from the perspective of protection from wrath itself. Christians are reconciled and

10. Compare my interpretation of Anselm of Canterbury to this sentiment in Georg Plasger, *Die Not-Wendigkeit der Gerechtigkeit. Eine Interpretation zu "Cur deus homo" von Anselm von Canterbury* (*The Necessity of Righteousness: An Interpretation of Anselm of Canterbury's* Cur deus homo).

protected from wrath. But this protection is based on the fact that the consequences of sin are carried by God himself. Jesus Christ who died for us is the nexus where the love-dimension of God's wrath in its deepest sense can be understood.

God is a wrathful God because of humanity; nevertheless, his care for his own creation prevents him from becoming cold or unconcerned. Instead, God puts himself at risk for us, he goes the way of death, and to give created persons life he allows himself to be forced out of the world in order to give that world a future. God's wrath is an expression of his mercy.

12

The Eternal Security of the Believer in Christ from the Perspective of Philosophical Theology

James W. Bryant

There is no doubt of the survival of the human soul beyond death in Greek philosophy. It is eternal, innately immortal. The Hindu idea of reincarnation is but one of several ideas of survival arising out of Greek philosophy. The Greek view of the innate immortality of the soul stands in stark contrast to the Hebraic-Christian view of the resurrection of the body. The former finds its roots in Plato and his idealistic dualism. At the top of his gradation of being is ultimate reality, ultimate good, pure form. At the bottom are ultimate unreality, ultimate evil, and pure matter. Both are eternal. The soul, being near the top of the scale of being, is eternal as well, pre-existent, everlasting, eternal in both directions, backward and forward.

Older than Greek philosophy and Greek logic, the empirico-logical mentality of Hebraic thinking may be traced to about 2500 BC and reaches its zenith in the Old Testament, written between 1400 and 400 BC. In anthropological thinking about AD 1900, Lucian Levy-Bruhl, the great French anthropologist, identified two categories of human thinking: logical and pre-logical.[1]

Shortly before 1940, William Foxwell Albright began to verbalize with clarity an objection to Levy-Bruhl's twofold classification of human thinking.[2] In all fairness to Levy-Bruhl, Albright notes that Levy-Bruhl

1. Levy-Bruhl, *Primitive Mentality*, 23.

2. Albright, *New Horizons in Biblical Research*, 24.

retracted his view in his famous *Carnets*, published posthumously in 1947 in the *Revue Philosophique*.[3] Nonetheless, Albright's third category may be fruitfully designated "empirico-logical" thinking. Some anthropologists contemporary with Levy-Bruhl had voiced objections, but Albright was apparently the first to suggest a third category of thinking.

Empirical logic, the logic born of experience, is as old as animals. A dog will soon learn to run across a square instead of going around the corner, and we all know what white rats can do with a little practice. Dolphins are proving to be extraordinarily quick learners. This is empirical logic on a very low level, but it is logic born of experience all the same. Nearly all ancient crafts were dominated by it, yet the ancients were no inventors. There were inventors in those days who proceeded by essentially the same methods as Thomas A. Edison, although they were, to be sure, more primitive and without benefit of the scientific discoveries on which Edison drew. But they used the same trial and error, through systematic application of which nearly all of Edison's inventions were made. (In order to invent the tungsten filament, according to report, he tried over a thousand materials in succession.) The ancients made thousands of pharmacopoeias consisting of medicinal plants, drugs, and other materials, which were developed by the ancient Egyptians and through them spread to modern times. The early Aztecs and early Chinese also had elaborate pharmacopoeias. In fact, some of the most important drugs used in modern medicine were taken over from folk medicine, for instance, quinine from Native Americans and ephedrine from Eastern Asia.[4]

The actuality of empirico-logical thinking is a fact in the phenomena of human history. Empirical logic comes into clearest focus with its masterpiece, the Old Testament. This type of thinking has persisted wherever humans seek to learn from experience. It is employed in the world of everyday activity with the best of results. "Sound empirical logic is still in general characteristic of the ordinary man in his everyday dealing with his fellows," says Albright.[5] It is out of empirical logic that the Bible was born, a written record of the revelation of God to humanity.

3. Ibid., 23.

4. Ibid.

5. Albright, *Archaeology and the Religion of Israel*, 35.

THE NATURE OF HUMANITY

The effect of Greek thinking on Christianity has been great. Although the New Testament was written by Jews and follows Hebraic thinking, it is written in Greek. Thanks to Alexander the Great, all his world was Hellenized to some extent. European and American thought is dominated by Greek thinking today. Western Christianity has never been exempt from its influence. Consequently, Western theologians have tended to shape their theology not just from the Bible, but also from a Greek mentality applied to the Bible. One of the tasks of Western theologians today is to reclaim the Hebraic thought pattern for the New Testament. Even though written in Greek, it is thought in Hebrew.

Nowhere does the effect of Greek thinking show itself upon Western theology than in the doctrine of humanity. From the second century AD forward Western theologians have allowed a Platonic view of the nature of man to invade their anthropology. The Greeks viewed each human as a pre-existent soul imprisoned in a material body. The body was material, pure evil and even unreal. But the soul was immortal, eternal in both directions, always existing and eternally surviving. Out of that understanding came the great arguments over the dichotomy or trichotomy of humanity. Is each human body and soul, or is each human body, soul, and spirit?

The Hebraic view of human nature is basically a unitary view. The authentically Hebrew thinker could not imagine the existence of a human being without its body: thus, the Hebraic emphasis on the resurrection of the body. Could the Hebrews have been influenced by the Egyptians in their understanding of the survival of the body beyond the grave? They certainly buried their dead like the Egyptians rather than burning them like the Greeks once did. This author thinks it was more than that. The revelation of God transpired in such a way that the God of the Bible was revealed as the God of the living, not the God of the dead. And yet he is called the God of Abraham, Isaac, and Jacob. Jesus himself uses this argument to support the Old Testament view of the resurrection of the body in Mark 12:26–27.

The classical view of humanity tends to treat humanity as innately immortal. The modern view tends either to make human immortality an impersonal, social thing, or else yields to naturalism, which obliterates immortality altogether. To this uncertain situation the Hebraic approach to the question of immortality speaks with relevance, clarity, and forcefulness.

THE UNITARY VIEW OF HUMANITY

The Hebraic approach to the unity of human being heightens the problem of immortality in Christian theology and occasioned its consideration in Judaism. Reinhold Niebuhr says, "The whole Hebraic-Biblical conception of the unity of body and soul and the meaningfulness of the historical process was bound to lead to this wrestling off the mind of later Judaism with this insoluble problem."[6]

In sum, while the Greeks viewed each human as an immortal soul imprisoned in a mortal body, the Hebrews viewed each human as a psychosomatic unity. In contrast to the Greek view, which presupposes a basic metaphysical dualism between form and matter, the Hebrew view presupposes the goodness and reality of the material world and its spiritual aliveness.

The Finiteness of Humanity

Coupled with this unitary view of humanity, the Hebrews accepted the finiteness of human life. This concept is a natural corollary to belief in an infinite Creator. Since creation is from God and therefore basically good, and finiteness is a mark of creatureliness, the Hebrew saw nothing evil about finiteness itself. Thus Neibuhr remarks, "The fragmentary character of human life is not regarded as evil in Biblical faith."[7]

These two concepts—unity and finiteness—were not the only causes of emphasis upon this life to the neglect of the life to come as found in Hebraic thought. The Hebrews were caught up in the rushing tides of history, as they still are in Israel today. They were enamored with the present because of its dramatic nature. But they did not neglect life after death because of an irreligious attitude. Rather, as Dean Stanley says,

> Not from want of religion, but (if one might use the expression) from excess of religion, was this void left in the Jewish mind. The Future Life was not denied or contradicted; but it was overlooked,

6. Niebuhr, *Nature and Destiny of Man*, 2:298.

7. Ibid., 1:168.

> set aside, overshadowed, by the consciousness of the living, actual presence of God himself.[8]

THE NATURE OF DEATH

However, to assert that the Hebrews emphasized this life while overlooking the life to come does not mean that they refused to think about death. It was a common, almost daily reality in ancient Jewish life. While they saw nothing evil about finiteness in itself, death was viewed as a corollary of evil, not good. In the words of Niebuhr, "While it is not Biblical to regard finiteness, as such, as evil it must be admitted that there is strong Biblical support for the conception of death as evil."[9]

Death and Sin

Theologically speaking, the universality of death finds two possible explanations. The first explanation is that death is simply a natural phenomenon. Some Old Testament theologians have adopted this explanation to say that, had Adam not sinned, he would still have died. This explanation ignores the connection of death and sin in the early narratives of Genesis, especially Genesis 2:17 and 3:3. Paul acknowledges this connection in Romans 5.

The second explanation therefore treats death as a consequence of sin. Without tracing the history of this doctrine, one who holds it may say with Karl Rahner, "Until we can know adequately why all living things, composed of many cells, and man in particularly, must die, the reason offered by faith (that is, the moral tragedy of mankind through its first parents) remains the only available explanation for the uncontested universality of death."[10] Possibly, the Hebraic concept of retribution contributed to the connection between death and sin, as pictured in Genesis and explained by Paul in Romans 5:1–12. The problem with death for the Hebrews was further complicated by their tendency to view death from a personal and individual viewpoint. Death spelled difficulty for the individual Hebrew because it indeed terminated life as one knew it and ended a person as one had been known by one's family.

8. Dean Stanley, as quoted in Knudson, *Religious Teaching*, 393.

9. Niebuhr, *Nature and Destiny*, 1:173.

10. Rahner, *On the Theology of Death*, 22–23.

A Positive Value of Death

The one relationship death did not end was the Hebrews' relationship to their God. That had been emphasized over and over by the biblical writers as a revelation, a word from God. Consequently, the Hebrews did not succumb to an utterly tragic view of death. They sensed a positive side of death. The word "sensed" is carefully selected. The ancient Hebrew had a veiled intuition that death was not final. One might be tempted to argue that intuition is not consonant with empirical logic. On the contrary, if one conceives of intuition as a supra-rational response to reality, it is quite empirical to employ intuition in arriving at the truth. This is one of the characteristics of Hebraic thinking. William Ernest Hocking (not at all in the Hebrew tradition) asserts that intuition is both real and empirical: "Intuition, as persistent awareness of, and reaction to, the real, is our most directly empirical relation to the world, the most universal, the most unrelenting."[11]

Hebrew intuition arose, in part, from a profound ethical sensitivity found in Hebraic religion. Coupled with this sensitivity was a positive understanding of the idea of retribution. The same God who punished the wicked would also reward the righteous. Thus, Job in the midst of his suffering could cry, "For I know that my Redeemer lives, and He shall stand at last on the earth; and after my skin is destroyed, this I know, that in my flesh I shall see God, whom I shall see for myself, and my eyes shall behold, and not another. How my heart yearns within me" (Job 19:25–27 NKJV). As Knudson says, "A profound ethical sense such as characterized the Hebrew religion from the beginning leads necessarily by an inner logic of its own [empirical logic] to the belief in an after-life."[12] So then, belief in a life after death was inherent in the faith and intuition of the Hebrews.

In Job's theology of death, there is a curious mixture of this life and the life to come, which is indicative of the problem the Hebrews had in thinking about death. In Job 19:25–27, as quoted above, Job says that after his body is destroyed, his eyes will see God. He thus demonstrates the utter inability of the Hebrews to conceive of human life apart from some form of bodily existence. If this seems unusual, consider the problem physical science has at this point of describing human existence. "It might be re-

11. Hocking, *Meaning of Immortality*, 195.

12. Knudson, *Religious Teaching*, 398.

membered with profit that natural philosophy finds it almost impossible to restrict the idea of the human body to what is covered by the skin."[13]

THE NATURE OF RESURRECTION

It is at the point of this inability that Hebraic thinking differs from Greek thinking about life after death. This difference is not to be understood just as idea of the immortality of the soul over against the resurrection of the body. Such an understanding describes the Greek view of life after death well enough, but misses the force of the Hebraic view. Yet Western Christian theology, traditionally, has spoken of the Christian view in terms of a "bodily" resurrection. Claude Tresmontant explains why classical Christianity adopted this terminology.

> In the New Testament we find the expression: "resurrection of the dead" (*anastasis nekron*), but not the expression of "resurrection of the body," since neither the idea nor the word are to be found in Hebrew. The resurrection of the dead is the resurrection of men [and women]. The Councils, in order to avoid a Platonic interpretation of resurrection, and to ensure that the "resurrection" of Revelation should not be confused with the "immortality of the soul" of the Greek philosophies, felt obliged to specify: *cum corporibus suis*. The addition was necessary in the circumstances because the biblical idea was being introduced into a world of dualist thought. Therefore, to give the full equivalent of what the Bible calls the resurrection of the dead, they had to specify that this meant the whole man, that is, in the Greek way of speaking, the soul *and* the body.[14]

The nature of the resurrection is centered about the wholeness of man. While Paul in 2 Corinthians 5:1–10 seems to indicate a separation of soul from body at death, he does not present a Greek view of immortality. As Cullmann and others note, such a separation was neither desirable nor permanent to Paul.[15] In Davies' words, "the separation of body and soul, for Judaism was not natural to man but the consequence of sin, and this implied that the reunion of soul and body in resurrection was involved in any doctrine of survival."[16] Davies goes further to suggest that Paul in

13. Rahner, *Theology of Death*, 105.
14. Tresmontant, *Study of Hebrew Thought*, 105.
15. Cullmann, *Christ and Time*, 238–39.
16. Davies, *Paul and Rabbinic Judaism*, 299.

2 Corinthians 5 actually teaches that the dead in Christ, while separated from their physical bodies, nevertheless assume some sort of embodied form. Yet, as Cullmann says, the exact term "resurrection of the body" is not biblical. The biblical term is "resurrection of the dead."

Toward a Biblical View

There is no scandal, speaking from a Hebraic point of view, in the idea of a resurrected body, as long as that body is understood to be the whole person. In the context of this understanding, the New Testament does teach a bodily resurrection in 1 Corinthians 15. Though some argue over the difference between a natural body and a spiritual body, a body is a body. The early Barth notes in his consideration of 1 Corinthians 15, "That by resurrection, anything else than *bodily* resurrection could be understood by Paul or by the doubters [of such a resurrection] is an assumption to be found nowhere throughout the chapter. It goes without saying that bodily resurrection is meant."[17]

Barth believes 1 Corinthians 15 to be the occasion of a struggle between this Hebraic concept of humanity as body and the Greek concept of humanity as soul. He sees the Corinthian doubters taking offense at Paul's view of resurrection because it involved a Jewish concept, which conflicted with their Greek ideas.

The immortality of the soul is placed in dispute by what Paul says here. Instead of the human soul, the Spirit of God appears in the resurrection. That which persists is not the soul (the latter is the predicate, which must give place to something else), but the body, and even that, not as an immortal body, but its transition from life through death to life.[18]

Non-Hebraic Influences

The Greek concept of innate immortality has not been the only non-Hebraic influence upon Western Christian theology at this point. Kantonen sees Christian philosophy as having been pressured from four influential sources: primitive animism with its idea of a ghost–soul, the Greek idea of immortality of the soul, the Zoroastrian concept of dual kingdoms, and the Hindu idea of retribution. The distinctive element of the biblical view of humanity is that his existence, "whether as body or as soul, is depen-

17. Barth, *Resurrection of the Dead*, 116.

18. Ibid., 196.

dent entirely upon God."[19] This is the very point of the Hebraic approach to the problem. As Robinson says so well,

> The important point to notice . . . is the particular quality of the hope resulting from the way in which it was reached. The hope of a future is made to depend on the relation of the soul to God. That relation is felt to have a mystical value, transcending the fact of death. We have here, as has been truly said, 'a strength of conviction of the reality of personal union with God, under which the thought of death as it were fades into the background and is ignored . . . This conviction of a personal relation to God independent of time and change, and not any particular theology as to the character of the life after death, is the lasting contribution of the Old Testament to the doctrine of a Future Life.[20]

Eternal Life

In the total biblical picture, whatever form humanity may assume at death, the assertion is that the person in Christ does not cease to exist at death. Rather, one enters into a new level of existence, which the Bible calls "eternal life." As Brunner says, "The result of our inquiry into the mystery of death is that for faith death is no longer the conclusion of life but the point of transition to eternal life."[21] He describes this eternal life by finding the clue to its existence in the resurrected Christ. The resurrected body of Jesus manifested its spatial limits and yet overcame the limitation of space. For Brunner, the time lapse between death and resurrection is not important. He asserts that the eternal God transcends the time lapse between departure and resurrection. Theologically, this position is tenable and is quite Hebraic, for Hebrew thought has no problem with a lapse of time. From the Hebraic standpoint, the debate over an intermediate state between death and resurrection is unnecessary. Biblical humanity is kept by the eternal and living God. And with the resurrection of Jesus, coupled with His post-resurrection appearances, the intuited thought of resurrection found in Job becomes hard, empirical thought as the disciples personally encountered the resurrected Christ.

19. Kantonen, *Christian Hope*, 32.

20. Robinson, *Religious Ideas of the Old Testament*, 96.

21. Brunner, *Christian Doctrine of Creation and Redemption*, 389.

REDEMPTIVE HISTORY AND RESURRECTION

When Augustine wrote his *City of God*,[22] he introduced a philosophy of history that was new to the philosophical world: rectilinear history, known simply as linear history today. It could be argued that this was perhaps the first Christian philosophy of history. This view of time is clearly biblical and Hebraic. Plato's view of time was a cyclical view. Mircea Eliade explains it in his writings as "The Myth of the Eternal Return," the sub-title for one of his books.[23] Cultures contemporary with ancient Judaism held to a cyclical view of history. The early Greek philosophers later expressed that same view. While early Mesopotamians did not articulate a philosophy of history, they did emphasize a particular view of history.[24] Their cyclical view emphasized the repetition of the cosmogony when stimulated by periodic, imitative rituals. In its religious setting, this cyclical view of history fostered an attitude of hope as long as life was going well. When agricultural crops were plentiful, health was sound, and foreign as well as domestic relationships were steady, these rituals gave the opportunity for periodic renewal and hope. But when things, events, and relationships were bad, the cyclical view led to despair because whatever happened was assumed to be beyond human control.

In the midst of the golden age of the cyclical view of history, a radically new horizon appeared to humanity. Judaism's rise brought with it a sense of linear movement in history. Later, when Augustine penned his *City of God*, the cyclical view had degenerated into nothing but despair. It would be easy to suppose that Augustine's linear view of history was a corrective to a degenerate view of time. But Judaism arose in the midst of the very high point or golden age of the cyclical view. James Connolly warns against distorting the grandeur of the cyclical view of history by examining its degenerate form of Augustine's day instead of its golden age of expression.[25] When Judaism began to hold a linear view, in the golden age of cyclical thinking, a radically new horizon in thinking was begun.

22. Augustine, *City of God*.

23. Eliade, *Cosmos and History*.

24. Ibid., 1–48.

25. Connolly, *Human History and the Word of God*, 3–4.

Disclosure Situations

A unique combination of elements occurred in early Judaism, which gave rise to the biblical sense of history. There was the element of what Alan Richardson calls "disclosure situations."

The distinctive character of Israel's history was that it was built around a series of disclosure situations, which through the activity of prophetic minds became interpretative of Israel's historic destiny and ultimately of the history of all humanity. It is to this distinctive feature that we should look for the beginnings of an answer to the question why it was Yahweh and not Chemosh who was recognized as the God of Righteousness and the Creator of heaven and earth.[26]

In the face of these disclosure situations, the early Jews reacted with an empirico-logical response and grounded their faith in the Divine will as they saw it expressed around them. This would account for the element of contrast between Israelite faith and surrounding faiths. According to Vriezen, Israelite faith was not static like Egyptian faith. It was dynamic. It was not dualistic like Babylonian faith, but monotheistic in a very practical sense. Nor was it grounded in natural and vegetative phenomena, as was Canaanite faith. Rather, Israelite faith was grounded in Divine will. Of this last contrast, Vriezen says, "This contrast is not to be taken lightly; for historically speaking it is the factor that more than anything else governs the religion of Israel."[27]

Promise and Fulfillment

Pannenberg surveys the whole sweep of Jewish history to propose the element of promise and fulfillment as giving rise to Israel's historical consciousness.

The disclosure of history in Israel appears to have different roots than those which Mircea Eliade holds responsible. Eliade connects Israel's discovery of a meaning of history with prophetic proclamation of punishment for the transgression of the people: "[H]istory gained meaning and coherence when these announcements were fulfilled in the historical destiny of Israel."[28] But Eliade's arguments do not touch the real basis of the Israelite consciousness of history. It cannot originate with the prophets'

26. Richardson, *History, Sacred and Profane*, 224.

27. Vriezen, *Religion of Ancient Israel*, 72–73.

28. Eliade, *Cosmos and History*, 149–50.

proclamation of judgment because the beginnings of Israelite historical writing, which can be recognized at the characteristic understanding of history for Israel, reach back into the time of David and Solomon.

The presuppositions of the historical consciousness in Israel lie in its concept of God. The reality of God for Israel is not exhausted by his being the origin of the world, that is, of normal ever self-repeating processes and events. Therefore this God can break into the course of his creation and initiate new events in it in an unpredictable way. The certainty that God again and again performs new acts, that he is a "living God," forms the basis for Israel's understanding of reality as a linear history moving toward a goal. But we have not yet thereby described the structure of this history itself.

Within the reality characterized by the constantly creative work of God, history arises because God makes promises and fulfills these promises. History is event so suspended in tension between promise and fulfillment that, through the promise, it is irreversibly pointed toward the goal of future fulfillment.[29]

Historical Certainty

It is precisely in the midst of history that Christian faith finds its certainty. The biblical person is caught up in a certainty of the moment as God works in his life. The magical powers of Moses impressed the Hebrews as much as they did Pharaoh (Exod 4:1–9). The crossing of the Red Sea represented a certainty of deliverance for Israel and a certainty of defeat for Egypt no matter how one interprets Exodus 14. This Exodus event became the central event in Israel's history and may be regarded as the key interpretative event in the Old Testament. As Vriezen says, "History as event, disclosure of the divine will, and a personal relationship, determine the course and character of religion in Israel."[30] The Exodus, with its subsidiary wonders, gave momentary certainty to Israel. Even when this certainty was often tried by hardship and attacked by doubt, there remained a continuity of certainty in Israel's faith and history.

29. Pannenberg, "Redemptive Event and History," 315.

30. Vriezen, *Religion of Ancient Israel*, 75.

Extended Certainty

It was quite natural for Israel to extend this certainty both backward and forward in thinking about history. Since Moses wrote what we now call the Book of Genesis, the Creation Narrative about the beginning of time was written after the Exodus. Since Yahweh was powerful enough to deliver Israel from Egypt, the Israelites had no difficulty in believing him to be powerful enough to create the heavens, the earth, and all therein. They easily extended the momentary certainty of the Exodus into the pre-history of the Creation Narrative. In later Judaism, this same type of empirico-logical thinking would enable the extension of momentary certainty forward to the prophetic statements about the future of Israel. In this backward and forward extension, momentary certainty became historical certainty.

Thus Israelite faith arose in empirico-logical response to the acts of God in history. This faith did not arise in full bloom; but as history continued, faith grew and deepened. Finally, the Jews possessed an entire history of God's acts with all the certainty derived therefrom. The Bible contains the record of that belief in response to the continuing revelation of God both in his promises and in his mighty acts. Wright says the Bible became "a confessional recital of His acts."[31]

A NEW CENTER OF HISTORY

With the coming of Christ, the history of God's Old Testament people, having been centered for thousands of years in the Exodus, suddenly became centered for God's New Testament people in the Cross and Resurrection of Jesus. The saving history of the Exodus now gave way for Christians to the saving history of the Cross. Conzelmann says,

> The church points not only to an event in the past, but also to the consistent tradition of the salvific event, to the church itself as a factor of the *Heilsgeschichte*. Its self-consciousness is a historical one from the beginning.[32]

The historical milieu in which this self-consciousness occurred was Hebraic. In adopting the Hebraic stance, the New Testament writers em-

31. Wright, *God Who Acts*, 85.

32. Conzelmann, "The First Century as Christian History," in *The Bible in Modern Scholarship*, ed. Philip Hyatt (Nashville: Abingdon Press, 1965), 217.

ployed a new center of history. Cullmann maintains that the midpoint in time for the Jews was always future as they looked for the coming Messiah.[33] If Cullmann means by midpoint the basic interpretative event of strictly Jewish history, one must object strenuously. The key event for Jewish history must remain the Exodus. In the New Testament, however, this key interpretative event is displaced by a new center of history, the Cross and Resurrection of Jesus Christ. In assessing either the New Testament alone or the Bible as a whole, the Cross and Resurrection, taken together, constitute the key interpretative event.

When one looks at Paul, a Hebrew of the Hebrews, he sees this shift to a new center of history quite vividly. As a Pharisaical Jew, Saul of Tarsus was thoroughly immersed in the Jewish idea of the Exodus being the center of history. No doubt he had an extended certainty in the truth of Moses' Creation Narrative and Isaiah's predictions of a coming Messiah. He had no idea that Jesus was that Messiah until he was confronted by the Risen Christ on the road to Damascus. The new center of history hit Paul between the eyes when he heard the voice of Jesus and was blinded by his presence. That converting moment became for Paul the starting point of certainty. Perhaps better than any other New Testament writer, Paul was certain in both directions. He was certain that Jesus was the Son of God because he rose from the dead and appeared personally to Paul. Consequently, Paul never doubted for a moment the virgin birth of Christ, his mighty miracles the Gospel writers recorded, or Jesus' prediction of his return and reign. Paul's extended certainty moved in a linear sense in both directions, backward all the way to creation, and forward into his personal return. At the heart of this certainty was the Cross and Resurrection. From his days as a persecutor of the Christian Way, Paul no doubt knew the body of Jesus was missing from the tomb. But he had no idea Jesus had really risen from the dead. However, once he met Jesus personally, he experienced no further doubts about Jesus' identity or power. It was Jesus' resurrection from the dead which convinced Paul that Jesus was who he claimed to be and could do what he had promised to do.

Resurrection and the Certainty of Everlasting Life

Paul connected Jesus' resurrection with the certainty of his own eternal life. While one might interpret Hebrews 6 as teaching the possibility of

33. Cullmann, *Christ and Time*, 83.

losing one's salvation, Paul did not write Hebrews. (He would never have identified himself as a second-generation Christian as the author does in Hebrews 2:1–4.) Notwithstanding, Paul uses the same kind of hypothetical argument in 1 Corinthians 15 to show the awful consequences if Jesus did not rise from the dead, an argument concluded with the clear and joyous assertion that Christ has risen from the dead and become the "firstfruits" of those who rise from the dead at the general resurrection. In this way, Paul connects the security of the believer in Christ with the resurrection of Christ. To Paul, to suggest that one could lose salvation is no different than suggesting that Jesus did not rise from the dead.

Theologically, this is a brilliant connection. It places the security of believers in Christ not in themselves, but in Christ; not in their faith, but in his faith. Theologically, the resurrection of Christ guarantees eternal life to all who believe in him. The unitary whole of the Cross and Resurrection stands clearly in the center of history. Belief in the Creation Narrative is no problem for the true Christian. Belief in Jesus' miracles become no problem. If Jesus could save Paul out of his lostness, he could certainly have healed the sick and raised the dead. Belief in Jesus' resurrection was no problem for Paul after his Damascus Road experience, where he had met Christ. Belief in Christ's return was no problem, for he who could rise from the dead and ascend into heaven by his own power can certainly return on his own power. Jesus promises,

> My sheep hear my voice and I know them and they follow me. And I give unto them eternal life and they shall never perish; neither shall anyone snatch them out of My hand. My Father, who has given them to Me, is greater than all, and no one is able to snatch them out of My Father's hand. (John 10:27–29 NKJV)

If Jesus was able to keep his promise to rise from the dead exactly on the schedule he promised, one would be hard pressed to argue that he could not keep his promise to keep those who had come to him in faith. How can one be certain about that? By being certain about his resurrection. How can one be certain about his resurrection? The same way Paul was certain, by meeting Jesus personally. The Gospel invitation Jesus gave is still open today, "For God so loved the world that He gave His only begotten Son that whoever believes in Him should not perish, but have everlasting life" (John 3:16 NKJV).

13

Eternal Security from the Perspective of Process Theology

DONNA BOWMAN

PROCESS THEOLOGY AND FOREKNOWLEDGE

PROCESS THEOLOGY IS A view of God, creatures, and the God-world relationship that emphasizes becoming rather than being. It takes its metaphysical cues from the work of Alfred North Whitehead and Charles Hartshorne in particular, and exhibits affinities to Bergson and Teilhard. Process thinkers find the impassible, simple, and unchanging God that Greek metaphysics bequeathed to Christianity in its first centuries to be inadequate to the Biblical witness, which speaks of God in reciprocal, dynamic, and complex language.

Accordingly, in what Hartshorne has termed a "neoclassical theism," God is reconceived as immanent in a shared dimension of reality (including a shared timestream) with creatures, rather than as transcendent in the sense of "qualitatively other" or distant. Creatures—human and otherwise—are not merely free because God has self-limited God's power or allowed creaturely freedom, but are free intrinsically, because it is the very nature of existence itself to be free. Hence, the actions of free creatures co-create each future moment with God.

It is impossible for the future to be foreseen or determined ahead of time, because the freedom of each creature at each moment builds the future. Foreknowledge is impossible because the future contains no actualities to be known—only possibilities (which can be known in a probabilistic manner). Like everyone else, God must wait to see what happens—although unlike everyone else, God knows perfectly the probable outcomes of each moment! God's power, then, is not coercive—to shape the future by force—but persuasive: to present possibilities, flavored with the divine value towards beauty and what Whitehead termed "intensity of feeling," to each creature at each emerging moment. God's perfection is perfect relationality (to be internally related to every possible other). Process thinkers assert that this is the metaphysical unpacking of the Gospel statement that "God is love."

PROCESS THEOLOGY AND SOTERIOLOGY

Taking up the question of the eternal security of the believer in this process context requires us to be clear about the definitions, or perhaps redefinitions, of the terms in question. The first topic that needs to be considered is salvation, since the phrase "eternal security" tacitly contains its continuation "in salvation." What we are talking about is the secure status of salvation for the believer who at any time attains this status—the safety of the believer from the peril of dropping out of the number of the saved. What kind of soteriology, then, emerges from process theology? This question in turn raises others: What do we need to be saved from? What is the meaning of sin, death, and the Devil for process theologians?

In this piece I have time for only a brief sketch of these large topics, enough to give a sense of how process thinkers have approached the questions; I refer the reader to the bibliography for in-depth treatments. I should also note that process theology is a fairly young movement, and while there are important systematic works in the field, a variety of interpretations and critiques currently carry on a vigorous conversation around these matters. There is no single dominant process orthodoxy. What follows should be interpreted as the attempt of one theologian to lay out an adequate, interesting, but by no means final synthesis, with some areas being more speculative than others.

Looking for clues to the identification and nature of sin, Christians have traditionally asserted that it is that which separates us from God. This definition follows from the treatment of sin in the Hebrew Bible, where it is first connected with impurity or uncleanness, without a clear distinction between ritual and moral impurity. In the eighth century BCE, we first hear the voice of the prophets drawing that distinction: sin, they assert, is moral failure, and this is what sets our faces away from God. Jesus certainly falls into this tradition, with his radical redefinition of the demands of the law as moral principles rather than ritual prescriptions, and Christianity has ever returned to those teachings of Christ for periodic liberation from legalism and ritualism.

Process thinkers deny that any creature can ever be separated from God in a metaphysical sense. God plays a crucial role in the coming to be of every moment of time, in the life of every creature. The separation, then, cannot be ontological, but it can be spiritual. Following a tradition of liberal theology and the social gospel, many process theologians find sin in the structures of human life that limit possibilities and impose their own heteronomous systems of value. To that insight I would add the individual sin of solipsistic autonomy: the rejection of one's resources in relationship in favor of a narrow self-interest. A meaningful relationship with God is openness to God's lure to possibilities of the creation of value that are unavailable to us in our reliance on private resources. To be saved from sin, then, I define as to be rescued from the limitation of possibilities, whether this arises from one's location in claustrophobic social structures that squeeze out novelty in favor of conservation and repetition, or from one's personal decision to shut out the multitude of voices in favor of the echo chamber of self-regard.

Few if any process theologians would affirm that we need to be saved from a literal Devil—a supernatural agent of evil—but most would agree with Paul Tillich's emphasis on the demonic as a real, effective category in our world. The demonic might be conceived as the evil that flows from creatures and societies—those deeds and structures that actively seek the destruction of beauty, goodness, and truth. Because freedom is intrinsic to existence itself, the possibility of the demonic cannot ever be removed from existence. God works continually to save us from the effects of the demonic by isolating evil agents, minimizing the harm that can be done by their actions, and reducing the number of "descendents" or "disciples" exposed to those evil value systems. We can work with God to achieve the same ends.

Death is not in itself an evil or something to be overcome for process thinkers. In fact, perishing—the end of the activity and subjectivity of creatures—is a constant fact of existence. As soon as each moment of existence is decided, with one possibility of its reality enacted and all others left behind, it is "dead" in the sense that it is no longer becoming. It is "brute fact," Whitehead says. But it is also "immortal," because it has become part of the changeless past. In this existence of perpetual perishing, the death from which we need salvation is not simply the end of subjective life. Instead, it is the triviality of our lives, their merely local effect, their tendency to lose power over time, that translates to "death" in the process sense. As long as something is effective, it is "alive," not subjectively but objectively. If it becomes ineffective, it is dead. Salvation from death is the eternal effectiveness of our lives, accomplishments, decisions, and contributions of value to the world.

PROCESS THEOLOGY AND THE MECHANISM OF SALVATION

Having sketched the realities from which we need to be saved, I now turn to the mechanism by which God saves us from the limitation of possibilities, evil agents, and the extinction of our effectiveness in the world. Whitehead describes God as an entity with two "poles" or aspects: a mental pole and a physical pole. Creatures share this nature as well. When I undergo the process of becoming, I move from my physical pole—the factual data of the past, exerting causative pressure upon each emerging moment—to my mental pole—the decision of order and valuation that I impose on that data. According to Whitehead, God's process is reversed. God moves from God's mental pole—a primordial decision that orders and values all possibilities—to God's physical pole—the factual data of free creatures, which God preserves in alignment with God's eternal will.

My salvation, then, occurs in three connected phases in my process of becoming. First, God presents me with possibilities ordered and valued in the primordial divine decision. This presentation of possibilities enters my view at each moment along with the factual data from my past. God offers me a vision of the meaning of that data for my present moment, and of the ways I might creatively transform that data into a future pulsing with life, beauty, and intensity of feeling. Without this divine influence on the initial stage of my process of becoming, I would be limited to the viewpoints available in my particular time and place. Surrounding myself with the causative influences of my past, I am prone either to slavishly accept without question the values of a powerful but provincial datum (my family, my community, the institutions that give shape to my life), or to consult only my own selfish interest as I arrange my world around myself at its pinnacle and center. With the lure of God's will, a viewpoint both universal and ubiquitous, I am freed from the limitation of my finite location and its resulting narrow worldview.

Second, God enables me to ascend to the honor of co-creator of the future. Without an infusion of order and purpose into the process of becoming, no progress can be sustained. All our individual efforts toward beauty and structure would be doomed to frustration, because without the divine work, their direction would be haphazard, chaotic, efforts along one vector immediately cancelled by efforts along another. Our isolation of purpose—similar to the situation of the "windowless monads" Leibniz described—prevents meaningful coordination, unless God's influence is common to all, luring us in particular directions. The future I make, then, exhibits order, structure, and the possibility for even greater order and structure building moment upon moment. My contribution is far from trivial—it is decisive. God's action provides the framework within which my creativity takes root and takes flight.

Finally, God eternally preserves and re-presents to the world my achievements of value. For many process thinkers, this is the meaning of "eternal life." Rather than the subjective existence of a continuing center of consciousness, eternal life is the everlasting effectiveness of my life, and the beauty I created, in the universe. I am not forgotten, nor is the result of my creativity allowed to die out by dilution, diffusion, and erosion through the repeated aggregations of data in an infinite series of becomings. The result—the decision or "fact"—created in each moment of my existence is embraced by God's physical pole and oriented in accordance with God's eternal will (the primordial mental pole of the divine). Thus included in God's everlasting becoming, my self affects the entire future by influencing the possibilities offered by God to the next emerging moment.

PROCESS THEOLOGY AND ETERNAL SECURITY

What then do process thinkers make of the traditional doctrine of eternal security? As I stated above, for many process theologians the assurance of eternal life—in the sense of a subjective continuation of my stream of conscious existence—is a moot doctrinal point. Orthodox defenders of the doctrine often have as their aim the guarantee for the converted of a home in heaven after earthly death. Eternal security, at its root, is the assurance that "no power in heaven, on earth, or under the earth, can separate us from the love of God" (Rom 8:39)—meaning that the regenerated believer cannot fall away back into damnation.

While the terms *salvation* and *damnation* certainly have a different resonance for process theists, and the guarantee of a heavenly home has no place for those process thinkers who reject the postmortem, everlasting subjectivity of each individual, the underlying intent of the doctrine continues to be affirmed in a Christianity informed by process categories. The pedagogical force of eternal security is twofold. First, the doctrine asserts that God keeps God's promises. In the Hebrew Bible, God enters into covenants with Noah, Abraham, David, and others; these suzerainty covenants (following a common Near Eastern model) involved promises by both parties, but were dictated unilaterally by the greater party, and cannot be dissolved unilaterally by the lesser party. In these covenants, God pledged special favors of protection, offspring, and status to the chosen people, who in turn promised obedience and worship.

Although the histories and prophetic works of the Hebrew Bible say that Israel failed to honor God as she promised, God, the initiating party to the covenant, never dissolved it. Its ongoing validity is attested by Paul in Romans 11, where he compares the Gentile Christians to a branch grafted onto the tree of Israel, and in Romans 11, Ephesians 1, and Galatians 4, where the adoption by the Spirit is contrasted to the natural heirs of the bloodline. The promise given to the patriarchs belongs now to Gentile Christians as well. God's promise is not void, then, but valid in an even greater expanse than human imagination could surmise.

Second, the doctrine of eternal security teaches us that salvation is God's work and not ours. If God saves, God can be trusted to be faithful to save whatever the future may bring. Our actions and attitudes as creatures, vile though they may be, do not compel God to turn away from us. The great Reformed theologian Karl Barth allowed no one to exceed him in serious consideration of the divine word of rejection. He made the dual realities of election and rejection the centerpiece of his theology. But when he concluded that rejection is a shadow-reality, and that God's freedom and power mean that God's *Yes* to creation overcomes even the most real, serious, and devastating divine *No*, Barth was giving voice to the principle behind eternal security. The sin, death, and evil that God overcomes in salvation do not suddenly become invincible when they affect us after conversion. God goes on working in the lives of believers, even when God's activity is invisible to all. As we are powerless to save ourselves, we are equally powerless to damn ourselves. God alone saves, and what God saves stays saved.

These two precepts guide process theology in its consideration of the security of salvation. First, God's faithfulness consists in God's eternal and unwavering purpose to foster beauty and intensity of feeling with the cooperation of creatures. God can be trusted to do everything in God's power to bring about this result. Process thought is often stigmatized as a theology of divine change—with the implication that the God of process theology wavers and waffles. What process actually asserts is that God responds to the realities of the world and creatively utilizes all available resources to meet its contingent needs, all the while steadfastly pursuing the unchanging divine will. This unchanging, primordial aspect of God includes the decision to include creatures in the divine fellowship—the determination to elevate and empower us. Thus the decision to save belongs to the eternal fount of Godhead, not to contingent responses to creaturely reality. The process God is faithful to keep God's promises, which are grounded in the divine decision to be God for us.

Second, our salvation is secure because it is not our work, but God's. Again, process thought is misunderstood as a doctrine of human power and divine weakness. Our ability to co-create the future is finite; it is limited by the accident of the data available to it, effective (on its own) only in the moment, unable to achieve cooperation or solidarity with others, dead and impotent as soon as the moment passes. God's salvation, however, means that our contributions are preserved and re-energized for each new moment. My life becomes part of God's glorious renewal of the world in God's self. To the extent to which process thought reminds us that our salvation is given to us and does become our own, through its focus on the creativity and accomplishments creatures are capable of in this system, it does reclaim theological talk of the power of the saved individual. But that ownership simply consists of the continuation of the value of my life in God's everlasting creative adventure. Without God's decisive action to offer salvation (in the lure to participate in the divine plan) and complete salvation (in the taking up of the result of my life into the divine consequent nature), my power would be irrelevant and of no avail.

CONCLUSION

Eternal security, though not a hotly debated topic in process circles, is a doctrine that process thinkers would do well to think through. It reminds us of the order of salvation, and the roles played in it by divine and creaturely participants. Its magisterium leads us to meditate on God's promise, God's faithfulness, and God's power to save. When considered in the context of a process understanding of human creativity, the doctrine invites us to examine our commitment to the divine will and places a renewed emphasis on spirituality and discernment. Thus Calvin's hopes are fulfilled, although in a form he never would have imagined: the doctrine confirming God's exclusive power over salvation frees us to act boldly and decisively in our proper sphere of human creativity.

FURTHER READING

Bowman, Donna. *The Divine Decision: A Process Doctrine of Election.* Louisville: Westminster John Knox Press, 2002.

Cobb, John B. Jr. *A Christian Natural Theology.* Philadelphia: Westminster Press, 1965.

———. *Grace and Responsibility: A Wesleyan Theology for Today.* Nashville: Abingdon Press, 1995.

Kraus, Elizabeth M. "God the Savior." In *New Essays in Metaphysics*, ed. Robert C. Neville. Albany, NY: State University of New York Press, 1987, pp. 199–215.

Ogden, Schubert. "'For Freedom Christ Has Set Us Free': The Christian Understanding of Ultimate Transformation." In *The Whirlwind in Culture*, ed. Donald W. Musser and Joseph L. Price. Bloomington, IN: Meyer Stone Books, 1988, pp. 200–213.

Williamson, Clark M. "God the Creator and Redeemer of Life." In *In Way of Blessing, Way of Life: A Christian Theology*. St. Louis: Chalice Press, 1999, pp. 99–130.

APPENDIX A

Testamentum Imperium

THE ARTICLES IN THE book first appeared in *Testamentum Imperium* (meaning "the great testament"), an online international theological journal that focuses on the eternal security of the believer, available at http://www.preciousheart.net/ti. The 2007 first volume contained eighty articles, and volumes are being planned for 2009 (on Divine Sovereignty and Human Freedom) and 2011 (on the Perseverance of the Saints).

Testamentum Imperium is the brainchild of Kevaughn Mattis, a young scholar from the Republic of Trinidad—a beautiful and proud two-island nation—who has been networking for the past five years with many of the top Christian scholars around the world on the topic of the eternal security. The whole collection of articles in volume one ranged from exegesis to theological construction. Eighty articles on the great testament of our eternal security—Mattis crossed the oceans through cyberspace and united a host in record time. What he has accomplished is indeed remarkable, for he has done this on his own, without the involvement of a team of scholars or the backing of a seminary or university department. The topic that he has selected—the eternal security of the Christian—has captured the attention of some of the best minds in a broad diversity of theological fields and denominational backgrounds.

In addition to the scholars in this book, here is a partial list of contributors to the 2007 issue of *Testamentum Imperium* just to indicate the diversity, together with their institution and country:

- William D. Barrick: The Master's Seminary, Sun Valley, California, USA
- Richard H. Bell: University of Nottingham, Nottingham, UK
- Kathleen L. Bruce: Graduate Institute of Applied Linguistics in Dallas, Texas, USA

- A. B. Caneday: Northwestern College, Saint Paul, Minnesota, USA
- James J. Ehrhard: Mid-America Baptist Theological Seminary, Cordova, Tennessee, USA
- Jan Gabriël van der Watt and Tiny van der Schaaf: University of Pretoria, Pretoria, South Africa
- Ruben D. Kwint: St. Matthew's Reformed Church, Trois-Rivières, Quebec, Canada
- Peter A. Lillback and Richard B. Gaffin: Westminster Theological Seminary, Glenside, Pennsylvania, USA
- David L. Mapes: Luther Rice Seminary, Lithonia, Georgia, USA
- Joseph A. Pipa, Jr.: Greenville Presbyterian Theological Seminary, Taylors, South Carolina, USA
- David W. Pendergrass: Baylor University, Waco, Texas, USA
- "Piff" Gregory C. Pereira: Baptist Theological College of Southern Africa, Randburg, South Africa
- Ronald L. Rushing: Pastor, El Camino Baptist Church, Tuscon, Arizona, USA

See the website for the complete list of authors and their bios and other writings. This is truly an international and interdenominational endeavor in Christian collaboration, led by one man who is much younger than all of the contributors and who is probably more savvy on how to use the internet for such purposes than most of them. The process he used speaks well of everyone involved, for though many of the authors have met each other, none of them have yet met Mattis face-to-face—but we desire to. What a feat!

Through Mattis' endeavors, one of the most cherished elements of our Christian salvation—our eternal security—is getting the attention it deserves. Each author makes a unique contribution. Would it not be wonderful that as the articles are digested by the theological masters and they muse and interact with each other, a consensus might develop on this important issue? And what additional contributions could be built upon these?

It has been my privilege and honor as managing editor to ride along from the early stages of this journal. I commend this collection with all my heart to all people, but especially to the household of faith and to the many captains of the vessels plying the ocean waves of theological scholarship.

Michael Glenn Maness
Managing Editor, *Testamentum Imperium*
Woodville, Texas

APPENDIX B

Complete List of Articles in *Testamentum Imperium* 1 (2007)

1. The Psalms: Eternal Security and Perseverance —Harold R. Holmyard III
2. "What My Father Has Given Me": Believers as God's Gift in the Gospel of John—J. Ramsey Michaels
3. The Security of the Believer as the Son's Fulfillment of the Father's Will—Shawn L. Buice
4. The Prayer of Jesus in John 17 and the Security of the Believer —Jon Balserak
5. Eternal Security and the Saving Love of God—An Exposition of Romans 8:31–39—Stephen Voorwinde
6. Making Your Calling and Election Sure: An Analysis of 2 Peter 1:8–11 —Verlyn D. Verbrugge
7. The Adoption Metaphor and the Security of the Believer —Francis Lyall
8. First Clement and Jewish Hellenism: Historiography and "Grace" in Light of Surviving Second Temple Motifs and First Century Christianity—Brandon G. Withrow
9. Predestination and Salvific Assurance in Early Modern Thought and Life—Kirk R. MacGregor
10. An Anthropological Look at Eternal Life: The Internal Changes Accompanying Salvation—Kirk R. MacGregor
11. Salvation from the Wrath to Come in the Present Epoch —Georg Plasger

12. The Eternal Security of the Believer in Christ from the Perspective of Philosophical Theology—James W. Bryant
13. Eternal Security from the Perspective of Process Theology —Donna Bowman
14. Salvation from the Wrath to Come: An Exposition of Romans 5:9 and 1 Thessalonians 5:9—Richard H. Bell
15. Everlasting Life in John and the Permanence of Salvation: The Life Metaphor in John's Gospel—Jan Gabriël van der Watt
16. Eternal Security and the Early Saints: Are the First, Second, and Third Century Christian Beliefs a Reliable Basis for Determining Soteriological Truth?—Peter A. Lillback
17. Jeremiah 32:40: New Covenant Promise of Eternal Security —Harold R. Holmyard III
18. Eternal Security and Perseverance: Ezekiel 33:12–19 —William D. Barrick
19. Delivered to Satan: 1 Corinthians 5:3–5 and 1 Timothy 1:18–20 —Paul Toseland
20. An Anthropological Look at Eternal Life: The Permanence of the Internal Changes Wrought at Salvation—David A. Depp
21. Security of the Believer—Ronald L. Rushing
22. The Pauline Concept of Union with Christ and the Security of the Believer—"Piff" Gregory C. Pereira
23. Eternal Security of the Believer—Douglas Kennard
24. Teleological Purpose and Eternal Security: How the Ultimate Goal of Salvation Ensures that It Is Forever—Keith Miller
25. Why I Am an Inclusivist—David W. Pendergrass
26. Believer's Security in Christ Jesus: Romans 5:1–11 —Joseph A. Pipa, Jr.
27. "Lest after preaching to others I become disqualified": Grace and Warning in Paul's Gospel (1 Cor 9:23–27)—A. B. Caneday
28. Foreknowledge, Predestination, Election, and the Final Destiny of the Believer—Jeff Alexander

29. Kept By the Power of God: The Lord as Guardian of Salvation —John A. Battle

30. Divine Sovereignty vs. Human Responsibility—Kenneth Boa

31. Eternal Security and the Missionary Message—Kathleen L. Bruce

32. Evidence of the Security of the Believer in the Old Testament —Jeff Chambless

33. Justification: Moral or Forensic?—Steven R. Cook

34. Redemption and Resurrection: An Exercise in Biblical-Systematic Theology—Richard B. Gaffin, Jr.

35. The Sealing Work of the Holy Spirit—Hal Harless

36. The Instrumentality of Faith in Securing Eternal Salvation —J. B. Hixson

37. Perseverance of the Saints and Christian Living: What Does the Lord Require of You?—Fisher Humphreys

38. The Consequence of Lazy Discipleship as Found in the Parable of the Eight Talents—Richard R. Klein

39. For His Name's Sake: A Study of Old Testament Passages in which God Had Mercy upon Israel for His Name's Sake—Ruben D. Kwint

40. Eternal Security for the Believer as Seen in Romans 8:1–13 —Robert Lancaster

41. Hermeneutics: The Distinction Between the Gift of Salvation and Future Rewards—Dan Lee

42. Perseverance and the Promises of God—Robert Letham

43. Romans 8:13 and the Security of the Believer—Fred R. Lybrand

44. Prescience, Predestination, and the Creator-Creature Distinction: Francis Turretin's Critique of Luis de Molina's *Scientia Media* —Marcus J. McArthur

45. The Perseverance of the Saints Encouraging to the Christian —C. Matthew McMahon

46. Lord's Prayer and Conditional Forgiveness: Abuse of Women and Forgiveness in the Lord's Prayer—Tiny van der Schaaf

47. Grace and Eternal Security: How the Gracious Nature of Salvation Ensures that It Is Forever—Forrest Weiland
48. Hebrews 7 and the Security of the Believer: Oath and Priesthood —Ron J. Bigalke, Jr.
49. Free Will and Eternal Security—Matthew Lynch
50. At the Moment of Salvation God Forgives All Our Sin: Past, Present, and Future—David L. Mapes
51. Why Did God Choose to Make Salvation Secure?—Jim McClarty
52. If Our Salvation is Secure, Why Should We Live Holy Lives? —Joseph Parle
53. Apostasy and Eternal Security—Gregory P. Sapaugh
54. If Salvation is Secure, Why Should We Live Holy Lives?—Eric Sowell
55. The Metaphor of "Sheep" and "Shepherd" and the Security of God's Flock—Daniel A. Warner and Doug Kennard
56. Assurance of Salvation—James J. Ehrhard
57. Hebrews 10:11–14 and the Security of the Believer —Timothy J. Finney
58. The Reformed Doctrine of Eternal Security—Iain Gordon
59. The Sealing Work of the Holy Spirit—Hal Harless
60. Christology and Security Dialogue—Harry Harriss
61. The Security of the Believer: Romans 6:3–11, 14—Daniel W. Hill
62. Understanding our Salvation and Security in Jesus through the Character of God—J. S. Hilliard
63. Forgiveness—The Way of Grace —E. Glenn Hinson with Liselotte Terrell
64. A Defense of Individual Election unto Salvation and Critique of Absolute Corporate Election—N. E. Barry Hofstetter
65. Denominationalism and Catholicity—Peter J. Leithart
66. The Security of the Believer—David E. Luethy
67. Assurance of Faith and Possession of Salvation—César Malan—from *Journal of the Grace Evangelical Society* 2:2 (Autumn 1989)

68. An Endeavor of Grace: A Struggle Against Social Sin
—Maake J. Masango

69. Perseverance of God's Love—Romans 8:31–39—Bruce A. McDowell

70. Seal and Deposit in the Family—E. Neufeld

71. An Anchor for the Soul: Hebrews 6:13–20—Eric L. Peterman

72. Security of the Believer—Evidences from Galatians
—Leonard W. Pine

73. Colossians 1:21–23—Charles H. Ray

74. A Study of 1 Corinthians 9:23–27—Charles H. Ray

75. The Eternal Security of the Believer—Aaron John Samuel

76. Eternal Security: The Believer as the Inheritance of God
—Ernest C. Seddon

77. Security of the Believer and the New Birth Metaphor
—A. Burge Troxel

78. Eternal Security: 1 John 2:15–17, 3:7–10, and 2 John 1:8–9
—Ed Vasicek

79. Perseverance of the Saints or the Security of the Believer
—Gene Wofford

80. Apostasy and Security—R. K. McGregor Wright

Bibliography

Albright, William Foxwell. *Archaeology and the Religion of Israel.* Baltimore: Johns Hopkins Press, 1942.

———. *New Horizons in Biblical Research.* New York: Oxford University Press, 1966.

The Anchor Bible Commentary Series (AB). 80+ vols. New York: Doubleday, 1956–2005.

Aquinas, Thomas. *Catena Aurea: Commentary on the Four Gospels, collected out of the works of the Fathers.* Oxford: John Henry Parker, 1845.

Augustine. *City of God.* Trans. Marcus Dods. New York: Modern Library, 1950.

———. *Tractates on the Gospel of John.* Trans. John W. Rettig. Washington, DC: Catholic University of America Press, 1988–95.

Baird, William. *History of New Testament Research.* 2 vols. Minneapolis: Fortress, 1992.

Balz, Horst and Gerhard Schneider, eds. *Exegetical Dictionary of the New Testament* (EDNT). 3 vols. Grand Rapids: Eerdmans, 1993.

Barnard, L. W. "The Early Roman Church, Judaism, and Jewish Christianity." *Anglican Theological Review* 49 (October 1967): 371–84.

Barth, Karl. *Kirchliche Dogmatik.* 4 vols. Zürich, 1942.

———. *The Resurrection of the Dead.* Trans. H. J. Stenning. New York: Fleming H. Revell Company, 1933.

Bauckham, Richard. *Jude, 2 Peter.* WBC. Waco: Word, 1983.

Bernard of Clairvaux. *De gratia et libero arbitrio.* In *Sämtliche Werke lateinisch/deutsch* I. Innsbruck: Tyrolia-Verlag, 1990.

Beyschlag, Karlmann. *Clemens Romanus und der Frukatholizismus: Untersuchungen zu 1 Clemens 1–7.* J. C. B. Mohr: Tubingen, 1966.

Blackaby, Henry. *Experiencing God: Knowing and Doing the Will of God.* Nashville: Lifeway, 1993.

Borchert, Gerald. *John 1–11.* NAC. Nashville: Broadman & Holman, 1996.

Bovell, Carlos R. *Inerrancy and the Spiritual Formation of Younger Evangelicals.* Eugene, OR: Wipf & Stock, 2007.

Bowden, James, ed. *Encyclopedia of Christianity.* New York: Oxford University Press, 2005.

Bowman, Donna. *The Divine Decision: A Process Doctrine of Election.* Louisville: Westminster John Knox Press, 2002.

Boyce, James Montgomery. "Galatians." EBC. Grand Rapids: Zondervan, 1976.

Breytenbach, Cilliers. *Versoehnung. Eine Studie zur paulinishen Soteriologie.* WMANT 60. Neukirchen: Neukirchener Verlag, 1989.

Brown, Colin, ed. *The New International Dictionary of New Testament Theology.* 3 vols. Grand Rapids: Zondervan, 1978.

Brown, Raymond E. *The Gospel According to John (I-XII).* AB. Garden City, NY: Doubleday, 1966.

Browning, W. R. F. *A Dictionary of the Bible*. 2nd rev. ed. Oxford: Oxford University Press, 2004.

Bruce, F. F. *The Epistle to the Hebrews*. Grand Rapids: Eerdmans, 1990.

———. *The Gospel of John*. Grand Rapids: Eerdmans, 1983.

Brunner, Emil. *The Christian Doctrine of Creation and Redemption*. Vol. 3 of *Dogmatics*. Trans. David Cairns and J. H. L. Parker. Philadelphia: Westminster, 1962.

Buckland, W. W. *A Textbook of Roman Law from Augustus to Justinian*. 3rd ed. Rev. P. Stein. Cambridge: Cambridge University Press, 1963.

Bunyan, John. *Grace Abounding*. London: Penguin, 1987.

Callan, Terrance. "The Syntax of 2 Peter 1:1–7." *Catholic Biblical Quarterly* 67 (2005): 632–40.

Calvin, John. "A l'église de Paris" (15 March 1557). In Vol. 2 of *Lettres de Jean Calvin: Lettres françaises*. Ed. Jules Bonnet. Paris, 1854, 122–26.

———. "A l'église de Paris" (16 September 1557). In Vol. 2 of *Lettres françaises*, 140–41.

———. *The Bondage and Liberation of the Will: A Defence of the Orthodox Doctrine of Human Choice against Pighius*. Ed. A. N. S. Lane and trans. G. I. Davies. Grand Rapids: Baker, 1996.

———. *Commentary on the Gospel according to John*. Trans. and ed. William Pringle. Grand Rapids: Baker, 1982.

———. *Concerning the Eternal Predestination of God*. Trans. J. K. S. Reid. Louisville: Westminster John Knox, 1997.

———. *Institutes of the Christian Religion*. 2 vols. Ed. John T. McNeill and trans. Ford Lewis Battles. Philadelphia: Westminster, 1960.

Cairns, Earle E. *Christianity through the Centuries*. 3rd rev. ed. Grand Rapids: Zondervan, 1996.

Carson, D. A. *The Gospel According to John*. In *The Pillar Commentary*. Grand Rapids: Eerdmans, 1991.

Cary, M., *et al*. *The Oxford Classical Dictionary*. Oxford: Clarendon, 1949.

Chandieu, Antoine de la Roche. *Histoire des persecutions et martyrs de l'eglise de Paris*. Lyon, 1563.

Charles, J. Daryl. "2 Peter." REBC. Grand Rapids: Zondervan, 2006.

Chesterton, G. K. *Orthodoxy*. Garden City, NY: Image Books, 1959.

Chrysostom, John. *Commentary on Saint John: The Apostle and Evangelist*. Trans. and ed. Sister Thomas Aquinas Goggin. Washington, DC: Catholic University of America Press, 1957.

Clendenon, E. Ray, gen. ed. *New American Commentary* (NAC). 35+ vols. Nashville: Broadman & Holman, 1992–.

Cobb, John B., Jr. *A Christian Natural Theology*. Philadelphia: Westminster, 1965.

———. *Grace and Responsibility: A Wesleyan Theology for Today*. Nashville: Abingdon Press, 1995.

Connolly, James. *Human History and the Word of God*. New York: The Macmillan Company, 1965.

Craigie, Peter C. *Psalms 1–50*. WBC. Waco: Word, 1983.

Cranfield, C. E. B. *A Critical and Exegetical Commentary on the Epistle to the Romans*. The International Critical Commentary. Edinburgh: T & T Clark, 1975.

Cullmann, Oscar. *Christ and Time*. Trans. Floyd Filson. Philadelphia: Westminster, 1964.

Daniélou, Jean. *The Theology of Jewish Christianity*. Trans. John A. Baker. London: Darton, Longman, and Todd, 1964.

Danker, Frederick William, rev. and ed. *A Greek-English Lexicon of the New Testament and Other Early Christian Literature* (BDAG). 3rd ed. Chicago: University of Chicago Press, 2001.

Davies, W. D. *Paul and Rabbinic Judaism*. London: SPCK, 1965.

de l'Espérandière, Merlin. "To Beza, from Longueville (Paris)" (10 January 1567). In Theodore Beza, *Correspondance*. Ed. Hippolyte Aubert, Henri Meylan, Alain Dufour, *et al.* 14 vols. Geneva, 1960–90, 8:29.

de L'Espine, Jean. *Excellens discourse de J. de l'Espine, angevin, touchant le repos & contentement de L'esprit*. Basel, 1587.

———. *Traitté consolatoire et fort utile contre toutes afflictions qui adviennent ordinairement aux fideles Chrestiens*. Lyons: Jean Saugrain, 1565.

———. *Traicté des tentations et moyens d'y resister. Composé par un docte et excellent personnage de ce temps*. Lyon: Jean Saugrain, 1566.

Derrett, J. D. M. *Jesus's Audience*. London: Darton, Longman & Todd, 1973.

de Zulueta, F., trans. and ed. *The Institutes of Gaius*. 2 vols. Oxford: Oxford University Press, 1946.

Diefendorf, Barbara B. *Beneath the Cross: Catholics and Huguenots in Sixteenth-Century Paris*. Oxford: Oxford University Press, 1991.

du Croy, Anthoine, Prince de Porcein. "Testament." In *Archives nationales, Minutier central*. Paris, 28 April 1567, 8:95.

Dunn, James D. G. *Baptism in the Holy Spirit*. London: SCM, 1970.

———. *Romans 1–8*. WBC. Dallas: Word, 1988.

Ehrman, Bart D, trans. and ed. *The Apostolic Fathers*. 2 vols. In *Loeb Classical Library*. Cambridge, MA: Harvard University Press, 2003.

Eliade, Mircea. *Cosmos and History*. Trans. W. R. Trask. New York: Harper and Brothers, 1954.

Enns, Peter. *Inspiration and Incarnation: Evangelicals and the Problem of the Old Testament*. Grand Rapids: Baker Academic, 2005.

Gæbelein, Frank E., gen. ed. *The Expositor's Bible Commentary* (EBC). 12 vols. Grand Rapids: Zondervan, 1972–92.

Grant, Robert M. and Holt H. Graham. *The Apostolic Fathers: A New Translation and Commentary*. 2 vols. New York: Thomas Nelson, 1965.

Green, Michael. *2 Peter and Jude*. TNTC. Grand Rapids: Eerdmans, 1968.

Grudem, Wayne. *Systematic Theology*. Grand Rapids: Zondervan, 1994.

Hagner, Donald Alfred. *The Use of the Old and New Testaments in Clement of Rome*. Leiden: Brill, 1969.

Harding, Mark. "The Salvation of Israel and the Logic of Romans 11:11–36." *Australian Biblical Review* 46 (1998): 55–69.

Harnack, Adolf von. *History of Dogma*. 7 vols. New York: Russell and Russell, 1958.

Harper, Robert Francis. *The Code of Hammurabi, King of Babylon About 2250 BC*. Chicago: University of Chicago Press, 1904.

Hartley, John E. *The Book of Job*. NICOT. Grand Rapids: Eerdmans, 1988.

Hatch, Edwin. *The Influence of Greek Ideas and Usages Upon the Christian Church*. Peabody, MA: Hendrickson Publishers, 1995.

Hays, Richard B. *The Conversion of the Imagination: Paul as Interpreter of Israel's Scripture*. Grand Rapids: Eerdmans, 2005.

Hendriksen, William. *John*. TNTC. Grand Rapids: Baker, 1953.

Hess, Richard H. *Israelite Religions: An Archaeological and Biblical Survey*. Grand Rapids: Baker Academic, 2007.

Himuro, Misako. "The Phoenix in the First Epistle of Clement to the Corinthians." *Renaissance Studies* 12.4 (December 1998): 523–44.

Hocking, William Ernest. *The Meaning of Immortality*. New York: Harper and Brothers, 1957.

Hodge, Charles. *Commentary on the Epistle to the Romans*. Rep. ed. Grand Rapids: Eerdmans, 1983.

Hodges, Zane. "Making Your Calling and Election Sure: An Exposition of 2 Peter 1:5–11." *Journal of the Grace Evangelical Society* 11 (Spring 1998): <http://www.faithalone.org/ journal/1998i/Hodges.html>.

Hofius, Otfried. "Erwaegungen zur Gestalt und Herkunft des paulishishen Versoehnungsgedankens." *Zeitschrift für Theologie und Kirche* 77 (1980): 186–99.

———. "Gott hat unter uns aufgerichtet das Wort von der Versoehnung, 2 Kor 5:19." *Zeitschrift für die neutestamentliche Wissenschaft* 71 (1980): 3–20.

———. *Paulusstudien*. Tübingen: Mohr Siebeck, 1989.

———. "Suehne und Versoehnung. Zum paulinischen Verstaendnis des Kreuzestodes Jesu." In *Versuche, das Leiden und Sterben Jesu zu verstehen*, ed. W. Maar. Freiburg: Katholische Akademie, 1983, 25–46.

———. "Versöhnung" (Reconciliation). In *Beilage zur Reformierten Kirchenzeitung* (1989): 2–4.

Holmes, Michael W., ed. *The Apostolic Fathers: Greek Texts and English Translations of Their Writings*. 2nd ed. Grand Rapids: Baker, 1992.

Hubbard, Robert L. Jr., ed. *New International Commentary on the Old Testament* (NICOT). 22+ vols. Grand Rapids: Eerdmans, 1976–.

Hyatt, Philip, ed. *The Bible in Modern Scholarship*. Nashville: Abingdon Press, 1965.

Jolowicz, H. F. *Historical Introduction to the Study of Roman Law*. 2nd ed. Cambridge: Cambridge University Press, 1961.

Josephus. *Antiquities of the Jews*. Trans. William Whiston. Rev. ed. Peabody, Mass.: Hendrickson, 1987, 27–542.

Kantonen, T. A. *The Christian Hope*. Philadelphia: Muhlenberg Press, 1954.

Keil, C. F. and Franz Delitzsch. *Commentary on the Old Testament*. 3 vols. in 1. Grand Rapids: Eerdmans, 1986.

Kelly, J. N. D. *Early Christian Doctrines*. Rev. ed. New York: HarperSanFrancisco, 1978.

Kingdon, Robert M. "The Control of Morals in Calvin's Geneva." In *The Social History of the Reformation*, eds. Lawrence P. Buck and Jonathan W. Zophy. Columbus: Ohio State University Press, 1972, 3–16.

Kittel, Gerhard and Gerhard Friedrich, eds. *Theological Dictionary of the New Testament* (TDNT). Trans. Geoffrey W. Bromiley. 10 vols. Grand Rapids: Eerdmans, 1964.

Knudson, Albert C. *The Religious Teaching of the Old Testament*. New York: Abingdon-Cokesbury Press, 1918.

Kostenberger, Andreas J. *John*. BECNT. Grand Rapids: Baker, 2004.

Kraus, Elizabeth M. "God the Savior." In *New Essays in Metaphysics*, ed. Robert C. Neville. Albany, NY: State University of New York Press, 1987, 199–215.

Kugel, James L. *The Bible as it Was*. Cambridge, MA: Harvard University Press, 1997.

Labrusse-Riou, C. *Themis: Droit Prive*. Paris: Presses Universitaires de France, 1997.

Lenski, R. C. H. *The Interpretation of St. John's Gospel*. Columbus, OH: Wartburg Press, 1942.

Levy-Bruhl, Lucian. *Primitive Mentality*. Trans. Lilian A. Clare. Boston: Beacon Press, 1966.

Lightfoot, J. B. *The Apostolic Fathers*. Grand Rapids: Baker, 1981.

Longman, Tremper III and David E. Garland, gen. eds. *The Expositor's Bible Commentary: Revised Edition* (REBC). 13 vols. Grand Rapids: Zondervan, 2004–.

Luther, Martin. "Letter to Elector John: Wittenberg, June 16, 1531." In *Luther's Works*. 55 vols. Trans. Jaroslav Pelikan *et al.* Philadelphia: Fortress, 1975.

Lyall, Francis. *Slaves, Citizens, Sons: Legal Metaphors in the Epistles*. Grand Rapids: Academie Books and Zondervan, 1984.

MacArthur, John F. "Perseverance of the Saints." *The Master's Seminary Journal* (Spring 1993): 5–24.

MacDowell, D. M. *The Law in Classical Athens*. Ithaca, NY: Cornell University Press and London: Thames and Hudson, 1978.

MacGregor, Kirk R. *A Central European Synthesis of Radical and Magisterial Reform*. Lanham, MD: UPA, 2006.

———. "1 Corinthians 15:3b–6a, 7 and the Bodily Resurrection of Jesus." *Journal of the Evangelical Theological Society* 49.2 (2006): 232–33.

———. "Hubmaier's Concord of Predestination with Free Will." *Direction: A Mennonite Brethren Forum* 35.2 (2006): 279–99.

———. *A Molinist-Anabaptist Systematic Theology*. Lanham, MD: UPA, 2007.

Macleod, Donald. *A Faith to Live By: Understanding Christian Doctrine*. Brooklyn: Christian Focus Publications, 2002.

Marot, Clément and Theodore Beza. *Les pseaumes de David, mis en rime françoise. Avec une oraison à la fin d'un chacun pseaume faite par M. Augustin Marlorat*. Paris: pour Antoine Vincent, 1566.

Mayor, J. B. *The Epistle of St. Jude and the Second Epistle of St. Peter*. Rep. ed. Grand Rapids: Baker, 1965.

Mazeaud, H., L. Mazeaud, J. Mazeaud, and F. Chabas. *Lecons de Droit Civil: La famille*. Paris: Monchrestien, 1995.

McGiffert, A. C. *A History of Christian Thought*. 2 vols. New York: Charles Scribner's Sons, 1932.

McGrath, Alister E. *Reformation Thought*. 3rd ed. Malden, MA: Blackwell, 2000.

Mentzer, Raymond A., ed. *Sin and the Calvinists: Morals Control and the Consistory in the Reformed Tradition*. Kirksville, MO: Sixteenth Century Journal Publishers, 1994.

Metzger, Bruce M., gen. ed. *Word Biblical Commentary* (WBC). 59 vols. Nashville: Word, 1983–2008.

———. *A Textual Commentary on the Greek New Testament*. 3rd ed. London: UBS, 1971.

Michaels, J. Ramsey. "Baptism and Conversion in John: A Particular Baptist Reading." In *Baptism, the New Testament and the Church. Historical and Contemporary Studies in Honour of R. E. O. White*. JSNTSup 171. Ed. S. E. Porter and A. R. Cross. Sheffield: Sheffield Academic Press, 1999, 136–56.

Moo, Douglas J. *The Epistle to the Romans*. NICNT. Grand Rapids: Eerdmans, 1996.

———. *2 Peter, Jude*. NIVAC. Grand Rapids: Zondervan, 1996.

Morris, Leon. *The Epistle to the Romans*. Grand Rapids: Eerdmans, 1988.

———, ed. *Tyndale New Testament Commentaries* (TNTC). 20 vols. Grand Rapids: Eerdmans, 1965–82.

Muirhead, J., trans. and ed. *The Institutes of Gaius and Rules of Ulpian*. Edinburgh: T & T Clark, 1880.

Muller, Richard. *After Calvin: Studies in the Development of a Theological Tradition.* Oxford: Oxford University Press, 2003.

Murray, John. *The Epistle to the Romans: The English Text with Introduction, Exposition and Notes.* NICNT. Grand Rapids: Eerdmans, 1959.

Newman, Barclay M. and Eugene A. Nida. *The Translator's Handbook on the Gospel of John. United Bible Societies Helps for Translators.* New York: United Bible Societies, 1989.

Neyrey, Jerome. *2 Peter, Jude.* AB. New York: Doubleday, 1993.

Niebuhr, Reinhold. *The Nature and Destiny of Man.* New York: Charles Scribner's Sons, 1955.

Nielsen, Charles M. "Clement of Rome." *Church History* 31.2 (June 1962): 131–50.

NIV Application Commentary (NIVAC). 42 vols. Grand Rapids: Zondervan, 1995–.

Oden, Thomas C. *The Justification Reader.* Grand Rapids: Eerdmans, 2002.

Ogden, Schubert. "'For Freedom Christ Has Set Us Free': The Christian Understanding of Ultimate Transformation." In *The Whirlwind in Culture*, ed. Donald W. Musser and Joseph L. Price. Bloomington, IN: Meyer Stone Books, 1988, pp. 200–213.

Olson, C. Gordon. *Beyond Calvinism and Arminianism.* Cedar Knolls, NJ: Global Gospel Publishers, 2002.

Origen. *Commentary on the Gospel according to John.* Trans. and ed. Ronald E. Heine. Washington, DC: Catholic University of America Press, 1989–1993.

Osborne, Grant R. "Soteriology in the Gospel of John." In *The Grace of God and the Will of Man*, gen. ed. Clark H. Pinnock. Minneapolis: Bethany House, 1989.

Pinson, J. Matthew, ed. *Four Views on Eternal Security.* Grand Rapids: Zondervan, 2002.

Plasger, Georg. *Die Not-Wendigkeit der Gerechtigkeit. Eine Interpretation zu „Cur deus homo" von Anselm von Canterbury.* Münster: Aschendorff Verlag, 1993.

Plath, Siegfried. *Furcht Gottes.* Stuttgart: Calwer Verlag, 1963.

Quasten, Johannes. *Patrology.* 4 vols. Westminster, MA: The Newman Press, 1962.

Rahner, Karl. *On the Theology of Death.* Trans. Charles H. Henkey. New York: Herder and Herder, 1961.

Richardson, Alan. *History, Sacred and Profane.* Philadelphia: Westminster, 1964.

Richardson, Cyril, ed. *Early Christian Fathers.* Philadelphia: Westminster, 1953.

Ridderbos, Herman. *Commentaar op het Nieuwe Testament: Aan de Romeinen.* Kampen: Kok, 1959.

———. *Paul: An Outline of His Theology.* Trans. John R. deWitt. Grand Rapids: Eerdmans, 1975.

Ritschl, Albrecht. *Die Christliche Lehre von Rechtfertigung und Versoehnung.* Bonn, 1889.

Robinson, H. Wheeler. *The Religious Ideas of the Old Testament.* 9th ed. London: Gerald Duckworth and Company, 1952.

Sanday, William and Arthur C. Headlam. *A Critical and Exegetical Commentary on the Epistle to the Romans. The International Critical Commentary.* 5th ed. Edinburgh: T & T Clark, 1902.

Schreiner, Thomas R. *Romans.* BECNT. Grand Rapids: Baker, 1998.

———. *1, 2 Peter, Jude.* NAC. Nashville: Broadman & Holman, 2003.

Snyman, A. H. "Style and Rhetorical Situation of Romans 8:31–39." *New Testament Studies* 34 (1988): 218–31.

Stott, John R. W. *The Message of Romans: God's Good News for the World.* The Bible Speaks Today. London: InterVarsity Press, 1994.

Swindoll, Charles R. and Roy B. Zuck, gen. eds. *Understanding Christian Theology.* Nashville: Nelson, 2003.

Tenney, Merrill C. and J. D. Douglas, eds. *New International Bible Dictionary*. Grand Rapids: Zondervan, 1987.

Torrance, T. F. *The Doctrine of Grace in the Apostolic Fathers*. Grand Rapids: Eerdmans, 1948.

Toussain, Daniel. *Prieres et consolations prises de plusieurs passages de l'Escriture, & des livres des anciens. Le tout accommodé à l'usage des vrai Chrestiens, & au temps auquel nous sommes*. Geneva: pour la veuve de Jean Durant, 1566.

Tresmontant, Claude. *A Study of Hebrew Thought*. Trans. Michael Francis Gibson. New York: Desclee Company, 1960.

Trumbower, Jeffrey. *Born from Above: the Anthropology of the Gospel of John*. Tübingen: J. C. B. Mohr/Paul Siebeck, 1992.

Vance, Laurence M. *The Other Side of Calvinism*. Rev. ed. Pensacola, FL: Vance Publications, 1991.

Van Unnik, W. C. "Is 1 Clement 20 Purely Stoic?" *Vigiliae Christianae* 4 (1950): 181–89.

Volkmann, Stefan. *Der Zorn Gottes: Studien zur Rede vom Zorn Gottes in der evangelischen Theologie*. Evangelische Verlagsanstalt: Marburg, 2004.

Voorwinde, Stephen. "Rethinking Israel: An Exposition of Romans 11:25–27." *Vox Reformata* 68 (2003): 4–48.

Vriezen, Theodorus C. *The Religion of Ancient Israel*. Trans. Hubert Hoskins. Philadelphia: Westminster, 1967.

Wallace, Daniel B. *Greek Grammar Beyond the Basics*. Grand Rapids: Zondervan, 1996.

Walton, John H. *Ancient Israelite Literature in its Cultural Context: A Survey of Parallels Between Biblical and Ancient Near Eastern Texts*. Grand Rapids: Zondervan, 1990.

Warren, Rick. *The Purpose Driven Life*. Grand Rapids: Zondervan, 2002.

Weiss, Johannes. *The History of Primitive Christianity*. 2 vols. New York: Wilson-Erickson, 1937.

Westermann, Claus, ed. *Essays on Old Testament Interpretation*. Trans. James Luther Mays. London: SCMP, 1963.

Williams, David J. *Paul's Metaphors: Their Context and Character*. Peabody, MA: Hendrickson, 1999.

Williamson, Clark M. "God the Creator and Redeemer of Life." In *In Way of Blessing, Way of Life: A Christian Theology*. St. Louis: Chalice Press, 1999, 99–130.

Wilson, R. McL. *The Gospel of Philip*. London: A.R. Mowbray, 1962.

Witsius, Herman. *De oeconomia foederum Dei cum hominibus*. Utrecht, 1694.

Wong, D. W. F. "Natural and Divine Order in 1 Clement. *Vigiliae Christianae* 31 (1977): 81–87.

Wright, G. Ernest. *God Who Acts*. Garden City: Doubleday, 1961.

Yarbrough, Robert and Robert H. Stein, eds. *Baker Exegetical Commentary on the New Testament* (BECNT). 8+ vols. Grand Rapids: Baker, 2004–.